T0060055

RUNNING TO GLORY

RUNNING TO GLORY

AN UNLIKELY TEAM, A CHALLENGING SEASON, AND CHASING THE AMERICAN DREAM

Sam McManis

LYONS
PRESS

Essex, Connecticut

An imprint of Globe Pequot, the trade division of
The Rowman & Littlefield Publishing Group, Inc.
4501 Forbes Blvd., Ste. 200
Lanham, MD 20706
www.rowman.com

Distributed by NATIONAL BOOK NETWORK

British Library Cataloguing in Publication Information available

Library of Congress Cataloging-in-Publication Data

Names: McManis, Sam, author.
Title: Running to glory : an unlikely team, a challenging season, and chasing the
    American dream / Sam McManis.
Description: Guilford, Connecticut : Lyons Press 2019. | Includes index.
Identifiers: LCCN 2019005201 (print) | LCCN 2019981360 (ebook) |
    ISBN 9781493041527 (cloth) | ISBN 9781493041534 (ebook) | ISBN
    9781493057801 (paperback)
Subjects: LCSH: Eisenhower High School (Yakima, Wash.)—Track and field.
    | Cross-country runners—Washington (State)—Yakima. | Cross-country
    running—Washington (State)—Yakima.
Classification: LCC GV1061.22.W2 M46 2019 (print) | LCC GV1061.22.W2
    (ebook) | DDC 796.4209797/55—dc23
LC record available at https://lccn.loc.gov/2019005201
LC ebook record available at https://lccn.loc.gov/2019981360

∞™ The paper used in this publication meets the minimum requirements of
American National Standard for Information Sciences—Permanence of Paper
for Printed Library Materials, ANSI/NISO Z39.48-1992.

CONTENTS

STARTING LINE

The sight, so unexpected and so compelling, that ultimately led me to become immersed in the all-consuming world of high-school cross-country happened in late afternoon, early October 2016, in my new place of residence, the blue-collar-poor but agriculture-rich city of Yakima, Washington. I was driving up 40th Avenue in one of the busiest strip-mall centers in a low-rise city replete with them. I had been distracted by the radio, the seemingly nonstop coverage on National Public Radio's (NPR) of the heated presidential race, and I failed to see that traffic had backed up to a standstill—a rarity in this town—traffic had backed up to a standstill. I stopped just in time and, once my heart rate returned to normal, stared ahead with simmering dread at the line of cars snaking up the hill, a passel of Subaru all-wheel drives, pickup trucks with dauntingly high ground clearance, and a few early-model, low-slung sedans that had seen better days but throbbed with heavy bass beats from blown-out speakers.

There emerged from the side of road, along a cracked and sorry excuse for a sidewalk, a hive of bobbing heads loping at a steady, almost metronomic pace—arms swinging and legs churning with impressive precision. Two hives, actually. First came a group of boys, about 10 strong and primarily Hispanic, nearly all shirtless and stick thin, their mahogany torsos gleaming slickly in the sun as they dutifully ground out a brisk pace. From farther up the road came a clump of girls, this pack a little more diffuse, their ponytails swishing, their stride more of a prance than a pounding, their collective mien jovial and chatty, save a short girl in front whose brown hair was gathered in a severe bun and whose full attention seemed focused on the task at hand.

The traffic light turned green just then, but I didn't make it through the intersection. This allowed me more time to watch these young runners at work. I figured it was the cross-country team from Eisenhower High School, located about two miles south of where I sat idling on 40th Avenue. The school is 70 percent Hispanic, with its share of DACA (Delayed Action for Childhood Arrivals) kids, and so low-income it qualifies for free breakfast and lunch for all students. And now it seemed clear Eisenhower also had some very swift runners. By the time they reached the bottom of the hill, near the intersection where I awaited release from the traffic snarl, they made a slight left turn and pooled at the base of a cul-de-sac along a road heading straight up, up, up a half mile to Yakima's only true "exclusive neighborhood" on the aptly named Scenic Drive. They milled about for maybe 10 seconds and then took off like an elk herd. At that point, though, so did I. The light had changed, and traffic flowed once more. But in that instant, I swiveled my head to the right and saw these runners, silhouetted by the sun, lower their heads as if in supplication and proceed in a long, snaking line up the steep incline. Unbidden, a half-remembered line from the poet Theodore Roethke came to me: "May they be taken by the true burning / May they flame into being!"

This is youth, I thought. This is sport.

This, too, is decidedly not football, arguably our new national pastime, our overriding obsession, all of that rah-rah *Friday Night Lights* highschool hoopla celebrated across the land each autumn. These, rather, were just kids out on a run, training for competitions that usually take place in the dew-saturated dawn of Saturday morning, long after the lights of Friday night, with the concomitant revelry and pageantry that high-school football engenders, have been extinguished. Cross-country, I thought in that moment, has to be the purest form of sport to be found. Run. Just go run. The fastest, the most fit, wins. Period. And the races, fittingly, traverse varying terrain—not the sheer monotony of circling a track. Like life, if you are of a metaphoric bent. Unpredictable. Uphill. Slightly dangerous. Often exhilarating. In cross-country, you never know what obstacles are around the bend, but you do know that you will have to deal with whatever comes, to push through, regardless of the pain involved. Cross-country runners love and hate the pain, perhaps in equal measure. The "love" part must dominate, because, if not, why else would they do it? Not for adulation. A cross-country runner is not going to be Homecoming King, not going to be the queen-bee popular girl, not going to have cheerleaders shaking pom-poms celebrating her or his sporting exploits. To run is to move through life with purpose, to keep putting one foot in front of the other until a clear destination emerges.

And for a school such as Eisenhower, many of whose students are children of farm workers and struggle to get by financially, the elemental nature of cross-country perhaps can serve as a socioeconomic and athletic leveler with those more affluent, predominantly white-dominated teams from schools in Seattle or Spokane or, heck, even just 70 miles away in the Tri-Cities of Pasco, Kennewick, and Richland. What's more, in a city saturated with fast-food joints and where bike lanes and sidewalks are merely rumors, these runners seemed to represent a rebuke, maybe even an answer, to the alarming rate of childhood obesity (37 percent) and type 2 diabetes (30 percent) endemic in the entire Yakima Valley.

All this I thought as I turned down the yakking pundits on NPR and just contemplated that brief, sublime sight of runners in the bloom of youth. Where, I wondered, is the literary paean to cross-country that, according to the National Federation of State High Schools Associations, attracts more than a million participants each fall? Who has written this sport's *Friday Night Lights*, that seminal 1990 book of sporting literature that later became a movie and TV show? Sure, in early 2015, Disney had released a movie, *McFarland, USA*, about a plucky band of 1980s Hispanic farm kids in California who, overcoming the requisite Disneyfied adversity, won a small school cross-country title. But that movie, "based on a true story," frankly was mostly the stuff of Hollywood, full of embellishment and brimming with poetic license and cheap sentiment. Where, I wondered, could one find the real version, the expanded and nuanced look at a minority high-school team that embraces this so-called minor sport and produces winning teams and quality students, year in and year out, for decades on end?

★ ★ ★

Turned out it could be found right there in the town I just recently had begun to call home. What I was doing in Yakima, after a lifetime in California—11 years in the Sacramento area and, before that, another decade or so in the Bay Area and in Los Angeles during my formative years—was to reinvent myself after three decades as a staff writer for daily newspapers, a media platform that, if not dying, was at the very least being moved into assisted living by its younger, hipper high-tech descendants. I had a vague, inchoate plan—grad school, English literature, and then what?—and my wife, a nurse practitioner, wanted to be closer to our daughter off at college in the western part of Washington State.

But something buried deep inside me stirred at the sight of those runners on that October afternoon. I could not shake the image. Part of it was, perhaps, a yearning for the past—both distant and recent. I had spent the first 10 years of my career as a sportswriter for the *Los Angeles Times* and, so caught up was I in covering the basketball Lakers and baseball Dodgers, I had never written about running, save some Olympic Games assignments. More recently, I had fallen hard for running as part of my early-onset midlife crisis, having twice qualified for and run in the Boston Marathon, as well as competing in races from 5Ks on the roads to ultramarathons on mountainous trails.

More recently, I had become enamored of prep cross-country after watching my daughter's high-school team from Davis, California, finish second in the state in 2014 and place 12th at NXN, the prestigious Nike Cross Nationals. Never underestimate how your children's obsessions can become your own. So taken was I with the sport during my daughter's career that I rearranged my reporting schedule, which required considerable travel, to make sure never to miss a meet in the fall. I would tell anyone who would listen, and even those who would not—those in the newsroom who mistakenly thought that the sport was boring and that you could only see the runners twice during a race (at the start and at the finish)—that there was much to see in a race, drama unfolding with each step. I wanted people to understand what cross-country was, what it meant to the participants. Instead I received, even from the sports department at my last newspaper, the *Sacramento Bee*, mostly blank stares and, sometimes, even outright scoffing. Minor sport, they sneered. Minor interest. Go back to the features department, bub, they snarled.

How to tell them that to nearly a million slim-hipped, concave-chested sporting misfits across the nation—and those who love them—there is nothing quite like the start of cross-country season? It means, for spectators, dressing in layers to be sloughed off like reptilian skin as the morning warms. It means leaning over the flag-lined barriers waiting for the first flash of fluorescent shoes to emerge from a tree thicket. It means counting like-colored singlets as the herd thunders past, trying to suss out where your team's top-five runners stand—lowest score wins in this most ass-backward of sports, points given out according to an individual's order of finish—compared to that hated rival in gaudy yellow and orange jerseys. It means waiting on that railing until your child or sibling or friend, passes with agony etched into her face, far back from the lead pack but plugging along undaunted. OK, maybe slightly daunted. It means shouting encouragement ("looking good," "finish strong") that neither you nor she really believes will help but nonetheless must be dutifully uttered. It means, as a fan, gamboling over downed trees and through weed patches to catch yet more glimpses of the lead pack as the three-mile race up dusty hill and down muddy dale (or, increasingly and lamentably, especially in college races, sanitized golf-course fairways) unfolds.

Yes, the most misunderstood thing about watching cross-country is that it has no real spectators, in the strictest sense. To be a fan is to *participate*. Coaches and parents have been known to clutch course maps and, with the perspicacity of field generals, plot out prime viewing points and speculate about the time and effort to alight there while making sure to make it back to the finish. Often, fans orbiting around the finishing chute will be as sweaty and out of breath as the competitors, having run almost as long, though certainly not as hard. What is most striking about witnessing a cross-country race on the prep level is its democratizing aspect. You see all types—tall and gangly; short and squat; some for whom puberty is a mere rumor; others sporting more facial hair than hipsters at a craft beer expo. In many states, for all but the championship meets, the number of runners to be entered is unlimited. Unlike in "ball" sports, cross-country coaches don't "cut" athletes. If you're there to run, they'll find a race for you. And at the front, among the elites, you are an audience to pure athleticism. Runners look at once vulnerable, even fawnlike, yet also hewn with ropy, striated muscles in the quadriceps and calves. Their strides are long and smooth, arms syncopated in a fluid cadence, inscrutable faces betraying neither pain nor fatigue. The girls' ponytails swing with a frenzy; the boys' pumping fists show a strength their slender frames mask.

I dare you to look at a finish line just after a cross-country race and not be amazed by the sheer grit, laser-focused determination, and raw emotion on display. Runners, often, are sprawled like fallen soldiers on the grass, limbs splayed, rib cages rising and falling rapidly. Occasionally, they must be assisted off the course, but the vast majority are so strong and fit that, though obviously winded, they walk off proudly, often arm in arm with exhausted teammates—and sometimes even with competitors.

That sight, runners utterly spent at the finish line, is every bit as iconic an image as an end-zone touchdown celebration or a gaggle of teammates greeting the walk-off home-run hitter at home plate or basketball players being hoisted up to cut down the net. And it's played out each Saturday morning in the fall, everywhere in the land.

★ ★ ★

Two days after that 40th Avenue sighting, I talked to my daughter on the phone from her dorm room in Bellingham, on the other side—the *preferred* side, she said—of the Cascade Range. I mentioned my glimpse of the Eisenhower runners and how it reminded me of her California prep cross-country team not so long ago.

"Dad," she exclaimed with daughterly exasperation, "you didn't know that Ike is one of the best programs in the state?"

"*Ike?*" I asked.

"Eisenhower, Dad. The president they named the school for?"

"Right, right, of course."

"Dad! They've got this coach who's been there forever, an Irish guy. You'd totally like him. It'd make a great story. Everyone calls him 'Mister.' His real name is Phil English. But everyone calls him Mister. Not Mr. English. Just *Mister.* The guys on my team [Western Washington University] know all about him. Everyone does."

I told her I'd check it out. And I was tempted. Really, I was. But at that point I was trying to sever my 30-plus-year ties with journalism, just as I had at some point divorced myself from sportswriting, seeing it as too trivial and celebrity-saturated, too bloated with narcissistic millionaire athletes and avaricious, plutocratic owners—in general, just not serious enough a subject to merit deep analysis. Yet another part of me, the youthful idealistic part long dormant, has always hewed to the hoary cliché that sports can serve as a microcosm of society.

I thought that, just maybe, I could find out a little more about this gritty new city I called home, a city that baffled me at first by its odd combination of high-desert aridity and agricultural richness, by examining one of its local sports teams. Yakima is, after all, hardly a place an outsider would peg as being part of verdant Washington, the so-called Evergreen State. Yakima, with a population hovering around 100,000, has long been derided by West-of-the-Cascades types (read: Seattle folks) as both a rural backwater and a depressed blue-collar town in which Hispanics outnumber whites. It has been called "Yaki-Vegas," a kitschy nickname that, according to its definition on Urban Dictionary, stems from its reputation as a city "riddled with crime and gang violence[;] the depressed area around and including the city are known for high unemployment rate and low property values." Not to mention high rates of childhood obesity and domestic violence. And not to mention its alarmingly low rate of high-school graduates. A kitschy billboard on Interstate 82 heading into the city proclaims, "Welcome to Yakima, The Palm Springs of Washington." A bit of an exaggeration, that. Palm Springs doesn't have a downtown of empty storefronts, blighted row housing, billboards featuring bail bond services and personal-injury lawyers. Yes, Yakima has its issues. But then you see these kids loping along the roadside, these runners looking so strong and confident and full of life, and hope for the town and its youth is buoyed.

★ ★ ★

One night, coinciding with the first mid-December snowfall, I gave into curiosity and Googled the Eisenhower coach, Phil "Mister" English. Up popped a photo of a proper, white-haired gentleman wearing a Donegal tweed hat; a very fit 60-something, his arms crossed over the slightest bit of paunch. He was surveying his team of predominantly Hispanic boys doing what looked to be stretching exercises. I learned from the web that the boys' team in 2016 had finished third at the state meet, one point out of second place, and that a surprising sophomore named Alfonso "Fonzi" Cuevas had shocked everyone by finishing fifth overall. The girls' team had finished far lower at the state meet, though that short, brown-haired, bun-wearing girl, Erica Simison, placed 10th overall—and the fact that most internet accounts mentioned how disappointing the girls' result had been only reinforced the program's high standards. More digging, and I found Coach English's school e-mail address. I hesitated only a few seconds before dashing off a quick note to him, expressing my nascent interest in writing about the program. I wasn't really expecting a response, or at least not a timely one.

Two days later, we met at a coffee shop, where this genial but flinty-eyed Irishman with an engaging lilt to his voice sipped hot tea and talked for two hours about the team, the town, the sport. He talked about runners who came from migrant families with not enough to eat, runners from previous years who had been undocumented DACA kids, runners who excelled beyond expectations and those who fell short. He talked about spending money to buy kids running shoes as well as to purchase food and storing it in a freezer underneath the track stadium. He talked about his upbringing, his emigration from a poor section in rural Ireland in order to run and attend college in 1970s America. He talked, too, about the sublime pleasures of running and how he's relished passing along that love to generations of youth ("yutes," he pronounced it in his Irish brogue).

By the time we parted, it was all set. Starting in summer, I'd be following the Eisenhower team—every practice, every meeting, every pre-meet pasta feed, every jouncing bus ride, every early-morning drills session, every evening video review—for the entirety of the 2017 cross-country season.

"You'll see," Mister said (and, yes, it felt silly calling him "Mister," but everyone uses the nickname), "that there's more to this story than just running. A lot more. But the running part's pretty interesting, too, all right."

Mister, as he is about so many things, was right about that. In a few months' time, I would find myself spending every day in the presence of the 32 members of Eisenhower's cross-country team. I would watch them run with a joy and effortlessness that might well be the very definition of youth. I would listen to their hopes and dreams and overhear their terribly urgent adolescent psychodramas. I would learn about their sometimes challenging home lives—single-parent families, migrant farmworker parents, the stress of familial obligations versus the desire to be first-generation college students.

Above all, I would experience, through new eyes, the sheer joy of sport, of striving for goals that may or may not come to pass, of a bunch of kids, both unremarkable and extraordinary, who flame into being.

HOME STRETCH

They gather in the dimly lit hallway outside the locker rooms, as they had so many times these past few months. Only, on this chilly early November morning, it is two hours later than their customary dreary, bleary-eyed predawn practices, precursors to their *real* afternoon workouts in which they run, do some drills, run some more, and then do even more running. They stand, too, not in their mismatched everyday workout gear but in what best can be described as running formal wear: long-sleeved T-shirts of tech fabric, emblazoned with "Eisenhower Cross Country" across the chest, letters tilted slightly to the right to denote motion and speed; basic black nylon sweatpants, cut sleek and tapered along the legs, nothing baggy, nothing sagging. Their hair is combed, their faces scrubbed. They look sharp. Look sleek. Most important, they look fast. Freakin' fast.

Whenever the Eisenhower boys' and girls' cross-country teams don this ensemble, it sends a message to their classmates, to teachers, to staff. It means they will be leaving class early to do that weird cross-country thing they do, to go off to some far-flung locale for a meet in which they will run over hills and through the woods, along dirt paths and over terrain ranging from soggy turf to rock-strewn roads. Few among their peers know where these meets take place, much less what exactly goes on there—*you mean, low scores are good?*—and nearly the whole season has gone by without a single cheerleader or pep-squad member deigning to show up and root for what is, by far, the school's most successful team. Hell, it's Eisenhower's *only* fall sports team to win its league and district titles and garner top-10 rankings in Washington's largest and most competitive division. No fewer than five trophy cases, holding 30 years of memorabilia from Eisenhower's seven state titles and 25 podium finishes, line the halls on the upper floor of the enclosed campus (most cases, not coincidentally, are directly outside the door to coach Phil English's science classroom); to the bulk of the student body, these adornments amount to little more than visual wallpaper.

But to the runners, nervously milling around waiting for their cue to start the procession, this day means everything. On this day, they will be leaving school for a 70-mile drive south to the Tri-Cities suburb of Pasco to prepare for the state meet. State! That's the verbal shorthand they all use. State!

As in, we need to make it to *State*.

As in, we have to stay healthy for *State*, so we're wearing these surgical masks around school for three weeks because Mister and our other coaches make us.

As in, can we somehow improve upon our rankings—fifth for the boys, eighth for the girls—and find a way to the podium at *State*?

As in, we know those white guys from Spokane—Central Valley and Lewis and Clark—may have more runners out for the team and more money for fancy running gear, and the trust-funders at that private school, Bellarmine Prep in Tacoma, have all the so-called advantages. But, hey, at *State*, it all comes down to who can run the fastest and, you better believe it, we brown boys and girls from the ag fields will bring it come Saturday and, no doubt, Yakima will *represent*.

As in, we've been working our asses off since June in 90-degree heat, through a scrim of choking smoke from summer wildfires, some of us coming to practice still sweating buckets after picking cherries all day, others overcoming injuries that would make any other student stay in bed for a week, all of us running mile after lung-searing mile through apple and pear orchards, cutting through jagged, high-desert canyons, and traveling on overnight trips to line up against the best in Washington and Oregon—all that to prepare for, yeah, you guessed it—*State*.

And now State is almost here. The chartered bus is right outside, engine idling, exhaust spewing, waiting to whisk them away. But Mister, well, he isn't about to let the moment pass without some school-wide recognition, some acknowledgment of all of the work his runners have put in these past months. So that's why they are standing in the hallway in the final few minutes before the bell will ring at 8 a.m. and first period will begin. Mister, as they all call their coach, Phil English, has planned a "send-off" for the team, a five-minute walk through the school cafeteria during the final minutes of the daily free breakfast time. Five whole minutes of glory, man. The pep band will play the fight song, the seniors on the team will hand the district and league championship trophies to the student-body president (before said trophies will find their way back into the cases near Mister's room), and the runners will toss candy and cross-country T-shirts to their captive pre–first period audience. The team tries to act cool, shrug off the ceremony. But they buzz with excitement. Finally, Mister arrives, lugging boxes filled with yellow T-shirts and bags of candy. The team digs in, holding candy in both hands and T-shirts under their arms. They are eager to get going on the bus, but the send-off is something no one wants to miss.

"A lot of you just throw the candy to the first 10 people you see," Mister says with customary clipped seriousness. "No! Don't do that. You have nothing left later down the line."

Near the back, seniors Rogelio Mares and Jesus Gonzalez lock eyes and smile. *Sheesh, really?* their looks seem to say. *Mister needs to school us how to throw freakin' candy?* Apparently so. For Mister never leaves anything to chance. This is a man, after all, who makes the kids wear surgical masks during flu season; a man who instructs them to take iron supplements to keep their ferritin levels in normal range; who buys a fancy device to give real-time readings of each runner's hematocrit levels to measure the oxygenation of their blood prior to workouts; who keeps the refrigerator and freezer in the team shed stocked with protein- and complex-carbohydrate-laden foods for runners to eat in that all-important 20-minute window after a hard run; who forbids them from ingesting any Halloween candy a few days before State because he feels processing massive doses of sugar could "shut down your pancreas"; who swaddles the runners' wrists with white athletic tape and has them carry Popsicle sticks in their closed hands during races to promote all-important arm swing and hand placement; who lately has taken to having each runner put a golf ball under her or his chin when doing uphill or downhill training to emphasize proper forward lean; who videotapes each runner's stride and breaks it down to the minutest detail to expose the tiniest inefficiency of movement; whose scientific approach to the sport is such that pre-running drills he introduced three decades ago now are standardized for every team in the state.

So, yeah, Mister is absolutely going to school them on candy-throwing strategy. And do the runners listen? You bet they do. Because they trust him. Because they know, despite his oft-gruff exterior and Catholic piety, he cares. Because, to some kids from single-parent families, he is as close to a father figure as they get. Because these mostly minority runners know just enough about Mister's own immigrant story—a rural, low-income childhood in 1960s Ireland; an adolescence spent running competitively, hoping his athletic ability would lead to a college scholarship in the United States; more than three decades in Yakima coaching first Carroll High School (closed in the mid-'80s) and Eisenhower to 11 state titles, total—to make them think he just might understand their lives, their hopes and dreams.

But such implicit trust does not mean that the runners fail to challenge him. There in the hallway, they win a concession. They will not have to wear the surgical masks while walking through the gauntlet of students for the send-off. Embarrassing enough that they must wear them in every class and even at lunch.

The runners are getting restless, shifting weight from one leg to the other in the hallway. The dull murmur of conversation from the distant cafeteria makes them antsy. ¡Vámonos!

"Hey, Mister," senior Molly Stephenson asks, raising her hand. "Can we just keep these shirts? It's annoying to see kids wearing our shirts around."

Fonzi Cuevas, the charismatic junior and most vocal member of the boys' team, perks up.

"Yeah," he says. "They take our T-shirts, but they still make fun of us."

And here Fonzi adopts a haughty, nasal tone, pretending to be a "typical" Eisenhower student: "They'll say, like, 'You're in cross-country? That's not even a sport.' And they say that while they're *wearing our shirts!*"

"All right now. Enough. You *are* passing out the shirts. That's what we've always done."

Mister speaks with finality, and the matter is quickly dropped. The runners know when to push things with Mister and when to back off. It comes with familiarity. Strangers might see English's half-smile, half-grimace and not know whether to take it to mean irritation or amusement or both. He has arresting blue-green eyes, made starker still by a shock of hair now considerably more gray than black. A slight overbite gives his smile a slightly feral—or maybe just devilish—quality, as if he is trying to put something over on you.

Now though, Mister's jaw muscles flex, and his temples throb. Impatience is mounting. Time to get the send-off going and then get going to Pasco, to State. He can hear the muted strains of the pep band waft over from the cafeteria. He flips his wrist over to glance at his watch, which he always wears facedown.

"OK, let's get moving. Girls first, then boys."

Mister does not just hand the trophies from Eisenhower's league and district titles to the four seniors; he gently bestows the hardware upon them with all due solemnity. Erica Simison and Molly Stephenson seem ill at ease, slightly embarrassed, hoisting two-foot bronze-plated statues of runners cast in mid-stride. They have earned it, all right, but to these veterans, State is all that matters. Rogelio and Moises Cook gleefully snatch the boys' title trophies, mock arguing about which one will carry the larger of the two.

When the runners finally take off, they don't exactly walk; they saunter, as if in a solemn procession, a la a wedding or funeral. No one smiles. Isn't this supposed to be a stirring event? A strange sight, indeed, for these are high-energy teens who do nothing lackadaisically. Perhaps they want to make the moment last. Perhaps they are wondering what type of reaction— or nonreaction—their appearance in the cafeteria will elicit. This is, after all, the morning of the big crosstown rival football game between Eisenhower and Davis High Schools, both winless in league play; banners adorn the hallway walls, and buzz about the game has echoed on campus all week. In any event, the send-off will all be over in less than five minutes, and then the teams can board the bus for Pasco and, in less than two hours, be among their "own kind," the wider cross-country family, at State.

Meanwhile, in the cafeteria, the band stops playing, and the last trays of breakfast food—sausages and waffles, McMuffin-like sandwiches and breakfast burritos—are cleared away, though a greasy aroma lingers. The commons area, which includes the cafeteria, is filling up now, 10 minutes before the first bell. Eisenhower has an enrollment of just over 2,000, and many linger in the cafeteria area to take advantage of the free breakfast provided at the low-income school. So a captive audience awaits the runners. Some tables have been moved from the center and some smooshed together so that a pathway could be formed for the runners to pass through. The band has its drum line and tubas and trombones on one side, its armada of saxophone players on the other. The cheerleaders, clad in blue skirts with red-and-white trim and wielding pom-poms like weapons, are out in force, not a single no-show.

Up on a second-floor balcony, where a four-foot, framed black-and-white photograph of the school's namesake, Dwight D. Eisenhower, looms over the student body from a wall, assistant cross-country coach Robert

Price, Mister's top lieutenant and father of Jonas, the team's fastest runner, stands with a microphone. He keeps glancing toward the mouth of the hallway, where the runners will soon emerge. At the first flash of blue-and-red rounding the corner, he shouts into the mic:

"Gooooood morning, Ike! At this time, we present to you your league and district champion cross-country teams . . ."

Scattered applause, primarily from the band members. A few pom-pom shakes but not exactly a heartfelt welcoming.

"They are heading off to State as they proceed here . . ." Price intones, and this time there is heartier clapping and even a few "woo-hoos" from students.

The runners now emerge from the shadows, Erica and Molly leading the girls. Each is holding a trophy somewhat precariously, Erica with the league championship cup that spans from just under her chin nearly to her waist, and Molly cradling the district trophy in the crook of her arm like a football. What isn't at first apparent, but is astonishing to anyone close to the team, is that Erica and Molly are holding hands—a show of solidarity and bonding noticeably absent for most of the season. Wasn't it just a few months before that these two were sniping at each other—nothing at all passive about their aggressiveness—at a tense team meeting up in the mountains at White Pass? Wasn't Molly calling out Erica—by far the team's best runner—for her haughtiness, and Erica, with her tight hair bun and Mona Lisa smile, was flatly stating that the girls' team—and that means even you, Molly—just doesn't care enough to train hard? Erica's 5-foot, 95-pound frame is one thing; her stature is quite another. She carries herself in a confident upright manner, wears to practice T-shirts from elite meets at which the other girls can only hope someday to compete. Molly, on the other hand, is 5-foot-6, solidly built, literally a farmer's daughter, who is garrulous and outgoing.

So their hand-holding while leading the procession? Maybe it is a sign of good things to come the next afternoon at State. The girls' team has spent most of the season unranked, struggling through injuries, illness, and personal problems. Mister fretted privately, early on, that the girls' team might not even win the league and district titles, breaking that 10-year streak Price boasts about on the PA system. The team's second-best runner, junior Dantzel Peterson, has struggled for two months with poor performances that Dantzel attributes to a lingering flu and chest-cold combination but that Mister and assistant coach Robin Bryson-Driver believe to be due to poor nutrition—namely, that Dantzel has not been consuming enough calories for the type of activities she is being asked to do. One of those classic teen overachievers, Dantzel is splitting her time between running and being a featured violinist for both the Yakima Youth Symphony and the all-state prep orchestra. She also is taking a bevy of difficult Advanced Placement (AP) classes and, as a devout member of the Church of Jesus Christ of Latter-day Saints, spends five mornings a week at Mormon seminary. Mister, well aware of the heightened risk of eating disorders among female cross-country runners, has taken note that Dantzel has lost close to five pounds during the season and seems as lethargic off the course as she has been on it, running in several races as much as two minutes slower than she had the previous season. But Dantzel rallied in the district meet, finishing only a few places behind Molly. As she follows teammates Madi Oliva and Sophi Rodriquez on the procession line in the cafeteria, she smiles brightly and tosses a few miniature candy bars to students—following, of course, Mister's mandate to spread the wealth.

"What these runners are holding, besides candy, are the championship trophies. Seniors Erica Simison and Molly Stephenson and boys Rogelio Mares and Moise Cook will hand the trophies to ASB President Brooklyn Cassel," Price shouts into the mic. "Brooklyn, where are you?"

Price has just finished announcing the girls' names, when the boys make their appearance. They approach with a certain swagger, amusing because most bear the thin, slightly gaunt frames common in runners logging up to 70 miles per week, week after week for several months. Somehow they manage to pull off a degree of bravado. Rogelio smiles broadly, his wide mouth extended almost to his ears. He is carrying candy, along with the district trophy, so, of course, one of his teammates has to crack something to the effect of, "Hey, try not to eat all of it, Rogelio." By now Rogelio is accustomed to the good-natured ribbing. Four years earlier, as a freshman, Rogelio was 40 pounds heavier and eight minutes slower over 5K as a runner; now, as a senior, lighter and fitter, he figures to finish among the top 20 runners at State—an amazing transformation that Mister relishes relating to audiences at his summer camp at White Pass, at school assemblies, and at the Yakima "Monday Morning Quarterback Club." Besides, Rogelio takes the ribbing because he, too, is always quick with a quip. He always exudes confidence, an easygoing attitude and ready smile belying an intense desire to succeed.

Mo, next to Rogelio, grasps the league trophy and raises it skyward when Price makes the announcement. At 6-foot-2, 160 pounds, Mo is not built like a cross-country runner; and, at heart, he isn't one. He was a state qualifier in the 800-meter in track, but through Mister's cajoling, he has developed into a solid No. 5 runner on the team. Mo knows (mostly because Mister has told him, again and again) that a good performance by him at State may make the difference between gaining a podium spot or finishing where the team was ranked (fifth), or even below. His countenance, therefore, seems pensive slightly more than 24 hours before race time. Angel Cuevas, the team's No. 4 runner, likewise has been pegged by Mister as a key to the race, but all week Angel has been as dispassionate as always, enigmatic, hard to read. Mister is only slightly exaggerating when he says that, in four years, Angel has barely spoken more than a paragraph's worth of sentences to him. But the guy has always run hard, if not always fast, and his fierceness will be needed, Mister believes, at State.

If Mo and Angel are expert at hiding their emotions, even with the student body now cheering for them and cheerleaders shaking pom-poms at them, the opposite is true with Fonzi. Always with Fonzi, what you see is what you get. When he races well, he is all smiles, ebullient, radiating joy as if lit from within. When he races poorly, his face all but collapses, his smooth forehead crinkling in worry lines, his eyes narrowing. In those instances, he loses his battle to fight back tears. He cries with impunity and pouts, but maybe half an hour later will be back joking and chatting up teammates. He is perhaps the most popular runner among teammates and well liked around school, showing a penchant for mimicry, dead-on comic timing, a vast pop culture and hip-hop knowledge, and smarts in school. Fonzi is the go-to guy when teammates have calculus questions, volunteering his tutoring services. Yet, lighthearted as Fonzi can be, he has to deal with a difficult home life. He is one of nine in a small three-bedroom house; his mother, Sonya, the lone breadwinner. Sonya Cuevas has taken in seven of her troubled eldest daughter's children in a foster-parent arrangement, and often, Fonzi has to assume domestic responsibilities most 16-year-olds never face.

But what has bothered Fonzi most this season has been his running. Last year, as a sophomore, he finished fifth at State and was heralded as a contender for state champion this year. But injuries and a growth spurt, coupled with an acute loss of confidence, have seen Fonzi fall to No. 3 among Eisenhower runners for most of the season, a precipitous and troubling drop in status. Much as he wants to believe he can repeat his breakout performance at State, Fonzi fears that last year's finish was a fluke, frets that he simply doesn't have the talent to consider himself elite. Sophomore Jonas Price has leapfrogged Fonzi all season and become a real threat to win State, which has hurt Fonzi's pride. Combine that with the fact that Rogelio, Fonzi's best friend, has beaten him at many meets this year, and the whole situation has plunged him into a funk.

If all that weighed on Fonzi, it doesn't show as he walks down the gauntlet. A brown-eyed girl, clearly drawn by his 1,000-watt smile, waves to Fonzi; and Fonzi, ever cool, runs a hand through his short black curls and motions for the girl to meet him at the end of the procession, where he'll hook her up with a T-shirt. He flashes those dazzlingly, wolfish white incisors at her, and she scurries off.

Mister follows closely behind, bringing up the rear with Bryson-Driver. The coach shakes his head at Fonzi being, well, Fonzi. Just in front of the coaches is Jonas, the last runner. This, undoubtedly, will be the only time Jonas Price will be so far behind the pack. He has emerged as perhaps one of Eisenhower's all-time best runners—and the damnedest thing is that the kid is just getting started. Like his father—but unlike his older brother, Ronan, who also starred at Eisenhower before graduating in 2017—Jonas is obsessed with running, totally smitten with the sport. That drive, more than the fact that Jonas is the only white runner on the boys' varsity, is what sets him apart from his teammates, who occasionally look askance at him when this scrawny sophomore, all bones and sharp edges, starts to call them out for not putting in the effort during practice. Fonzi, though slightly envious of Jonas's ascension, has defended Jonas's youthful outbursts, because Fonzi knows just what an effort it takes to be an elite runner and, after injuries and other circumstances, to try to stay one. But Jonas, unlike Fonzi, has had a nearly flawless season, each performance building upon the previous one. And he is not shy in stating his goal: nothing less than winning the state individual title. His teammates haven't razzed him about it; in fact, they nod in assent. They see how hard he trains and how fast he runs and, you know, the guy just might do it.

Now Jonas seems annoyed at being stuck near the back of the send-off. He inches his way up to the middle, next to his buddies, brothers Jonathan and Nathan Valenzuela. Just then, overhead, his dad wraps up the spiel.

"So at this time," Robert Price shouts, like a frenzied game-show host, "team members, what are you going to do?"

No one responds. The candy bags remain ziplocked, except for those of some girls who jump the gun. Mister winces. Hasn't he given them explicit instructions? Kids, these days.

"Throw candy, you knuckleheads," Price shouts. "One . . . two . . . three . . . Throw! Throw it!"

Flying shrapnel of miniature candy bars sprays the crowd. This, finally, gets the intended reaction from the students, who roar and scuttle along the ground to retrieve the offerings.

"Strike up the band!" Price intones. "Let's go to State."

The drum line, on cue, does multiple paradiddles. The band director raises his arms and points skyward, and then the brass kicks in, big time. The band powers through the fight song, not once but three times. The trombonists lift their instruments up and down, the tuba players' fingers work furiously, and the sax line swivels back and forth in unison. The cheerleaders do their steps and kicks. Mister stops to offer a T-shirt to one, but she ignores him, focused as she is on her routine. Fonzi has found his intended T-shirt recipient, but when other students try to hit him up, he raises both hands, empty palms up, to show he's run out of swag to bestow.

The runners, at last, do what Mister instructed and evenly distribute the candy to the waiting hands of students. OK, actually, the boys rear back and fire candy as far toward the hallway as they can. After the band's final rendition and the obligatory chant of "go, fight, win, Ike" to put an exclamation point on the send-off, the team reaches the double glass doors at the front of the school, and the runners are considered sent off.

"Let's go out this way," Molly, up front, says. "It'd be awkward to walk back through after all that."

So, as the first-period bell rings, the runners circle around the perimeter of the campus to where the chartered bus is parked at the back of the school. As they board, many of the boys are still guffawing at their candy-throwing antics, some boasting about hitting guys squarely in the forehead with treats.

The mood, however, swiftly becomes subdued as Mister walks aboard and takes his customary seat in the front.

"Masks on!" he barks.

And the runners rummage through their backpacks and dutifully fit the masks over their mouths and noses as if they're surgeons preparing to remove a gallbladder. After all, slightly more than 24 hours remain before the races, still time to come down with a cold and blow the team's hopes at State. Mister isn't taking any chances. It has been a trying season and, more than anything, Mister wants it to end with the runners feeling good about themselves. Even if the boys' and girls' teams do not improve on their ranking, even if they aren't able to knock off one or two of those rich-kid teams, all that matters to him in the end is whether they run well and to their capabilities, harboring no excuses or regrets.

Mister thinks that, all right, and plans to tell the runners that very thing in meetings later that night. But, come on, this is Phil English, the feisty, bare-knuckled Irishman, born competitor. He wants to *win*—or at least prevent others from doing so. And because of the fighting spirit, the pursuit of excellence, he has imbued in his runners, they will not buy this "just run hard" stuff either. They haven't trained for six months just to be happy to qualify. Let 'em loose on the course. See what happens.

With a pneumatic whoosh of finality, the bus doors close. Next stop, Pasco.

PRESEASON

CAMP GHORMLEY

Sometimes you just have to get away, to escape the heat and wildfire smoke-congested sky and, well, just flee the oppressive sameness of another Yakima summer. That funky reggaeton song "Despacito" is still playing on every car radio in town. Crank it up once more, why not, and hit the road.

This is late August, after all, only a scant few weeks before the Eisenhower High cross-country team will embark on another season brimming with high expectations and freighted with responsibility to live up to past success. Training is getting serious now—OK, *more* serious—so it seems to be the perfect time to seek higher ground, where the temperature drops and stately pine trees rise up, where the runners and coaches can spend three days together without the distractions of family obligations or jobs, whether it be Angel Cuevas picking cherries and peaches in a scorching orchard, or Antonio Heredia packing apples in a cold warehouse.

Among team members earlier in the summer, the buzz was that Mister might do away with the Camp Ghormley trip this year. Some wondered whether the week in July spent up at the White Pass ski area, alongside many teams from throughout the state and as far away as Alaska, would be it as far as retreats were concerned. But that's all it was—just talk. They know Mister. They know that Phil English doesn't discard tradition so easily. There were a few years, granted, when the team eschewed Camp Ghormley, the Christian retreat at 4,000 feet on the way to White Pass, in favor of other venues. But, sure enough, in the waning weeks of August after completing workout after workout at the same series of parks orbiting

Eisenhower—Gilbert, Franklin, Carroll, Randall, Chesterley—with occasional forays out to "the Rez," the orchards lining the Yakama Nation tribal lands, the Eisenhower Cadets are on the march. They come on this morning, as they do every year, with enough gear to last a month, everything from sleeping bags and snacks to drawers full of T-shirts and shorts for the twice-daily workouts. Too much stuff, Mister grouses. That, too, is expected. Mister, every year, faux-grouchily grumbles at his runners that they "bring so much it looks like you're running away from home," and the runners just smile and nod knowingly because Mister has stayed true to form. And for a group of mostly low-income teenagers whose home lives can be easily uprooted or may lack stability, such consistency in an authority figure can be both comforting and exasperating.

So they meet on a Friday afternoon in the school parking lot and fling their duffle bags, backpacks, and sleeping bags into the bed of Mister's hulking red Ford F-350 pickup before squeezing into the cab. Or they choose to stash their gear in the bed of assistant coach Robert Price's slightly less hulking but nearly identical red Ford F-150 and cruise winding Highway 12 with the track-and-field banter of Price dad and son, Jonas, riding shotgun. New people always make note of how Mister and Price own similar trucks, and they make the obvious joke that the protégé is trying to be a "Mini-Mister," but by this point, the team hardly even takes note. Some runners, mainly the girls, opt to ride in assistant coach Robin Bryson-Driver's Subaru Forester, or the media-savvy among the crew catch a lift with Fonzi's mom, Sonya Cuevas, who got roped into driving on this, her only day off from work. The advantage, many say, of this latter choice is that Fonzi has full radio hegemony and he remembers to bring his aux cable to blare hip-hop. Much better, the guys say, than Mister's lame 100.9 Cherry FM, playing '80s hits, though no one, of course, would dare make the comment to Mister, who in any event hasn't made the slightest effort to stay up-to-date with current pop culture. When the boys go off on one of their extended riffs about the video game *Injustice League 2*, they might as well be talking about life on Mars for all Mister knows about it. That is the way the team likes it. It would be somehow inauthentic, or just plain weird, if Mister were to change his ways at this late date and try to make a vain stab at youthful hipness.

The gaggle of runners milling around and giggling is as usual, but at 2 p.m. sharp, as the itinerary notes, they hit the road. The mood this year is not quite as festive as usual. There are microscopic rifts on the team to be mended, challenges to be laid down, goals to address. Every season has its issues, naturally, but this time Mister considers it more pronounced. It both is and is not easy to be a runner for one of the state's top cross-country programs, to run for a coach whose teams at Eisenhower (and earlier, the now-closed Carroll High) have won 11 state titles, 10 state runner-up places, 42 district titles, and 43 league titles. Easy, because as coaches, the runners have at their disposal English, one of Ireland's top distance runners in the 1970s who helped Washington State to podium finishes in NCAA cross-country nationals three times; Price, a former 1992 Olympic trials steeplechase competitor who won eight state prep team and individual titles in cross-country and track running for Mister at Carroll High; and Driver, the 1988 state champion at Eisenhower and Division 1 runner at the University of Texas. And, in Mister, who has a master's degree in exercise physiology, the runners have exposure to the latest theories in biomechanics and efficient running movement and all sorts of contraptions and measurement devices that he often pays for out of his own pocket. Mister's contacts in the running world are such that Eisenhower is one of the few schools in the state that receives partial sponsorship from the running-shoe manufacturer Brooks, and Eisenhower occasionally receives returned or factory-rejected shoes from a Seattle running store. When a Cadet runner cannot afford a new pair of shoes, Mister simply jogs to a locked room, dubbed "Mister's shoe closet," above the school gym and finds a pair to give the kids. If Mister rummages around and cannot find the right size, he often goes to the local sporting good stores and shells out a hundred bucks of his own money to take care of the problem. In fact, resting on the floorboards of Mister's truck on the trip to camp are two Nike boxes for Jesus Gonzalez, who has literally worn holes through trainers he's used for more than a year and who for the past few days had the indignity of wearing a pair of white-and-pink girls' Asics because they were the only shoes in Mister's closet that fit him.

So, yes, being part of this program has advantages. But running for Ike also has its stressors. Mister, as his sobriquet implies, can be a taskmaster whose expectations, some feel, are higher than the Seattle Space Needle. In the community, too, Eisenhower simply is expected to win its league and district titles every year—mostly because, well, it always does—and make a strong bid for a top-five state place. At times, too, the team's Hispanic runners, especially, on the boys' side, feel as if they are carrying the expectations of Yakima's significant migrant community. Perhaps to be expected from a school whose mascot is a ramrod-straight soldier holding a rifle in parade-rest position, the program is run with great discipline. Mister employs a series of tedious and rote, but beneficial, drills, many of which he developed himself but some he cribbed from visiting Eastern Bloc countries in the 1980s, to teach proper running form. Such exactitude of purpose and laser focus on performance can be wearying to teenagers, and many feel obligated to try even harder because Mister has helped them out by providing food, clothing, shoes, and even help with family issues. Runners don't want to disappoint Mister, and they feel not winning would mean letting him down, though Mister professes to anyone who asks that "maximum effort," not winning, is what he wants from his kids.

And it is primarily effort, or a lack of same, that figures in the "issues" the team will be trying to hash out starting at its Friday night meeting and continuing nearly nonstop until returning to Yakima on Sunday afternoon. The situation with the girls' team is particularly fraught, given that the same interpersonal relationships and performance issues that saw the girls barely retain their district title (by a scant three points to crosstown rival Davis High) last season have lingered. To wit: Erica would run up front, and then you had to wait a *looong* time for the next Eisenhower runner. Erica Simison, one of the 4A division's top returners, is at least a minute and a half faster than any other Ike girl and a good three minutes ahead of the team's fifth and final scorer. In cross-country terms, the Ike girls' "gap" between first and fifth is way too big. Of course, the issue is not to have Erica slow down but to try to get the others to move up incrementally so they can at least see the top of Erica's hair bun for part of a race. And, on Erica's part, she seems to harbor no interest whatsoever in helping her teammates improve through encouragement or bonding. All summer, she has either run with the boys' pack or run by herself, telling the coaches and her teammates that running with the girls would hurt her. Mister can understand her thinking, but where he differs is in Erica's attitude, which he sees as haughty and elitist. He wants to run her easy days with the girls, and Erica has done that for a few minutes on some summer days before inevitably opening up a gaping distance between her and the rest. He also wants her to deign to at least warm up and do drills with the girls, but so far she has mostly refused. Beyond the Erica divide, and all of the teenage psychodrama it entails, the girls have a commitment problem, in Mister's estimation. Many skipped vast stretches of summer workouts. Dantzel, the second-fastest runner, was at a three-week summer Mormon reunion in Utah and, when she returned, complained of tiredness, which Mister suspected to be a combination of not consuming enough calories and/or low ferritin levels. Dantzel, both a hotshot violinist and runner, continues to deny a problem exists. Minelly

Sereno spent nearly a month visiting relatives in Mexico; and others, such as Madi Oliva, Izzy Gutierrez, and Sophi Rodriguez just blew off nearly all of the morning workouts. Mister detects a disturbing pattern, one he's never had to face before in his coaching career because, on balance, he's had more success with his girls' program than with the boys'. The close call on the girls' district title last year hardly seems to faze the returning runners, Mister feels, and that is the problem. Do they even care about Eisenhower's tradition, as well as its streak of 10 straight district crowns? "Tell you what," Price says, "if they lose Districts this year, you'll see screaming headlines in the local paper. It'll be a big deal."

Ike's boys, for their part, face subtler problems that may be beyond their power to fix. The team is nothing if not bonded and together. All but Jonas, who is white, and Mo Cook, black and adopted from Haiti as an infant, are Hispanic and from similar socioeconomic backgrounds. Many come from single-parent families, often extended families, with absent fathers and challenging, if not severe, money issues. But their circumstances aren't what particularly bonded them; rather, it is their love of running, love of video games, and overall esprit de corps that extends to the Eisenhower campus, where they lord it over their domain—the unofficially designated "cross-country table" in Eisenhower's spacious indoor lunch area. What concerns Mister is that the boys may be *too* comfortable with each other, will not push one another in workouts and races in the manner that separates great teams from the merely very good. There is little worry up front, where the über-focused Jonas and mentally tough Fonzi often battle it out, but the fire and intensity of the rest of the pack need work, according to Mister. Rogelio, coming off a breakthrough track season in which he finished third in the district 3,200 meters, beating the injury-plagued Fonzi, has stayed with the top two all summer, but the question remains: Will that be enough? The Ike boys are ranked third, behind Central Valley (from the Spokane area) and defending champion Bellarmine Prep (from Tacoma) in the preseason poll; and to beat either rival, Eisenhower will have to improve its placing of its fourth and fifth runners—as well as keep the nonscoring sixth and seventh runners in contention in case someone up front is having an off race. And Mister openly wonders, *Do they want it enough to make the effort, or will they be content with another third-place "podium" finish, like last season?*

All that will begin to be hashed out this weekend, in a series of team meetings in the Christian retreat's main lodge, where an imposing 30-foot cross hangs from the alpine ceiling near a stone fireplace. When Mister stands before the cross to lecture, it always gives him a somewhat messianic appearance. The teams will have some structured fun, of course. There is the annual Giant Jenga showdown between the boys and girls, and the lively debate over the design and slogan for the coming season's T-shirts. But there also will be some soul-searching. Runners already have been not-so-silently stressing about Mister's individual meeting with each runner to go over goals, explore deficiencies, and applaud a few positives. Over the years, many a tear has been shed at these tête-à-têtes; many a head has been hung. But also, many a runner has emerged with a sense of purpose, a new spring in her or his step, a renewed commitment to personal and team goals.

Right now, though, as the convoy rolls into Ghormley's tree-lined gravel roads and stops next to the log-cabin dining hall, the runners are told to stow their gear in two rooms with six bunk beds each. The girls cop the dorm room closest to the door; the boys are left with the one way in the rear, the coaches' quarters wisely serving as a buffer. It is a mad scramble for the choicest bunk, and Mister can only hope that the workout that is only 15 minutes away—"15 minutes, I mean it guys, 15; meet outside!"— will be as lively. He and the other coaches retreat to the lodge to set up a printer and connect Mister's HP laptop for the one-on-one interviews that will commence on Saturday. They look more like corporate executives at a retreat than prep sports coaches. Camp, to Mister, is all business.

* * *

Mister unrolls the butcher paper and deputizes Ivan Alfaro, a former Ike runner who is deaf, mute, and 80 percent blind but has served ably as an assistant coach the past four years, to tape it to the wall, one sheet on each side of the fireplace. Each team, as if on some corporate retreat, will brainstorm overall team goals, both for times and place, for the season, breaking it down meet by meet as well. The last item, clear at the bottom of the list but looming large, is one word: *State*. Before handing out the Sharpies to the runners with the most legible handwriting, Mister lays down the ground rules in a short speech and then promises to remain mum until the task is completed.

"We want to take stock where we are right now," Mister says. "With that, *why* are we where we are. If we don't know where we are, that's not going to be very productive. The discussion with the girls needs to be different than the boys. Two different circumstances. If we leave here and everybody's not quite clear on why we're doing what we're doing, that's not very productive."

The runners do not dare look away from Mister. Nobody has his or her smartphone out, partly because only those with Verizon coverage have service but mostly because they know from experience that Mister demands full attention. Then again, Erica is braiding Molly's hair, a thawing in relations between the two seniors; Dantzel is drawing a pencil sketch of a house and garden; and sophomore Nathan Valenzuela is fighting the urge to nod off. Yet Mister is on a roll, and most appear genuinely interested, if not enthralled.

"If we're going to have the success that some of you want—I don't know if all of you want it, but some of you—then we're going to have to do something different than we've ever done before. That's what training is all about. You do something you never thought possible. Understand?"

Heads nod.

"We can't move forward without this. We've put two sheets of paper on the wall. Evaluate where we are. Go to it. We'll meet back up in a while and go over it together."

The boys' conversation is animated and, frankly, loud. There is much cross talk, a few playful slugs in the shoulder, and high fives. They have no disagreements over goals, though a few times personal records are debated. Fonzi unearths the results of the 2016 races that Mister has hole-punched and put in three-ring binders for each runner, and he shouts out each runner's time and what other teams, such as Central Valley, Lewis and Clark, and Bellarmine, ran as well. Too bad the Sharpie doesn't have an eraser because, soon, the sheet of paper is riddled with cross-outs. Still, within 10 minutes, the boys are done. The penmanship might have been weak, but the goals are lofty. In each invitational, the boys list a top-three or top-five finish as a goal and predict some heady individual times, such as three sub-16-minute finishes and two more sub-16:30 at Fort Steilacoom, the first major invitational in late September; and top-three team finishes both at the Sunfair Invitational, which Ike hosts, and the Richland Invite. For the Districts, one simple goal: "Win and qualify for State." For State? No exact team-finish prediction, but an ambitious goal to have their top-five (scoring) runners all finish under 16:10 on the 5K course. If that happens, assuming Fonzi and Jonas place among the top-10 individual finishers, Eisenhower will have a shot at upsetting Central Valley and that school's impressive display of "pack" running.

Across the room, the girls are much quieter—and taking much longer. Erica is fidgety, mostly because she is planning to leave with Bryson-Driver right after the meeting to return to Yakima in order to take the SAT (Scholastic Aptitude Test) in the morning. (She will return Saturday afternoon in time for the traditional and vertically challenging 12- or 16-mile run up Bethel Ridge Road.) But Erica also doesn't like what she hears. When several girls list as a goal to get in better shape, Erica huffs. "The season's *starting*. You should be in shape *right now*." Molly chimes in, "How about to get in *better* shape?" Awkward silences punctuate the girls' huddle.

At last, Mister intervenes, drawing the two groups together. He tells the boys to sit tight; they are going to evaluate the girls first. He doesn't say it, but everybody knows: This will take a while. The first problem is that the girls' sheet is only partially filled out. Perhaps meaningfully, and certainly conspicuously, they have left the sheet blank under the heading "State." Mister lets that omission slide for a moment and looks at what the girls have put down next to the two league meets. They write for the first meet, "Top 3 in top 5—varsity (all) top 25," then put an arrow to the second and write, "Hold on to those spots! League Title!"

"Are you sure that's going to be enough to do it this year?" Mister mutters.

Molly purses her lips.

"We think so, Mister, don't you?"

"Well . . . let's go to the districts. You say 'varsity district champs.' Great, but you don't say how you are going to do it."

Some snickers come from the boys' side of the room. Mister shoots the group a raised-eyebrow rebuke, and Price barks, "Can it, guys!" The boys, in what later will be considered a first for them and a tremendous achievement in self-control, remain silent for the next half hour while Mister attends to the girls.

"Let's talk about Erica—again," he says. "Like I said at White Pass over the summer, how do you think not having her run with you is going to affect the team? She's not going to be jumping into the boys' race once the season starts, right?"

Sophi: "Molly's really stepped it up and pushed us."

Molly shakes off the compliment. She admits that her summer training lacked intensity and focus.

"I think we all have a good understanding of where Erica is and why she doesn't run with us," Molly says, trying to will her voice into a deadpan but failing.

"But that's not the way this team can function, though," Mister says. "If she continues to train with the boys, she's going to wreck her season. She won't be able to recover. She's not physically as strong as those guys. It's counterproductive. By all means, she'll run some workouts with the JV boys during the season, but not what she's doing right now. It *will* affect the team. Remember, Dantzel, you spent a lot of last year trying to run with Erica [in workouts] and you benefited from it. Now she's no longer there. Yeah, you're running with Molly, all right, Dantzel, but are you getting the same type of workout?"

Dantzel rakes her hand through her shoulder-length blond hair, which falls so that it partially covers her face.

"Is that a rhetorical question, Mister?"

Izzy, team cutup, laughs. She is the only one to do so. "We're bringing up literary terms now?" she asks. No one answers. They apparently know the question is not rhetorical.

Mister clears his throat.

"A compromise has to be reached," he says, "and we'll have one before we leave camp."

Dantzel parts the curtains of her hair. "There's such a big gap," she says. "It's hard. It's either I'm going to kill myself today trying to stay with Ric [Erica] or be dead in the workout tomorrow. You get so tired. It's hard for me to, like, step over the edge but not die. I feel it's hard to even go after her [Erica] for a little while."

"Sometimes," Erica says, voice even, gaze steady on Mister, "I'll start off with them, and then it's like, what's going on? Then the boys took the first part of summer easy, so I was able to run with them."

"But, Erica, the boys' easy day is still going to be hard for you, and that's really dangerous. You aren't getting enough recovery," Mister says.

"I've just gotten so used to a pace over the summer. Just the sheer change of pace [with the girls] is like, what am I doing? The term steady is really different between me and [pause] someone else."

"You see their steady as going slow?"

"Yeah, Mister. It's probably not slow to them, but it feels extremely slow to me."

Mister pauses, scans the girls in chairs and sitting cross-legged on the floor. He sighs.

"Sometimes," he says, "it is slow."

Several girls wince.

Mister changes the subject.

"Going back to what Dantzel said, if the gap is that big, do you girls have any idea how far you're going to be back in the race? The team is not going to be successful if there's that kind of gap. Now, let's talk about your confidence level, girls."

The girls all look away. Mister squinches his bushy gray brows and raises a hand.

"Where does the low confidence come from, from us or yourselves?" Mister's voice is soothing, a broguish lilt, not at all accusatory.

Sophi breaks the stalemate and levels her gaze at Mister.

"We're busting our ass in a workout and are dead in the end, and we know we worked hard, and then it's hard to hear from you that's not good enough, you could've gone faster, your form could've been better. It's a lot of criticism," she says. "It's always just what goes wrong."

Dantzel emerges from her hair once more.

"There's no communication. . . . Everybody might not want to tell how they are feeling because a coach might not understand. This girl might've had something happen to her that day. She might've given everything she had in her entire body in practice, giving it everything she's got. And it might not be perfect, but that's all she's got. And then the coaches come over and say, 'You aren't running fast enough, your arms aren't going.' That's when the girls go, like, 'Ugh. I've given you all I have.'"

Bryson-Driver opens her mouth to speak, but Mister has beaten her to it.

"From our perspective, I don't think we ever ask you to 'run harder.' I never use that term. The whole focus is on technique. Speaking for the coaches in our defense, it appears as if there's very little effort is changing technique. It starts with the drills. No fatigue is involved. We'll never tell you, 'run harder,' in the middle of a race or a workout. That's counterproductive. What we will tell you is to fix something so that [breakdown] won't happen. What we felt last year is that the effort in making the change wasn't there, and a lot of it was due to immaturity. It's got nothing to do with running hard, Dantzel. I agree with you, 100 percent. All you can do in a day is what you've got."

Dantzel does not back down. She puffs out her cheeks, slightly reddened. "But you do tell us when we're exhausted and tired after a hard workout— just mentally, just trying mentally to move our body forward—you're telling us we're uncoachable and our form is crap and all this stuff. But all we can think about in workouts is just to get through it. You don't understand."

"OK," Mister counters, "but what about before the workout even starts? In drills. There's no fatigue at all doing drills. We work on this, and it appears there's no effort from you girls at all. How do you think we're going to interpret that? We're not asking you to do something you can't do. We're asking you to make a change. If your perception is that we're generating this low confidence, if that's your perception, then it's reality. And it is an issue. But success has to be important to you. If it isn't, you're going to have that cascade effect all the way down. What you're going to find is, the excuses come in. We got a lot of this last year, a lot of 'I don't feel well.' When you tell us that, what do you expect us to do with that?"

"Maybe nothing, Mister," Dantzel says. "Just let them run the workout and do what they need to do."

"But if someone says I don't feel well," Mister continues, sighing audibly, "we're going to stop her workout. Some of you are using that excuse every day. It's common. A litany of excuses. . . . It's finding ways of not being able to do things. You have to understand how many times this was used last year. Be honest."

"What happens if we're not crying wolf?" Izzy asks. "What if we really are struggling?"

"That's when we stop the workout."

Another pause. Dantzel furtively wipes a lone tear from her cheek. Mister hitches his pants and points toward the boys.

"Let me tell you about Tony," he says, meaning Antonio Heredia, a senior who this year is vying for the seventh and last spot on the boys' varsity. Tony, all of a sudden, becomes very interested in the pattern of the wood planks in the floor.

"When he was a freshman all the way until last spring, Tony would give up mentally. He admitted that to us. You might know it as mental toughness. How hard you are on yourself. Running is not easy. Running hard, running fast, is not easy. You have to be in total control of your mental state in order to push your body. He readily admitted, when any type of pain set in, he'd find an excuse not to finish it. He'd go to the bathroom during workouts. Everybody knows this ploy. Tony knew it, and he had to overcome it. Some of you are in that same situation. . . . The first thing is to recognize it, like Tony, and overcome it. The thing with running, on a regular basis, is, you have to push yourself so that discomfort gets pushed back, pushed back, pushed back. If, at the first sign of discomfort or pain, you cave in, you'll never go beyond the first step. You'll never run fast because you're shutting down at the first sign of pain. It's like those PE classes where they have kids run a mile. A hundred meters in, half the class is walking at the first sign of discomfort."

Both sides of the room, boys and girls alike, laugh. It is more of an anxious release of emotion, as if to say, well, at least we aren't as bad as the kids in PE.

"The summer training can't be regained at this point, girls. We can only move forward. Hopefully, when you come out of this camp, you have to know yourself. If there are teammates who don't care about the success, and you're somebody whose whole future depends on it in terms of a college scholarship, we've got a problem. If they don't really care, they should be doing something else. Running is too hard not to care."

Mister claps his hands together and walks toward the boys, some slouching so much in their chairs that they are horizontal. Erica pops up, motions to Bryson-Driver to take her home so she can get some sleep before the SAT. The girls' portion of the meeting has run more than an hour, and Erica will not get back to her home until 10 p.m. The test starts at 8 a.m. "No problem," she says. "I'll be fine." Her teammates, however, look shell-shocked. Many stare at the floor as Mister starts the boys' portion of the meeting.

It is, in comparison, anticlimactic, utterly lacking in dramatics. If anything, the boys are harder on themselves than Mister is. They castigate each other for not running hard enough over the summer, even though nearly all of the top runners made every practice. Mister nods curtly.

"There's probably a half a dozen teams that have worked harder in the summer than you have," he says. "That's the reality. It doesn't mean they are going to be there at the end of the season. But at least right now."

"We didn't want to push ourselves enough," Fonzi says. "We were used to the easy workouts the first few weeks of summer. We kept that up most of the summer."

Jonas: "Not acceptable."

'Let's look at your sheet," Mister says, pivoting. "You put down as a strength 'team bonding.' Why?"

Jonas nearly jumps out of his chair.

"Because there's no one new on our team. Everyone knows everyone."

"True," Mister says, "but that doesn't necessarily mean relationships have improved. Sometimes, somebody new on a team can actually help chemistry. Do you see anything that's the downside in the relationships?"

Jonas is ready to challenge him. "But we've been having team bonding, breakfast and volleyball in the park."

"But, Jonas, how do you think no change in the team is going to affect the *running*? What's the problem, guys, in that when it comes to training and racing?"

Jesus mumbles, "You get too comfortable?"

"There you go. Exactly!" Mister brightens. "Who's the hammer on the team? Who pushes you?"

Fonzi doesn't hesitate. Brow furrowed, "I'd have to say Jonas."

Mister nods. "You're running along, and it's supposed to be a hard workout and then, you're leading the mile repeats, and maybe some guys aren't feeling it that day, but that's what needs to be done—a hard mile repeat. When you're doing it, no one's going to like you for pushing them, whoever that person is. It doesn't have to be Jonas. When you all get comfortable with yourselves like that, that's the fear. When you're supposed to be hitting 4:45 mile repeats, and you're at 5:10 because you don't want to push the pace, that's the problem. While the workout's going on, you don't have to like anyone on the team. When the workout's over, you're back to normal."

The boys look perplexed. Isn't being a tight-knit group, one that works together and plays together, supposed to be a good thing? Sensing some skepticism, Mister elaborates: "You can't maintain the same chemistry on a team for very long, anyway. People change. It's almost impossible. A season is as long as it gets with one type of chemistry, and then you start over again and have to build it. I'm asking you guys to push each other."

"My other question is down there at the bottom," he says, pointing to the all-caps "STATE." "You gave time goals and all that, but, what else? What's the team goal?"

Fonzi barely lets Mister finish the question.

"Win a state title," he says, and then he shoots a glance to the right, where Jonas sits, elbows on knees, nodding vigorously. Fonzi looks away and then, in a softer voice, adds, "Win state as a team. As a *team.*"

Robert Price sidles up behind the group. He has remained silent throughout the exchange, perhaps not wanting to upstage Mister or because his son is on the team. But now he feels compelled to speak about his favorite subject: pain.

"When pain comes, you have to fight those thoughts and stay focused," he begins. "You have to be able to do that in races, and you have to do it on your own. We can't be in that particular spot on the course when you need an extra yelling at. You've got to compartmentalize what you're doing in the here and now. I think you guys are kind of competitively immature. When the going gets tough, you say, 'Ughhhh.' When there's 400 meters to go, that's 60 seconds of pain. You've endured more in cross in repeat miles than that. But when somebody pushes the pace on you, it's 'Ah, I don't wanna do that.' That's where you've got to make that decision."

Nobody says anything. The boys look straight ahead. The clock strikes 10 p.m., a full hour after the battle-of-the-sexes Giant Jenga game had been scheduled. Mister, finally, seems to be wrapping it up.

"For both groups, this can feel like drudgery at times," he says. "You want to enjoy the process along the way. There will be good races and bad races along the way this year. Whether you win State or whatever, the world isn't going to end. It's just the journey that you're on.

"Whoever goes to the line at the state meet, you're going to have to do something you've never done before. Mentally, are you ready to do that? Will you train yourself over the next three months to do that? If this is what you want, then that's what you're going to have to do. Sometimes, when you don't feel like it—it's a Monday afternoon, and we're into long repeats in the middle of October and it calls for the entire six [repeats] under the five-minute pace, and you're not *feeling* it—can you force yourself to do it? Can you be that dedicated? Can you be that mentally tough?"

Rhetorical question or not, Fonzi pipes up.

"Hell, yeah!"

The room explodes in laughter, two hours of tension erased just like that.

It will be lights-out soon. The Jenga game is postponed to the next night.

★ ★ ★

Scene: A wooden dining room table on the back deck of the lodge, looking out on a tree-lined hillside sloping downward, two hawks circling overhead and the distant swoosh of the creek flowing down below. Three chairs are placed on one side of the table, a lone chair on the other. The runner being queried will sit in that single chair and face Mister in the middle, flanked by Price to his left and Bryson-Driver to his right. Centered on the table is Mister's laptop, open to a folder containing the notes he took at last season's one-on-one runner interviews, detailed time goals and ferritin (iron) levels, and ratings of effort over the summer months. He will hand each runner a printout of last season's goal and then ask the same questions. The whole setup resembles nothing so much as a job interview or, more accurately, a performance review. Then again, the look on the faces of nearly every runner as they shuffle in to take a seat speaks of concern and anxiety, as if being summoned to the vice principal's office to explain themselves.

Rogelio Mares, wearing a tank top over his slim frame and sporting an impressive three-day growth of facial hair, almost qualifying as a full-fledged beard, is first. Rogelio knows what Mister will hone in on: how in both his sophomore and junior seasons, he bombed at the state meet. Last year, he was Eisenhower's seventh finisher, after being a top-five scoring member most of the season. Rogelio knows the question is coming, and it comes right away.

Mister: "Can you put your finger on what happened?"

Rogelio: "Just brain dead. Or, what do you call it, lizard brain."

Mister laughs. He's had Rogelio in science class. The kid, obviously, has retained the fight-or-flight lecture.

Mister: "I think the lizard-brain thing kicked in, all right, but can you remember what were your thoughts during the race?"

Rogelio, slumping in the chair: "Last year, I was just trying to finish the race, basically. I was dead, basically. Tired. Just trying to get the race over with."

Mister: "When did fatigue set in?"

Rogelio: "You know that uphill, before Mile 2?"

Mister: "Both races each year were almost the same. Your technique came apart. When you have no arm action, you have nothing to turn over the legs, and every stride you took then was going from bad to worse. They were just streaming on by now. I think you understand now how important technique is. You had kind of a breakout season in track last spring. You've made great strides. You beat Fonzi (in the 3,200 meters). I know, going forward, you're hoping the same thing won't happen this year at State. It won't as long as you shut down the lizard brain and, in the first part of the race, you are relaxed and then 'race' the second part of the race."

Rogelio: "Right, Mister."

Mister: "What's your goal? Place on the team?"

Rogelio, smiling: "I'm good where I'm at right now [behind Fonzi and Jonas], helping the team."

Mister, shaking his head: "You may be shooting a bit low. You're running well. OK, anyways, what's your biggest fear?"

Rogelio adjusts his thick-framed glasses, looks down at the sheet of paper showing last year's goals: "Probably having the same thing happen as last season. Starting off great and then doing really bad toward the end of the season. I don't want that to happen again."

Mister closes his laptop with a decisive snap, smiles broadly: "Rogelio, your rise as a runner has been incredible in your high-school career. From being overweight and not being able to beat the girls' JV team to being top three on a very good varsity team. Just keep doing what you're doing, OK."

Rogelio nods.

"Can you go bring in Molly, please?"

Molly bounces to the back porch, wearing a sweatshirt and jacket but still mentioning that she is cold. Her hair is wet from a shower after the afternoon workout. She smiles broadly and says, "Let's do this." A senior, this will be her fourth one-on-one with Mister. Having missed the second half of her junior season with a stress fracture in her right leg, Molly knows Mister is going to ask her about her health.

Mister: "What is your greatest weakness?"

Molly: "Form, probably. The leg that tweaks out when I stride. I think about form, I do. You don't think so, but I do."

Mister rubs his temples: "I think one of your greatest weaknesses is, you don't pay attention to details well. Technique. Blood tests for ferritin. These are the details you aren't good at. Technique, I know you've worked on it, but deep down, I don't think you think it's important. When you get in a race, you run hard. I think your mental state going into a race is super-important. If you don't think you're going to do well, you aren't. Would that be accurate?"

Molly: "Yeah."

Mister: "What's your role in team chemistry? Where do you and team fit in with Erica?"

Molly sighs. This again: "It's a lot better now than last year. Last year, she just . . ." (pause) "she just saw us as trash, and she'd go with the guys. Now she's kind of getting better to try to cheer us on and be more positive."

Mister looks up quickly from his computer screen: "Really?"

Molly: "Yeah, a lot better than last year."

Mister: "Do you have any concerns going forward?"

Molly: "I'm really concerned we're going to lose our [league and district] title, to be honest. That's big."

Bryson-Driver: "Have you talked about that as a group?"

Molly shakes her head: "It seemed counterproductive to say, 'We're going to lose our title if you don't improve.' We don't straight out say it."

Mister: "How important is that to you, keeping the title?"

Molly: "Pretty important."

Mister: "How important to the other girls?"

Molly: "I don't think they realize it's an issue, that the title is in kind of jeopardy. They just see it as, 'Oh, Eisenhower is the best. We always get league and district.' I don't think they realize it's *them* that has to work harder to get the title."

Mister nods curtly and then buries his head in the keyboard. Molly feels as if she's being dismissed.

Out comes Angel Cuevas, a senior, the No. 5 runner from last year who hopes to vie with Rogelio for the third spot. For the first time in his four years, he has been coming to summer workouts, even though he worked in the orchards picking cherries and peaches from 6 a.m. to 3 p.m. alongside his dad and two brothers. Mister has said half-jokingly that he's heard Angel mutter only three sentences all summer. He is laconic, no doubt, even around teammates. But he is quick with a smile, and he blushes when Price tries to break the ice by teasing Angel about his girlfriend, Nayeli Barron, a sophomore on the girls' team.

Mister: "You aren't nervous about this, are you?"

Angel: "No."

Mister smiles: "You're ahead of last year at this stage. What are your goals?"

Angel: "Top three. Maybe after mid-season."

Mister: "What about a place at State or time at State?"

Angel: "Probably 15:40, around there."

The pitch of Mister's voice rises: "That'd put you at top 16 at State. Top 16 would put you on the podium."

Angel stares straight at him, dispassionate.

Mister, smiling: "What's your greatest strength?"

Angel: "Pushing myself to, well, with the help of you guys, to keep up with the other guys. I end up falling behind because I sometimes space out."

Mister perks up. This is the first time in four years Angel has opened up: "Let's talk about that. Pound for pound, you're the strongest kid on the team. We've noticed you're better than ever this year, running with the [top] guys. When you drop off, what's going through your mind?"

Angel: "I don't know."

Mister sucks on a stem of his reading glasses: "That's good for us to know. In the future, when you're dropping off, we can just beat you, and we'll get your attention."

Angel smiles.

Price: "And the beatings will commence!"

Mister: "I think when the field is big, you get kind of distracted. One way to deal with that is to lock onto someone like Jonas or Fonzi. That becomes your target. You are obviously a key piece of the team. We probably need you to run No. 3 or 4, but not be 30 or 40 seconds behind those top two guys. You gotta be right there with them, challenging them."

Angel: "OK, Mister."

Dantzel, a junior and the second runner on the girls' team, shuffles to the chair, arms crossed. A breeze has picked up, and sunset is fast approaching. She looks peaked from the 12-mile hill run a few hours before, and she has mentioned to the coaches that she has felt fatigued in many workouts. Then again, for someone like Dantzel, a straight-A student in AP courses, a violinist strong enough to play in the all-state symphony, and an active member of the Church of Jesus Christ of Latter-day Saints, she may just be overextending herself. It showed in her lackluster performance during track season. In her freshman year, Dantzel was seriously underweight, and Mister prodded her parents to take her to a sports nutritionist to evaluate her eating habits, calorie intake, and monitor her ferritin level. In 37 years of coaching, Mister has had a few girls struggle with eating disorders—"but not a lot, because we try to catch problems early," he's said. The coaches have been careful not to label Dantzel as having an "eating disorder," and the word *anorexia* has never been uttered either in her presence or among themselves. But Mister is well aware of rising statistics of eating disorders among female high-school athletes, particularly runners. He mentions to the coaches a recent Norwegian study that showed that 13.5 percent of all female athletes had some form of disordered eating, 24 percent when broken down to endurance sports. Mister and Bryson-Driver both have been cognizant of the "female athlete triad"—disordered eating, amenorrhea (loss of period), and osteoporosis—that plague female distance runners.

So Dantzel knows what's coming. In fact, she'd told teammates that Mister is going to bring up "the fatigue thing." She is not wrong.

Mister: "You say that you've got a lot of things going on, and you do. From time to time, you haven't done a great job of balancing things. I think you're in denial as to how healthy you are, Dantzel. Your parents would agree with me on this. Cross-country your freshman year, you weren't eating enough. You were severely anemic. Your body changed a little bit, you had a good season last year, but there's no doubt in my mind you were anemic last spring. No doubt. The signs are there. Right at the end of track, I said, 'Get tested.' But you never did. That's why you're in denial. You knew you were anemic. You just didn't want the numbers to show it. This is an area you're fighting us on all the time. Yesterday, you said, 'I'm just exhausted.'"

Dantzel: "Yeah, I am tired."

Mister: "But we haven't even *started* yet."

Dantzel stares at her hands folded in her lap: "Yeah, exactly."

Mister: "Does this make you uncomfortable, talking about this aspect of it?"

Dantzel: "I hate talking [about] eating, yeah."

Mister: "Most of the time there's a physical reason why people aren't performing well. People who are dedicated, like you, it's not mental. It's physical. Why does it make you uncomfortable?"

Tears fill Dantzel's eyes, and one slides down her right cheek. Price rises to fetch tissues; Dantzel's chest fills, and she exhales: "You know I'm a perfectionist, so it's something I can never beat."

Mister: "You mean the anemia part?"

Dantzel: "Running. Everything else in my life—academics, I can work my tail off and get ahead. Violin, you can practice for hours and get ahead. But running? I feel like it's just my body, and I can't do anything about it."

Mister: "It's your *body* that's letting you down?"

Dantzel accepts three tissues from Price: "I work out really hard, and my body feels dead, and I don't know what to do about it. I'm taking iron. I'm eating healthy, trying to sleep."

Mister: "Let's take one of these at a time. The eating healthy. You're a picky eater. Would you agree with that?"

Dantzel nods.

Mister: "If it's a vegetable, you'll eat it every day of the week. There are aspects of the vegetable diet that are great, but there's only so many nutrients in it. It's an incomplete diet."

Dantzel: "That's the thing. That's how my home is. That's how I've grown up. My mom's trying to go vegan so that's like, a fight, when you have to come home and cook your own meat and produce your own protein. She helps, but that's how it is."

Mister lowers his chin and looks over the frames of his glasses: "Hold on, when I met with your parents a year ago, they were on the same page as I was about you consuming more calories."

Dantzel: "It's hard. I try to."

Mister: "If you're training at this level, your body has to have this. You aren't consuming enough calories."

Dantzel cries harder now, frustration making her voice crack: "It's not like I don't eat."

Mister: "But it's not enough. It's all vegetables, carrots."

Dantzel: "I eat other food. What do you want me to eat then?"

Mister: "For what we're running, go on a diet of 4,000 calories."

Dantzel: "I can't consume huge amounts of food."

Mister: "Spread it out over the course of a day. . . . We're having this conversation because your body's failing you. It doesn't have enough energy to do the work you're asking it to do. This has been an issue since you're a freshman."

Mister and Dantzel spend the next 20 minutes discussing the principles of nutrition for runners, and Mister tells her that if her ferritin test (iron levels) comes back low, her training will have to be curtailed. If it registers in the normal range, he says, "Then we'll know it's just not consuming enough calories, and we'll deal with that."

Mister: "What are your goals for this year?"

Dantzel: "Try to get this team closer. I'd love to do better at State. Get top 30 [individually] or something. I'd love to connect the whole team and get us together. Some people have told us they don't even want to do it next year. There are people who come to practice and go, 'Oh, I don't want to be here. This is too hard.' . . . Natalie Stephenson, a sophomore, is such a great runner, but she just chooses not to. There're other girls who I look at and think, 'You are so strong, yet you choose not to use your talent.'"

After conversing nearly an hour, Dantzel looks utterly spent. She stands slowly, senior citizen slowly, and shuffles back inside. She leaves two unused tissues on the table. An extended silence follows, the three coaches staring into the trees. This will be an issue all season. Mister has fretted about it.

Interviews continue for the next two days, the coaches glued to their perch on the porch for hours at a time. By design, they leave the interviews with the program's top three runners—Jonas, Erica, and Fonzi—for last. They want to, in running parlance, finish strong.

FONZI

He fell, but he did not face-plant. The whole thing wasn't that embarrassing. Shocking? Yes. Unfortunate? Absolutely. But neither demoralizing nor devastating. Sure, all of the other runners had taken off, and there lay Alfonso Cuevas prone on the grass by himself for a few seconds, a few precious seconds.

This was the 2016 state meet championship race in Pasco, Fonzi's sophomore year, and he had psyched himself up and was all ready for a breakout performance, redemption for his disappointing 71st place finish at State as a freshman, when inexperience and lack of confidence got the better of him. Now, faced with a situation that might have daunted a runner with less grit and mental toughness, Fonzi knew what he had to do. It was what he'd seen his mother do, time and time again, in the face of obstacles and adversity in the family's sometimes chaotic home life.

Get up. Dust yourself off. Move forward.

And, like a shot, Fonzi was back on his feet and off in hot pursuit.

★ ★ ★

Sonya Cuevas works for the Washington Department of Fish and Wildlife as an administrative assistant. She has tweaked her schedule so that she can get Fridays off, which means she works four 10-hour days. With seven kids still at home in their modest three-bedroom ranch house near downtown Yakima—two of her own, Alfonso, 16, and Caris, 9; and her eldest daughter's five children, whom Sonya has custody of via foster care—Sonya needs more than the full-time day-care provider she employs for the younger ones. She likes to keep a close watch, so when she settles into her cubicle each morning, she props up her smartphone next to her computer monitor and clicks on an app that opens her motion-activated home monitoring system.

"I like to keep track of them," she says, a slight smile brightening her stern countenance. "Sometimes, I'll see something and have to call home to say, 'Hey, you need to quit doing that.' That makes them think, 'Well, maybe she is watching us, so we better behave.'"

Sonya knows what people might think: Here's yet another "helicopter parent," one of those hovering, overly involved types who smother rather than mother. She does worry about being "that kind of mom," but anyone who knows her circumstances perhaps can understand her need to stay connected and keep a tight rein on her family.

It hasn't been an easy home life for the Cuevas family, what with Alfonso and his sister, as well as Fonzi's nieces and nephews, all under one roof. Sonya is estranged from her husband, Alfonso Sr., who lives in the Tri-Cities and does not have much contact with the family, rarely making the hour drive north to Yakima. He has no driver's license, no car, no steady job. He has never seen Fonzi race, not even at the state championships in Pasco, one of the three cities in Tri-Cities. About her husband, Sonya will only say, "We keep in contact with him, but [because] I have foster kids, kids, you have to pass a background check; he can't have contact at the house because he's had some trouble. He's from LA, the Pomona area, and he's kind of, you know, involved in stuff. If you were to see him, your perception would be: gang member. He's got tattoos all over. He's had a rough life."

Two of Fonzi's three older sisters, older than he is by eight to 12 years, have had trouble finding their way in life as well. All five of the foster children in Sonya's care were born to her eldest daughter, who is 28. (Sonya's second-oldest daughter has a child and lives on her own, while her third oldest is married with two kids and serves as Sonya's backup, emergency day-care provider.) The children under Sonya's care range from a 13-year-old boy, Tatum, to a 5-year-old girl, Mierica, as well as the newest addition, an infant, Royal. It's a full house, but Fonzi, since seventh grade, has managed to squirrel away his own room. That's a big concession his mom made to him, an acknowledgment of Fonzi's teen need for a modicum of privacy. But it means that the others have to double or triple up, according to gender, in rooms throughout the house. "That's been crucial," Fonzi says. "It can get a little tight in the house, but it's all fine. But, man, Chuckie [who is 6 and in the first grade], he drives me crazy. Oh, man, he's a handful. You tell him something, you turn around, he ends up doing what you told him not to, and you're like, 'Chuckie, I told you not to do that!' And he's like, 'I know, I know.' And I'm like, 'OK, just go sit down.'"

Fonzi can decompress by shutting himself off in his room, where he'll put in his earbuds and listen to his favorite rapper, Kendrick Lamar, or the gangsta rapper XXXtencion. Or he'll join his teammates online to play *Injustice League 2* on Xbox or *Clash Royale* on the smartphone. He loves adventure movies and some sci-fi, but his favorite genre is comedies— the wackier, the better. His all-time favorite, the one that never ceases to crack him up, is a Wayans Brothers flick called *Little Man*, about a robbery scheme featuring a dwarf pretending to be a baby and . . . well, it's too complicated for Fonzi to flesh out the plot, but he recommends just seeing it. His room is sacrosanct to all but his mother. And when it's homework time, even after a 14-mile day when Fonzi just wants to curl up and sleep, Sonya makes him do it in front of her at the kitchen table while she cleans up the younger children's mess. Fonzi's a good student, though he claims not to be "book smart." Still, he is taking AP literature, honors chemistry, world history, and, as an elective, photography. He has aced AP calculus and is on call to tutor teammates with math deficiencies. The course load, Fonzi says, is not too bad. He still gets plenty of time to chill and zone out on his Xbox playing online video games against his cross-country "boys."

Sonya, though, has precious little escape, cramming a 40-hour work-week into four days and then tending to seven kids and never missing one of Fonzi's races, except those that are out of state and require hotel stays, which she frankly cannot afford. She's in her early 40s, but her face remains mostly unlined and her hair jet-black. If she's under stress—and she is, oh, certainly, she is—it doesn't readily show. She laughs. "Right! Have you heard of Clairol?" she asks, touching her hair.

Sipping coffee, the left side of her face resting in the slightly calloused palm of her hand, Sonya is not shy in detailing why she keeps Fonzi on a tight rein. The plights of her eldest daughter and her estranged husband, their descent into gang involvement and "bad choices," she delivers with surprising lack of melodrama and with a candor that shows she has long since come to terms with her reality.

"My oldest girl started getting into trouble her sixth-grade year at Franklin [Middle School]," she says. "Back then, Franklin had a lot of gangs, the blue versus the red. My daughter ended up getting in the wrong group of people. I guess it made her feel she was accepted, but, whatever, that's where I started losing her, sixth grade. She never completed that grade. She was constantly running around, leaving home. I'd constantly have to chase her, looking for her, trying to bring her back. It was totally chaotic. I don't even know how I worked during that period.

"My three older girls, I was so involved just with trying to keep them from bad surroundings that there wasn't time for normal [parenting]. With my older one, I don't blame myself. It was a choice of hers, but now she's really struggling to get back to where she needs to be. She's never been there. All she knows is the partying. Whereas, my second daughter, she has only one child, lives on her own, has her own car. She still comes to me for stuff, but I'm OK with it. My third daughter, the one who's married and has her own family, I feel I kind of ruined it for her. She doesn't know how to cook and isn't a great house cleaner. It could be because I was busy chasing around the others and I just did everything for [her]. I never taught her to cook and clean.

"Lately, this past six months, I've told Alfonso, I said, 'We need to start teaching you to cook. We need to teach you to wash your own clothes, clean your room, and teach you to drive.'"

And how well is Fonzi doing on the domestic front?

"Well," she smiles, ruefully, "he's a boy."

★ ★ ★

Vertical and ambulatory again, Fonzi looked ahead at the pack retreating into the distance. The first thing he thought was, *Don't panic*. So, of course, he panicked. But just a little bit. It was crazy, he thought, that no one stepped on him, impaled him on their spikes. They just casually eluded him as if he were just another course obstacle. He did notice, up ahead, that a few runners from rival Tahoma were waving their arms at the race starter, holding the gun, asking him to fire a second shot to bring the group back because a runner is down. No such luck. The race proceeded.

Fonzi was on his own, a feeling alien to him, given that he belonged to such a tight-knit Eisenhower team and had a mother as close to him as any mother and teen son can be. All he could think of was, just get to Ronan. That would be Ronan Price, Ike's top runner. But that meant weaving his way through almost the entire pack, first the stragglers already well off the pace and then the congested middle pack, which included a couple of his teammates, Angel Cuevas and Ulysses Ayala and Mo Cook. He didn't have time to even exchange a word or a nod with them. Fonzi was on the move, redlining it, running hard, heart pounding at almost maximum effort. Whether he would tire and fade before reaching Ronan near the lead pack, he did not know. The immediate concern was simply to reach his teammate, the runner off which Fonzi always keyed his pacing. Fonzi had yet to finish ahead of Ronan in a race but was incrementally narrowing the gap on the more experienced senior.

But now this—a mad dash just to catch up.

Something Fonzi seemingly had been doing his entire young life.

★ ★ ★

When Sonya finally had a boy after three girls, she naturally spoiled him. Couldn't help herself. He was just so cute, chubby, and cuddly, with a wonderful disposition. She didn't think herself overprotective but, rather, just protective enough, given the domestic circumstances.

At Fonzi's six-month well baby check-up, the pediatrician discovered something amiss with the boy, something that the attending physicians in the delivery room had missed at birth, when this strapping boy weighed in at a hefty eight and three-quarter pounds after an understandably trying labor for Sonya. At that newborn examination at the birthing center, they had laid Fonzi flat on an exam table, as is customary, prodded and probed, listened to his heart, and pronounced him a bouncing baby boy.

"Whenever they examine a baby, they lay them down on the table, and Alfonso's murmur I guess was in the lower chamber, something like that, so when he laid down, it muffled that murmur," she says. "They never caught it."

But at that second exam, Fonzi was crying and colicky. Sonya fretted. This was unlike her little Alfonso, always so docile and accommodating. No way he would lie on the exam table this time. Sonya fretted some more. So unlike her baby. She finally gathered him and propped him up in the crook of her arm. That's when they found a heart murmur, the tiniest hole in the lower chamber. Sonya tried to remain calm, but she could barely absorb the doctor's explanation. Something about how the murmur couldn't be detected at birth because Fonzi was lying flat and that, in a way, it was fortunate he was fussy now and needed to sit up, because the murmur in the lower chamber was loud and clear at this point. Sonya took the news with surprising aplomb, considering. Just keep him active, the doctor told her. If you do that, there is a great chance the heart murmur will close on its own. Keep his heart pumping, and he'll be fine.

But Fonzi wasn't being active enough in the next few months. By nine months, he weighed 35 pounds—about 15 pounds heavier than what the World Health Organization deems a "large baby boy." If Fonzi wasn't obese, he certainly was headed there, like so many babies born in the Yakima Valley. But Sonya kept trying to follow doctor's orders. It helped that he walked early, before turning one. He started to slim down in his toddler years, but it was the weirdest thing—Fonzi's motor skills seemed off. They kept putting balls in his right hand, but he'd throw awkwardly, elbow askew, what in a less-enlightened time might be described as "throwing like a girl."

"When he was little I taught him everything right-handed and I thought, oh my God, he's going to be so slow [developmentally]," Sonya says. "I tried to get him into special ed. He'd always pass his pen back and forth between hands. Forming letters was difficult. The people I took him to said he was really smart. They thought it was a developmental thing. Sports, he just totally sucked at them when he was little. I worked with him and worked with him at home only to find out—he was left-handed!

"After that, he just took off. Everything he tried, sportswise, he did excellent."

Heart murmur aside, keeping Fonzi busy in what she called "positive" group activities was crucial to her plan for him. She thought of her estranged husband's history and of her eldest daughter and the daughter's associations with gangs, and she felt she needed a different approach.

"I was a little worried because Alfonso is my only boy, so I was like, 'What's going to happen to him?' My [eldest] daughter's into really bad stuff, and his dad was, you know. I didn't want to wait for my son to be like that. So I just put him in every sport I could think of. Every sport. He really took first to basketball."

When he started playing sports is when he picked up the nickname Fonzi. Sonya encouraged it, not because the name Alfonso reminded her of her estranged husband of the same name, but because people were always messing up the name, calling him Alonzo or some such thing. Sonya once sat Fonzi down and showed him YouTube clips of the original Fonzi, from the 1970s TV show *Happy Days*, but "he wasn't really impressed; he didn't quite get it." In any event, Fonzi was the star of the YMCA league by age 7, and Sonya was bursting with pride. Not only had her son thinned down and become healthy and found "positive" friends, but he was a darned good player. She was driving him home after one particularly stellar game, replaying the highlights, when Fonzi made a declaration.

"Mom, I don't like basketball."

"What?"

"I don't like it. It's not that fun."

"Well, what do you like?"

"Soccer, mom."

Actually, in retrospect, it made sense to Sonya.

"Where we live, it's a whole bunch of low-income families, and all the kids go over to the school [Garfield Elementary], and all they do is play soccer," she says. "It turned out, Alfonso was very, very good at it. He made the U-11 [under age 11] 'premier' team as an 8-year-old, and he was good. The coach used to use Alfonso as an example of how to run."

One afternoon in third grade, when Fonzi's class headed out to PE instruction, the teacher surprised the kids. He not only had a whistle around his neck, but also a stopwatch in one hand. Every student at Garfield, they were told, would be timed while running around a course set up along the fence line of the play fields. Many kids groaned. Some tried to get out of it, citing injury or illness. Fonzi was pumped. So were a few of his soccer-playing friends. None had ever formally run, as in a race, as in being timed. But they ran all the time, up and down the soccer fields at Garfield. Fonzi took off like a shot when it was his turn. The PE teacher, whose father was a longtime supporter of Eisenhower's cross-country and track programs, kept looking down at the watch and up at Fonzi dashing over the grass back toward him. He had, by far, the fastest time of the day. Later that night, the PE teacher called his father and said that "Mister" might have another good one coming in five or six years.

Sonya beams at the memory, adding proudly, "I saw the guy [teacher] recently, and he said nobody has beaten Alfonso's times at Garfield yet."

The only person not overly impressed? Fonzi. He was so enamored with soccer that he gave no thought whatsoever to running as an actual sport, rather as a means to an end. It was just something he did while chasing after the ball. Fonzi played center-mid on the soccer pitch, a position that requires lots of running, both sprinting and sustained movement. By age 13, he was playing on a team that traveled the region playing against other top teams. But because his mom wanted him to participate in at least one sport all the time, lest "bad influences" encroach, Fonzi decided to run cross-country and track at Franklin Middle School—just to stay in shape for soccer, nothing more. Fonzi had made tentative plans to go to Davis High—school kids in Yakima can choose either high school, regardless of where they live—because it had a better soccer team, even though Sonya was pushing for Eisenhower, because its math program was purported to be superior and she wanted Fonzi in every honors class the school offered.

A funny thing happened when Fonzi started competing in middle-school races. He won—and kept winning. He even won the middle-school section at the meet Eisenhower hosted, the Sunfair Invitational, catching the attention of the Eisenhower runners and coaches.

"I'd become pretty full of myself back then, because I was undefeated in middle school," Fonzi recalled. "The Ike guys even came to watch me run and talk to me about coming there. It was pretty crazy."

Miguel Vargas, one of the veterans on the 2014 Eisenhower cross-country team who came, en masse, to check out the hotshot 13-year-old, remembered the scene in the 1.5-mile race at Franklin Park.

"One of our guys said, 'There's this kid, Alfonso, he's really fast,' and we had practice at Franklin, so we thought we'd check him out," Vargas said. "He was one skinny little boy who was, like, 200 meters in front of everybody after only about 800 meters into the race. We were all like, 'This kid is going to be good.' Fonzi was just running effortlessly. And he was wearing Vans shoes, too!"

Sonya Cuevas doesn't recall much of that race, other than the reaction from Eisenhower boys.

"They were yelling, 'Go, Fonzi, go,'" she says. "That just happened to be Alfonso's best race of the year. And it made me feel good that these kids sought him out. I could see he was a little taken aback by the attention. He was a little intimidated. He's not sure what to think when people are cheering for him and making a big deal."

★ ★ ★

He caught up with his teammate, Ronan, nearing the first mile. The two were just off the lead pack. He was tired, utterly spent. But a strange thing happened once Fonzi matched strides with his teammate. His adrenaline rush subsided, and Fonzi could breathe again. He could relax into a steady, reasonably hard pace. He found, amazingly, that he had energy left. Tons of energy. He had never felt this strong before, never. Mister's race plan called for Ronan and Fonzi to be in the top 16 after the first mile of the 3.1-mile race and then to systematically pick off runners from there.

In the second mile, Ronan and Fonzi reached a big uphill that stretched almost half a mile. By this time, Fonzi had fully recovered and merely had the normal in-race pain and exertion to deal with. He had told himself, while walking the course with the team the previous afternoon, that this would be where he'd make a move. *Runners die here*, he thought, *but I'm going to surge and then let the downhill after that carry me*. He took off, in 14th place at this point. As he crested the hill, Fonzi saw Mister leaning over the flag barrier shouting something to him. All Fonzi could hear was the word "go." He went. He just tucked his chin and pumped his arms even harder than usual.

Up ahead, Fonzi saw runners dangling off the lead pack, faltering a bit. He saw them, and he passed them, including two from rival Central Valley. His world had been reduced to tunnel vision by this point, during this mad sprint to the finish, but he had the presence of mind to know that his sophomore rival, Riley Moore, from Richland High was just ahead. Fonzi had lost to Moore at every invitational this season, and last season, as well. The two were Snapchat friends and, privately, Fonzi wanted nothing more badly than finally to beat Moore. Up one hill, down another, and Moore was history. He had turned to look back at the rapidly approaching Cuevas and fell. By the time Moore arose, Fonzi was gone, out to pick off some other bobbing heads in front of him. He could hear some Eisenhower supporters yelling, something about Nate Pendleton, one of the state's best runners, being within striking range.

He pumped his arms harder.

* * *

Mister looked askance at this fresh-faced freshman. Of course, he knew all about Alfonso Cuevas and his middle-school running exploits. But what in the Lord's name was the kid doing wearing Vans sneakers and soccer sweats to the first practice? No, this would not do. And he told the kid as much. Fonzi, for his part, was intimidated and cowed.

"Mister was like, 'We need to get you some real shoes,'" he recalls. "So he got me some Brooks. I'm like, 'Yeah, these fit.' But they felt weird at first. I was like, 'Man, I really want to take these off and run barefoot or something.' But Mister was like, 'Keep them on.'"

He kept them on. And he got used to them. The veteran Eisenhower runners welcomed the touted freshman—until he started unduly pushing the pace in practice.

"They were getting mad and saying, 'Who does he think he is?'" Fonzi says. "When the workouts started progressing, they really schooled me and taught me a thing or two."

But the older guys admired Fonzi's toughness.

"He was always so mentally strong," Ronan Price said.

"For me, it's all mental," Fonzi says. "I don't think of it as physical. I think, 'I have to stick with this guy.' I mean, I'm a very tough person, mentally. I don't like losing. I like to stick in those packs, even when I'm hurting. I have last-minute surges. I can take the hurting."

What he has trouble dealing with is failing. Maybe not failing, per se, but not living up to the performance standard he has set for himself. His state championship race as a freshman is a case in point, according to his mother. Fonzi finished a distant 71st that day, still good enough to help Eisenhower finish third overall. But he expected so much more.

"I kept seeing all these other Eisenhower kids going by near the finish line," she says. "Finally, I could see him, and he was mad. I could tell. His facial expression, you can always tell with Alfonso. . . . When he's [doing well], his eyebrows come down, and he's concentrating. But this time he just had a scowl on his face. I used to take video at the finish. I don't like to take [video] anymore because I catch myself [on tape] saying things I shouldn't and that get him mad. I say things like, 'Where's he at?' I record things and get caught up in the emotions. Alfonso does not like it."

But during Fonzi's breakthrough sophomore season, the videos the coaches recorded during races showed a runner who, consistently, was going about a minute faster than the previous year, a runner who was seriously challenging the senior, Ronan Price. At the district meet, the qualifier for the state championships, when Fonzi finished in second place less than a second behind Ronan, he was overwhelmed by the attention. People slapped his back; teammates fist-bumped him, and a few even gave bear hugs. Sonya had brought her whole extended brood, from the ones still in strollers to the toddlers orbiting her to the slouching middle schooler.

Fonzi's grandfather, Chuck Ortiz, Sonya's dad, started coming to the meets that year, too, when his health permitted it. Ortiz had led a hard life—a high-school dropout, addicted to drugs, a diabetic who had lost part of his biceps muscle from years of intravenous drug use and needed dialysis for kidney failure. But Sonya says her father had "found religion" and was cleaned up, so she didn't balk when he wanted to come to the meets. And he loved watching Fonzi race. But it became a little awkward for Fonzi after races, Sonya says, when her dad's voice would start to quiver addressing his grandson. "See, my dad, he never felt he'd done anything great in his life, and he sees Alfonso and he gets emotional. He'd say, 'That was an awesome race, Alfonso,' and then he'd start crying. I'm not sure Alfonso likes that attention."

Because, as Sonya says, "We don't come from a very athletic family." Fonzi's success, therefore, is a big deal to those close to him. So, too, with his academic success—nearly straight As. Sonya, who earned an associate degree from Yakima Valley College, is the only member of her family who went to college. So the fact that Fonzi was now getting recruiting letters from universities was exciting to her and other family members.

"Yeah, he got a lot of 'Way to go, Fonzi' comments around here," she says.

The positive reinforcement sometimes weighed on Fonzi, though. He felt the burden of expectations in those well-meaning comments. He tried not to dwell on the pressure, but it was there.

"I've been feeling that since I got into high school, because I think the farthest my sisters made it was sophomore year," he says. "Me just being here now is doing better. My freshman year, I wasn't that good with grades, and she (his mom) told me, you have a good chance of being the first kid to go to college. So that part really motivates me."

And when Fonzi's motivation waned, his mother was there to crack the whip.

"She's strict, but she does it for my well-being," he says. "She's usually tough on me when I'm slacking off or even during the season. You can tell that I can be not very serious sometimes [at practice and meets], and she gets on me for that. She cracks the whip on grades, too. I'm not too 'book smart,' but I know my stuff. She knows when I'm slacking off. She goes, 'You gotta get this in and this in,' and I'm like, 'Mom, I just ran, like, 12 miles today. Can I just get a little sleep before doing it?' I know personally, it's all me that's doing the pressuring. Coaches and teammates have been great. My mom, she takes the pressure off sometimes. Reassures me. Every time after races, even if it's a good one, I'll find something to be like, 'Aw, I wasn't able to do this.' She always tells me the good part. I always forget that. I can get easily frustrated."

Fonzi's sunny outward demeanor can mask some of the family challenges he faces. He occasionally struggles to come to terms with not having his dad involved in his life and having a troubled older sister. It can depress him, Sonya says. Sometimes, in dark moods, he frets about his genetics, wonders whether he may have inherited a penchant for bad behavior from his father, worries that at some point in his life he may succumb to the same fate as Alfonso Sr. Mention his father, and it is as if a veil descends upon Fonzi's face and his demeanor. Asked what his father does for a living, Fonzi looks at his shoes. "I don't know," he says, in a near whisper. He doesn't talk much about him, even with his close friends, such as Rogelio.

"I try not to let Alfonso think that because his father's lifestyle isn't the correct way, or even went the way he wanted it to, it shouldn't impact his life," Sonya says. "I don't want him to think that just because someone else's choices in life were not great, it should impact his. I told him it's a proven fact that just because a certain person lives a certain way and they have a child doesn't mean that child is going to be that way. He worries."

Fonzi, for all his joking with teammates and easy banter with teachers and other adults, is a private person, Sonya says.

"I try to keep our relationship really close," she says. "That's where my joking [with him] comes in. I can kind of ease up on what I want to say if I joke with him. I don't know if I'd say I'm a typical mom. I'll just go down to his room and sit with him and hug him, joke around. I didn't do that with my other kids, but Alfonso is just totally different. He's got like his own little bubble. He likes to be left alone."

When his running was going well, such as the fall of his sophomore year, Fonzi felt pressure to maintain his so-called elite status. When his running was not going well, such as the spring of his sophomore year when his track season was hampered by lingering ankle issues due to foot pronation, Fonzi felt a different type of pressure. A pressure to get back to where he once was. Sonya, the summer before Fonzi's junior year, already saw it taking a toll. He'd get a little moody, withdraw into himself more, burrow into his room where the bib numbers lining his walls from successful races served as a constant reminder both of what he could accomplish and what now was expected of him. A lot to place on a slim 16-year-old's shoulders.

"Expectations are higher," she says. "Everyone's making a big deal about him after State last year."

Then again, sometimes for all of Sonya's good intentions, she admits she has added some pressure as well.

"My mom, before races, she'll come up and say to me, 'Here, have something to eat,'" Fonzi says, laughing. "She'll say, 'Have some almonds, Alfonso, I hear they are good for you.' And I'll say, 'Mom, it's 20 minutes before my race, I don't need any almonds.'"

Sonya remains unapologetic.

"Yes," she says, "but then I'll go through his bag and find the almonds not even opened and I'll be like, 'Son, this could be why you didn't have that oomph at the end of the race. Oh, he just loves when I say stuff like that.'"

★ ★ ★

He was hugging the shortest possible route to the finish. Running the tangents, they call it. He was close enough, at one point, that spectators behind the roped-off areas could almost reach out and touch him, until the runners reached the home stretch, where the fans receded to a respectful distance, and the runners bore in on the finishing tower. Eighty meters left. Parents were screaming, people's voices so intermingled that, to the runners, it came off as a dull roar.

Fonzi had passed the red singlet of Daniel Maton of Camas High, whose older brother and sister are elite college runners. Fonzi had passed the white singlet of Pendleton, and now he was honing in on the giant, long-legged, fair-skinned Dawson Besst, of Tahoma High, with the big green "T" on his chest. Got him too.

Scrunched among all of the spectators craning their necks looking for runners stood Sonya Cuevas. She peered ahead and caught a glimpse of a brown-skinned, blue-shirted runner approaching in fifth place. He had white tape on his wrists, and black Kinesio tape running up his right arm, a ploy by Mister to make sure Fonzi remembered to get good arm swing. She exclaimed to nobody in particular, "Is that a Mexican?" It wasn't Ronan, was it? She glanced over to where her father, Chuck Ortiz, and his friend were standing. Tears were streaming down Chuck's face. That's when Sonya knew, *My God*, it was indeed Fonzi, the fifth finisher. Sonya quickly reached into her purse, grabbed her phone, and caught the last few seconds on video of the best race of her son's young life.

★ ★ ★

Nearly a year later, that 2016 race at State seems, if not surreal, slightly in the realm of fantasy for Fonzi. His poor track season, brought about by his ankle injury due to foot pronation issues, makes it seem to him that it was some other kid with his name who finished fifth the previous November. And his continued problems during summer conditioning—adapting to the plastic orthotics placed in his shoes to correct the foot problem and struggling to keep up with surging Jonas and even the much-improved Rogelio—have done nothing to restore Fonzi's confidence.

How did Fonzi's times deteriorate so much from the fall to the spring of his sophomore season? Literal growing pains, Mister says. He grew an inch or two, and it threw off his form. He started pronating, his right ankle collapsing inward with each footfall. This caused not only shin and

Achilles pain but also served as, in Mister's words, a "braking mechanism" slowing down Fonzi's push-off on every step. By early summer, Mister felt Fonzi needed orthotics to correct the imbalance. Landing an appointment with a physical therapist or podiatrist often can take months, even with the best insurance, but Mister, of course, has connections. The husband of one of his former runners is Yakima's most sought-after physical therapist, and Michael Kane agreed to see Fonzi, to videotape his stride, and, if need be, fit him for plastic orthotics that would realign the arches.

What Kane saw in Fonzi's gait was classic pronation.

"I have been studying foot and ankle mechanics and gait for a long time," Kane said. "Sometimes the structure of your body can affect how it functions. But most people don't think about how their feet might influence the rest of their body. Once their foot hits the ground, then it's a closed system where your tibia and fibula sit on top of your foot and ankle, and the femur sits on top of the tibia, and the pelvis sits atop the femur. So if the foot does something odd, it can create a chain reaction all the way up to their knees, hips, or backs. When I did the video, you can see clearly his foot is really collapsing and pronating excessively. It's making his gait really inefficient. The goal is that the orthotic was to help eliminate the compensation he is doing. If I identify areas that are tight or aren't functioning optimally, I might add a few things, but Mister already does a lot of those functional things to get them stronger."

In a way, for Fonzi and Mister, it was good news. It was something that could be fixed in time. Or so they hoped. But, as with most teenagers, Fonzi showed impatience. He wanted it rectified immediately. Instead, he struggled all summer to adjust to the hard plastic shoe liner, developing blisters that lasted nearly a month.

"The whole thing was pretty weird," Fonzi says. "When they cast my foot, it felt like paste on the bottom of my shoe. Have you ever had braces? It's the same thing. He said my feet were pretty bad. He said even when I just stand there I pronate. He noticed both ankles were collapsing in, the right one a little more. He showed me some photos. He told me, 'You're exerting more energy because of this. That's why you are having pain and why you can't keep up with the workouts.' He was explaining all this stuff, and it just made sense. Now I'm just waiting to get better."

* * *

It turns out to be a prolonged wait, a summer-long wait. And now, on the cusp of the season, here Fonzi sits across the table from Mister during the obligatory camp "interview," still bummed by his lack of progress, and he's sure all of these issues will be brought up. Which is why Fonzi, for once, isn't smiling—in fact, he looks a little pained—as he lowers himself to his chair on the back deck of the lodge at Camp Ghormley. Mister begins the interrogation.

"What are your goals for cross, Fonzi?"

"Hopefully I want to get under 15 for a race, 14:50s sounds nice, for three miles, maybe 15:20 for 5K."

"What about state placing?"

"I want to get top 10 at State."

Mister takes off his reading glasses and looks Fonzi in the eye. Fonzi doesn't blink.

"But you were fifth last year, Fonzi."

"Yeah, well, there's a lot of factors to that."

"Like what?"

"Falling."

Mister barks out a laugh. Actually, more of a chortle.

"You expect to fall again?"

Bryson-Driver smiles broadly.

"You *hope* to fall, Fonzi?" Mister continues.

"Hope not," Fonzi says, looking directly at Mister and not smiling.

"Explain that."

"How do I put this? Me getting top five was . . ." He lets the sentence dangle.

"A fluke?"

"Yeah. I really don't feel like I deserved that spot. There were a lot of things that helped me get there and a lot of things other runners did that helped too. Let's say, a little after the second mile, that gradual downhill. I just listened to you to go down the downhill, and no one really pushed me. I was lucky that happened."

"What do you mean you were *lucky*?" Mister asks, incredulous.

"Because they didn't go with me. I was surprised no one went with me on my downhill."

"There is very little luck involved in finishing fifth in State after falling at the start line. I don't know where you're coming from with this 'luck' thing."

"Do you think I doubt myself, Mister?"

"OK, you did surpass all expectations last year, but, nonetheless, *you did it*. If you can do it once, you can do it twice. You need to give that some thought."

In the silence that follows, Bryson-Driver fills the gap.

"You came prepared to race that day at State," she says, "and they did not, Fonzi. You need to start to think of yourself differently as a runner."

"OK."

"What's your greatest fear?" Mister asks, his boilerplate question for all Ike kids in the preseason interview.

"Not getting back in shape or being able to run like I did last year."

"Do you lack a bit of confidence right now, do you think?"

"Yeah, I do."

"OK. How are you going to overcome that?"

"I have no idea right now, honestly, Mister."

"Let me help you there. It'll probably be in workouts you'll get confidence from."

"Yup."

"The good thing is you have a teammate who will run with you, and that's Jonas—and, to some degree, Rogelio as well."

"Yup."

"But let's go back to that top question. What are your goals other than just time? You were fifth at State as a sophomore. That finish alone catapults you into the elite status of distance runners in the state of Washington. But do you see yourself as one?"

"No, I don't."

Mister's voice rises in surprise: "Why not? You really think that was a fluke?"

"I don't know. Just how I act in workouts and how other races have been, I don't think I'm an elite runner, at least not yet."

"OK. All right. Would you want to be one?"

For the first time, Fonzi cracks a smile. His face lights up, the crinkled forehead becomes smooth once more.

"Of *course*."

Now Mister smiles too.

"Lots of changes take place for guys between their sophomore and junior years, Fonzi," he says. "Mentally and physically. Hopefully, in a short amount of time, your doubt will be put to rest once and for all. There should be no reason why you shouldn't have a stellar year. I don't see any drawbacks. No reason at all. Understand?"

"Yup."

ERICA

At the foot of Bethel Ridge Road, on the final full day at Camp Ghormley, there was Erica Simison, and then there was everyone else.

The boys stood clumped together, bobbing on the balls of their feet, chatting about *Injustice League*, eager to get going yet dreading the climb that awaited them—seven miles straight up, seven straight back down. Most were bare-chested, given that the temperature was holding steady at 87 degrees, surprisingly hot even for late summer at 5,000 feet elevation. The girls lingered way in the back, adjusting the knots in their ponytails and taking final sips of water before their 12-mile journey, six up and six down. No one spoke. Earlier, at lunch in the camp cafeteria, the afternoon hill-climb workout loomed like an unwanted visitor; perhaps if they ignored it, it might go away.

And between these groups stood Erica, all 5-foot, 95 pounds of her, wound as tightly as her hair bun. She saw me, the journalist who had been following the team all summer, off to the side stretching.

"You doing this run?" she asked.

"Yeah, I guess. I'm a masochist for hills," I replied.

"Good. You can run with me."

"OK."

Her invitation struck me as one not of politeness to the newcomer but of necessity.

"Great. But I'm not into 'chatting' much."

"No problem."

Mister slammed the door of his truck, hitched up his khaki shorts, and sent us on our way. Then he and Robert Price and Bryson-Driver drove off to the five-, six-, and seven-mile marks up the winding, steep road, where they'd park and provide water and inspiration. All they provided at the start, however, were billows of blowing dust coming off their tires.

Almost from the start, Erica and I left the girls behind. Not even two-tenths of a mile into it, we couldn't see the girls' pack when we reached the first switchback and could look down the hill. Then again, we also couldn't see the boys' varsity pack, which had taken off and left Erica and me behind. This is the training dilemma Erica has long faced. Unlike most on the girls' team, Erica has been running competitively since the second grade, and her times at Eisenhower often are two minutes faster than her next best teammate. This has made training hard for Erica: too slow to stay with (most of) the boys; way too fast for her teammates. So she had mostly trained alone, which both pleased and grated on her. It pleased her because she was not an ebullient extrovert who went out of her way to make friends; it grated because training alone was hard, in that no teammates were around to push her, to help keep pace. Adding to this tension was that Erica had made little effort during her four years at Eisenhower to bond with her teammates, mostly because she did not view cross-country as a team sport. Sure, sure, officials tally up the places of each runner and award team titles, but she had always believed that if you ran your own race well, took care of your own effort, that team stuff would take care of itself. A rah-rah runner she was not. She admitted that. Arrogant and standoffish was what many of her teammates thought. Misunderstood was what Erica thought.

About a half mile into the climb, when we reached a relatively flat plateau around a sharp turn, I thought about breaking the silence. Until that point, the only sound coming from either of us was the labored breathing of a steep ascent and the repetitive scuff of shoes on a rock-strewn dirt road.

"How'd the SATs go?" I managed to gasp out.

Erica had left camp the previous night to return to Yakima to take the SAT test on Saturday morning, and she'd been a little anxious beforehand, as a strong score would help when college cross-country coaches would be looking to recruit her and give her financial aid and partial scholarships.

"Good," she said. "Think I did all right."

She kept looking straight ahead. After a minute or so, she added, "My hips feel a little tight now."

"Could be because you sat at a desk for four hours taking a test."

"Maybe."

End of conversation. Back to business. Back to climbing.

Some climbs begin gradually and proceed steadily in steepness and lung-burning intensity so that, like the proverbial lobster placed in luke-warm water and slowly boiled alive, you almost—*almost*—don't feel it all that much until suddenly you do. Some climbs, however, hit you all at once, effort and pain from the first step. This was one of those latter runs. Erica stared straight ahead, mostly, but I needed some distraction. I looked around. I saw a cloudless expanse of blue sky—nice change from the smokiness of Yakima—and felt a warmth on my shoulders that made me wish our first water stop wasn't at the five-mile mark. Still, I mused, these were perfect conditions in which to suffer, Mister's attempt to toughen up his team.

That is what you know awaits you on hill-climb days: suffering. But it's a pleasurable suffering, a suffering borne of inspiration, suffering with a purpose. It requires a certain mind-set on climbing days, a well-culti-vated discipline. This will not be an enjoyable run. You will feel as if your lungs are being scoured with a Brillo pad, your legs alternating between a hot-poker burning and a dull heaviness; either way, the effort to lift the knees, expand and contract the hamstrings, quadriceps, calves, and glutes is accomplished only by sustained force of will. Your arms, metronomic pistons that move seemingly on their own on less challenging courses, now need to be goaded into action. Your steps no longer seem certain, each footfall a negotiation with the terrain—a slight lunge here to avoid a gnarled, exposed root, a stutter-step there, a push off a boulder embedded in the soil. Yet you keep moving. For the benefits to be had in a hill climb come from enduring, not conquering, the pain, from the sheer stubborn-ness of the toil involved. The one thing you do not want to do, under any circumstances, is stop. To stop is to succumb.

Erica and I slowed our pace, slowed considerably as the first and sec-ond miles were behind us, but we maintained a relentless forward motion. I realized then what perhaps Erica's teammates had known: It wasn't "fun" to run with Erica. She made you work. At three miles, we had caught and passed Mo and Tony, who had been dropped by the rest of the varsity pack and seemed to be struggling. They grunted to us as we passed. Erica didn't seem to notice.

Then we reached a longer flat stretch, time to exhale. Erica shook out her arms for just a few seconds and then resumed her pumping. The

burning from my lungs to throat had dissipated, the feeling slowly returning to my legs, while my arms relaxed and my scrunched shoulders sighed.
These false summits, these caesuras in the symphony of your run, always
end too soon. But even this respite, this break from the grind of the climb,
renewed me enough to carry on to the next steep section. My vision alter-
nated from straight down at the ground, my world reduced to the perpetual three feet of trail directly in front of me, to the occasional glimpse
skyward to the destination, not yet visible. Erica just kept grinding away,
machine-like, seemingly impervious.

But it was on this stretch when a curious thing happened: Erica initiated
a conversation. Or, more accurately, she resumed (and amended) a conversation we had had a few weeks before, concerning the issues raised during
a contentious girls' team meeting at Mister's White Pass summer camp, held
a few miles west on Highway 12 from where we currently were running.

"God, it'll be good to have someone to run with next year," she said,
and for the first time she turned her head and looked my way. "It's going
to be weird in college when I'll have girls my level to run with."

"Yeah, I'll bet," I gasped.

"I mean, it was fine this summer because the boys weren't running all
that hard, and I could keep up with them," she added. "But now I'm back
running by myself. I mean, if I run with them [the girls], that does nothing
to help me."

A few more turns and we would reach the five-mile water stop. I
asked, haltingly, "Did you think the coaches were kind of hard on you at
White Pass?" referring to the July team meeting in which Erica was all
but labeled as selfish for not running or doing drills with her teammates.

"Every time we have one of those meetings, I'm like, 'Should I say
something? Or should I just sit back and do what I've been doing for three
years?' For three years, it's been my own thing. I think everyone kind of
knew that I always see it as myself in running. You know, the guys always
make a joke out of it, saying like, 'Oh Erica, does your back hurt?' They
mean from carrying the team on my back. Stuff like that."

I nodded, and she continued as we trudged upward toward the last
mile and the turnaround.

"I expected Mister's reaction. I'm still kind of working on thinking of
it as a team thing. Not everyone can think of it that way because they don't
really want to make themselves better as strongly as maybe I do. I've never
seen cross as doing it for someone else, because I've always been doing it
for myself. I've always been that way."

Given Erica's stated aversion to "chatting" on a run, this qualified as a soliloquy. When silence resumed, labored breathing the only sound, my mind drifted back to the scene in July at White Pass, in which the girls met around two pushed-together tables and tried to hash out their differences, with Mister and assistant coach Robin Bryson-Driver serving as (mostly) silent witnesses.

★ ★ ★

At White Pass, Erica didn't mince words. She thought her teammates' effort during summer training was lacking—something of a joke, really—and she leaned both elbows on the table and told them so.

"I know you guys probably think I'm crazy, starting to train super-hard way early. But I think after camp is the time to slowly start turning it up. I think you guys are really freaked out about burning out; it's just mental. After camp, you guys should focus on picking it up."

Bryson-Driver, legs crossed and staring at the floor but hearing every word, winced at Erica's repeated use of "you guys" instead of the more inclusive "we" when talking to teammates.

Erica, lips pursed and arms crossed, had more to say.

"You guys lack the competitive edge. . . . I mean, we're not like a state title-winning team. But we should at least do the best we can with the talent level we have."

Dantzel shook her head. "I feel we should *act* like we are, though. Because the more you act like you are, the harder you'll work."

Erica resumed: "We were very close to losing [the district title] last year. We went 1-2-3 last year at districts and *still* almost lost. That was scary."

After a lull, Mister stood and addressed the table. He, at last, made an explicit reference to the underlying problem with the girls' team.

"How," he asked, "are you going to come to terms with the big split between Erica and the rest of the team?"

All eyes, seemingly, turned to Erica.

"It took me a really long time, three years, to think that, you know, [my teammates] go through the same exact thing I'm going through [in a race]," she said. "I mean, we're all the same. I'm not different in any way. We're all females. We're all human. I don't know, I kind of forget they can improve and have bad days, and it's just different levels. I've been doing this for a really long time and it's like a super-big thing to me, and I always forget that this isn't, like, their life. I still don't really think of this as a team sport because I've just been always thinking, if you just focus on yourself, then that will improve the team score. It's been rough trying to think of it as a team thing. I'm *trying*."

"Erica," Mister quickly responded, his voice softening despite his sucking-on-a-lemon expression, "that speaks volumes right there, though. If you don't think of it as a team sport, then a lot of your actions, well, that's the way it's going to be reflected. You understand, though, what you're saying?"

"It's hard because I also have my parents saying, 'Oh, just focus on yourself.' It's hard because I know I don't spend a lot of time with you guys because I'm either doing my own thing or running with someone else. But I still love cheering you guys on in races. That's like my favorite thing, screaming and yelling when you run."

Mister would not let the subject go.

"How do you see the rest of the team performing, Erica? In terms of the workouts? Do you make a mental disconnect between yourself and the team?"

"I'll say, 'Oh, good job, girls,' whenever I pass them or see them, but usually I'm just trying to focus on whatever I'm doing," Erica replied. "I'm oblivious to whatever's going on. I'm just trying to run my own workout and such."

"That's a two-edge sword, Erica," Mister said, scanning the group. "The rest of you, what we saw last year was all the different reasons why you couldn't do something. That's got to improve."

Molly piped up: "It's not like we say, 'Oh, we're going with Erica.' It's like, we want to go this pace. Me and Dan are working together in practice. It's not like our goal is, we want to be with Erica. We can't."

Erica: "When I'm running with the boys and feeling OK, that's such an energy rush and confidence builder as well. I think, hey, I'm running with this person I couldn't imagine running with before."

The meeting broke for lunch shortly thereafter. They did, it should be noted, eat as a group, Erica included.

Lingering in the buffet line, Mister and Bryson-Driver spoke sotto voce about the meeting.

"This is something that needs to be resolved, quickly," was all Mister said.

Bryson-Driver, the former Eisenhower individual state champion in 1988 whose team finished second that same year, was more animated. She pushed her glasses back up on her nose and puffed her cheeks before exhaling.

"I just don't understand that thinking," she said of Erica. "When I ran, it wasn't about how *you* were doing. It was the team. Not me, me, me. It was the same situation when I ran. I was at a different level, but the girls got along and worked hard, and I made a big effort with them.

"Erica talked to me at last year's state meet as we were going over the course beforehand. The year I won the state title, we lost the team title by two points. Erica asked me, 'What it was like to win the individual state championship?' I said, 'Honestly, Erica, I was thinking about the team, and I was down because we lost by two points.' Even now, I think about that more than winning the [individual] title. Erica said, 'I can't understand that. You were the winner.' It's a different personality and mind-set, I guess."

A few days later, back in Yakima, many of the girls were still talking about what happened at the meeting. No one begrudged Erica her talent and dedication. Not a single Eisenhower runner, boy or girl, had trained as hard and with as much intensity. Her inward focus and lack of concern for teammates rankled some, especially Molly. She and Erica, as the only returning varsity seniors, had a cordial relationship and sometimes could be overheard talking about TV shows they liked. But they differed in approach. Whereas Molly, and Dantzel as well, would shout out encouragement to struggling teammates at practice, Erica was mostly silent, all business, concentrating on her time splits.

"I feel like it was me and Dan and the other girls versus Erica, that's sort of what it got down to, *again*," Molly said a few days after the meeting, her face crimson either from the run or from her memory of the Erica meeting. "A couple times, me and Dan looked up at each other whenever Erica said she doesn't look at it as a team sport. She's been saying that for years, and Mister's just been letting that happen. So that's why we were happy Mister finally said something to her about it. This was the first time he's spoken about it to her and the team.

"I get that she's better than us. I'm completely fine with that. But she doesn't need to vocalize it, is what we're saying. It's her personality; she's not a leader. We know that. We said to her [after the meeting], 'You don't need to tell other people they are not important to you.'"

★ ★ ★

Back on Bethel Ridge Road, we neared the summit—or, at least, the six-mile turnaround. When you find yourself getting closer, when you dare to take a quick backward glance to assess where you are going from where you have been, it can be a shock to notice how civilization has fallen away, how far down "down there" is, just how far you have traveled, step by step, and it can lift your spirits and propel you forward.

Erica stopped for water at the turnaround. Even she was breathing hard by this point, rivulets of sweat running down her frame, but I still figured that she would want to get going on the downhill right away. But she lingered. She waved me over to the side of the road, where, looking down about 4,000 feet from whence we came, we took in a gorgeous view—a vast tree-lined expanse below—and reveled in the sight of the late-afternoon sun glinting off Rimrock Lake.

"When we came up here last year—no, two years ago—somebody took our picture with us staring into that view from this spot," she said. "It was so cool. I used it as my background photo on Facebook."

On the trip down, Erica retreated to silence once more. Her body seemed to move in sync via muscle memory, years of practice making her movement almost automatic. Her mind seemed far away, deep in contemplation. A mile back down the road, we passed Molly and Dantzel chugging upward. Sweat matted the girls' brows, and their heads and backs were bent forward, leaning into the uphill as if pilgrims in supplication. We saw them before they saw us.

"Good job, girls," Erica said to them as we passed.

I smiled and looked Erica's way, but she had already resumed her mechanical movement, eyes fixed straight ahead, always straight ahead, as if willing herself to keep moving forward.

★ ★ ★

To begin to understand the gulf between Erica and her teammates, you had to look at her background. And that meant, first, looking at the photo on the Simison family refrigerator. It explained a lot.

The snapshot showed Erica at age 7, just a tiny little thing, competing at the Sunfair Invitational kids' race. Her forehead barely cleared the orange plastic netting placed around the course. Her bib number, 2663, extended from her clavicle to her waistband, covering her black T-shirt that reads "Davis Cheer." She was wearing regular cotton shorts and a pair of tennis shoes, not fancy running trainers.

Her dad, Eric, just loves this picture. And relishes talking about it.

"That was Erica's first race," he says. "First of many."

He smiles, the same slightly wan, slightly crooked smile as his daughter. Erica looks like her dad—same olive complexion, same high cheekbones and full, dark eyebrows—though he is slightly taller at about 5-foot-6. He is the keeper of the cross-country memorabilia in the family. Much of the basement in the family home on Yakima Avenue in the historic district is devoted to Bryan and Erica's running exploits. Eric had strung wire along the walls and threaded both of the kids' bib numbers for races, as a Buddhist would do with Tibetan prayer flags. Eric saved every news clipping, every medal and ribbon, his kids earned. And there were a lot.

He loves to recount Erica's first Sunfair appearance. She had come to Yakima's Franklin Park a little late that day to watch her big brother, Bryan, eight years her senior, run for Eisenhower. Erica and her mom had been at a Davis High School cheerleading event earlier in the day, hence the seemingly mixed allegiance.

"It was a one-mile race for third, fourth, and fifth graders, so Erica was too young," he says. "But Phil said, go ahead and put her in. You could just tell she kind of liked it. I think she finished in the top five that day."

Erica—surprising, for her—does not remember either her time or place. But the experience made a big impression on her. In fact, in her room, she still has a photo of herself between Amy-Eloise Neale, the Sunfair champion that long ago day, and Mayra Chavez, Eisenhower's top runner and Erica's role model.

"I thought it was so cool. I grew up watching my brother race," she says. "I thought, 'Wow, these runners are like gods. They are incredible.' I grew up thinking, I hope I'm at least half as good as they are some day."

"I suspected, after that day," Eric adds, "that she'd want to go to other races."

And not just to watch her brother.

Erica became something of a prodigy, one of Washington's best youth runners. Eric saw a lot of potential early on in his daughter but says he didn't push her. Erica, he says, always asked to compete.

"She wanted to do it," he says. "She kind of figured out that, 'I might be OK at this running thing,' and kids are drawn to something that they are good at sometimes. Gosh, I remember she raced at the Bellevue Invite and placed in the top three against adult women in the open race. She went to the Richland Invite. There were 250 girls in the middle school race, and in her sixth grade year she got second. She raced the [Washington-Oregon] Border Clash for four or five years, the 'future clash' kids race, and she did great."

Eric and Pam Simison never feared that Erica would burn out, as can happen to some young phenom runners who do too much too soon. That's because she was always so exuberant about racing. The way young

Erica figured it, if she had to tag along all over the state to watch her big brother race for Eisenhower, she might as well join in the fun.

Turned out, Bryan was the one experiencing burnout, though Eric and Pam didn't know it at the time. Bryan was Eisenhower's top boys' runner in 2008 and second fastest in 2009. He still holds two of the top 15 fastest times ever for Eisenhower boys at the state meet. Such performances earned him a scholarship to run at New Mexico State University. What they didn't know until several years later was that Bryan was feeling the strain of expectations and simply wasn't enjoying himself. Eric is an electrician, Pam manages a hospital pharmacy, and they needed that scholarship money back then to send Bryan to college. Looking back, they say, it may have put pressure on him.

"Bryan really didn't feel like he had that option not to run," Pam says. "Not because we were making him feel that way, not to my knowledge, but we just didn't offer it to him. We didn't remind him that it's just an extracurricular activity that he didn't have to do."

"Bryan," his dad adds, "didn't care much about the running, but he liked how he felt when he did well. He liked the reward. You couldn't get him to do anything offseason, anything at all, as far as racing. We found out after he graduated that there were a bunch of Sundays Mister wanted him to run a half hour, easy, and he didn't do that. But with Erica, right from the start, if a coach or somebody like that said to balance greasy BBs on your eyeballs, she'd try it."

Erica would be by her dad's side at all of Bryan's races, tugging on his sleeve, asking to learn about strategy and tactics. Bryan, like Erica, was a diminutive runner, and Eric pointed out to his daughter how Bryan would be aggressive at the congested start, would use his elbows to find room to run. Most elementary-school kids look for a playground to gambol in on a cross-country course, anything to avoid the chaos of herds of runners thundering by and parents bleating out encouragement. But Erica sought out the competition. Watching her brother was something of a primer for her future self.

"I said to her, 'You watch Bryan, Erica. He's looking where he's going to go, making sure he didn't get boxed or pushed out, picking a line." And Erica paid attention. And she asked questions. Now she's very aggressive in a race. In a pack, she's not afraid to let those elbows out and tap people on the arm, make sure they keep their space. Erica knew how to race because she's been doing it for so long."

Pam says that once she and her husband learned of Bryan's burnout— he no longer runs, not even recreationally—she took it upon herself to lower the burner to simmer when it came to Erica, to remind her that they have no expectations of her on the course or track.

"I flat out told her, 'Remember, Bryan had some challenges, and I'm worried that you'll burn out too.' Erica said, 'No, I'm not going to be like Bryan. I'm confident I can do this.'"

What is a caring parent to do when his child is so hell-bent on competing? Do you hold her back and risk frustrating her? Or do you plunge headlong into the sport and risk burnout in the future?

The Simisons chose the second option, mostly because Erica was always there with her running shoes at the ready. Other parents and perhaps some coaches may have felt that Erica was running too much too soon. But the family pressed on. By the time Erica hit fifth grade, she was routinely beating the middle-school kids: sixth, seventh, and eighth graders. That fact that Erica was even racing against the older kids at that point was the cause of some controversy.

"It all started," Eric says, "when I was helping to set up a middle-school [cross-country] race with a guy named James Thomas who did all the timing and setup for all the running events in Yakima. I remember him asking me, 'Want to enter Erica?' I said, 'Can we?' He said. 'We run the meet, we can enter anyone we want.' So we made a number for her. But I said to him, 'She shouldn't get a ribbon or a place in the race. Her run won't count.'"

That first race, Erica finished second among eighth graders.

"So then track season rolls around, and James and I are setting up middle-school meets, timing them. We started putting Erica in the 1,600 [meter race]. They'd run the boys and girls together. Erica finished second in the first two races. Then, in the third race, at Franklin Park, she won it. Beat a seventh grader, Megan Glenski [future Eisenhower standout runner]. The coach at Franklin comes up to Erica and us and says, 'Who's this? What school do you go to?' And Erica turned to me like, 'What do I say, Dad?'"

The coach was told that Erica was a fifth grader at Whitney Elementary School and that she would occasionally join the workouts of the neighboring Wilson Middle School track team.

"Well, the coach, she got all upset," Eric continues, "called the school district athletic coordinator, and then he called Wilson's coach, told him Erica couldn't practice with them and said Erica couldn't compete either. The guy made a big deal out of it. I did some research, and there are numerous occasions they let fifth graders compete in middle school and eighth graders in high school. Typically, it was small schools in rural areas.

I wrote a letter to the school district guy and I titled it, 'Nowhere to Run.' The letter basically said that, in this day and age when we're trying to get kids out from behind a screen or TV, and here we have a child who wants to do more, you're telling kids, no, do less. What kind of message is that? You have a kid who wants to push herself beyond normal for her age, and what harm does it do? She ran for no trophy, no medal, no ribbon. She was nonexistent. She just wanted to run. He sent back some bureaucratic letter, blah, blah, blah."

Miffed, Eric contacted the media, a sportswriter from the *Yakima Herald-Republic*, and told him the whole story.

"The writer told me that Erica obviously had a lot of talent, but did I really want to go public with this thing? I eventually backed off and I thought, you know, in less than a year, she'd be in middle school herself. Erica understood what happened, but she did enjoy whipping those kids who were older than her."

Even in middle school, Erica kept the same coach—her father.

"During junior high, the coaches don't really train the kids," he says. "They just want them to do something, like play Frisbee, whatever. Erica'd come home, and I'd say, 'How'd the workout go?' And she'd go, 'What workout? We kind of fooled around.' So I coached her at Franklin [Park]. But at the end of middle school, Daddy's not your coach anymore. That had been the plan. She knew in third grade what she wanted. She said, 'I'm going to Eisenhower and running for Mister.' It was, like, predetermined. Not by us. She was dead set on going to Ike and running for Mister. It's something every young runner around here does."

Erica fondly recalls her early years in the sport. What sticks out most in her mind is the relationship she built with her dad.

"My dad just loved to watch me race when I was little," she says. "One of the first community races I did, I think it was in Spokane, and I think I finished fourth, he was so excited he started crying. He gets so into it. I guess it might be because I'm the last kid [left at home] or the only girl. He's been super-chill about everything. And he supports me even now. Sometimes in the summer when I won't be able to make practice, I'll call him and tell him, 'I'll be running at Franklin tonight,' and he loves to come over and just watch me. That's our way of bonding."

★ ★ ★

Erica does not cry, her mom says. What's more, she does not *believe* in crying. She's not philosophically opposed to the concept or anything. It's fine, if that's how you choose to get your emotional release. But that display of emotion is just not for Erica.

Not exactly stoic, more like strong and formidable, Erica faces obstacles and setbacks head-on. If she shows an emotion in tough times, it's more likely to be anger or annoyance. Or, when in a celebratory mood, she'll crack an almost Mona Lisa–type smile. No hoots and hollers from this young woman.

The brunt of Erica's emotions ofttimes is her mother. Whereas Erica said she long ago bonded with her father over their shared interest in running, her relationship with her mother has been more complicated.

"She has this thing where she thinks crying is a weakness," Pam says. "She didn't get it from me. She gets kind of angry and she'll lash out at me in [some] moment. But she's not a girl you'll find sobbing and people consoling her. She does not like that at all. I don't know how to explain it. She's always been that way."

Erica says her relationship with her mom has evolved, gotten better.

"My mother's always like, 'You need to socialize more with the girls' team. Be more sensitive,'" Erica says. "She's always saying how insensitive I am. Growing up, I didn't have ways to bond with her. We kind of had a strained relationship, the normal teenage stuff like, 'Oh, Mom, blah blah blah.' But as I've grown up, I'm dressing differently. She loves that. She once worked at Nordstrom. She is kind of a fashion diva. Before, I would always just wear running clothes and not do my makeup. Now I'm dressing up more. She just loves it. Now we're able to bond."

Still, Pam is worried that Erica's lone-wolf tendency on the cross-country team has had an alienating effect—both on Erica and the team. As a mother, though, Pam's primary concern is Erica and her socialization. She and Eric have had heart-to-heart talks with Erica about her solitary ways, her go-it-alone attitude, and it's caused a minor familial rift.

"It does matter to me," Pam says. "I'm a lot more observant of things like that than my husband. Things like that don't bother him much. I find myself in the position of constantly saying things to her about [socializing] and that caused a little strain in our relationship. She just didn't like what I was saying. So, Eric was the good parent because he didn't offer anything. I was the one saying stuff about socializing.

"I was the one always saying, 'Do you want to have somebody over? Do you want to go to the movies?' It's interesting. She's very content to be home. Her social time is school and running, and then she's done socializing, whereas you hear of other people going off to a football game or other events. Honestly, you cannot tell if she's had a bad day at practice. I will maybe come at her from another direction or overhear a conversation she has, but you cannot tell. She hides it from us very well. . . . I try to be creative, like, 'Oh, who showed up for practice today?' Get her talking like that. I think she knows I'm on her side. But I also point out, 'Not everyone is like you.'"

Erica is hardly friendless. Her best friend at Eisenhower is fellow senior Paul Perrault, scion of a major Yakima Valley hops producer, Perrault Farms. Her boyfriend is Ronan Price; the two started dating in her junior year during cross-country season. But Ronan now is at Eastern Washington University, so that's one fewer close confidant for Erica during the school day.

Her daughter's social life may have been an issue to Pam, but Erica seems utterly unconcerned. Like most teens, Erica is into binge-watching TV shows—*Orange Is the New Black* is a favorite. She plays video games, on occasion, but does the bulk of her socialization texting by phone. Often, after getting home from practice, Erica will draw a bath and loll in the warm water for more than an hour, texting all the while. She has yet to drop the phone in the water, though Pam fears that day will come eventually.

"I try not to push," Pam says, "but I do tell her, 'You can always have friends over. Just tell us first.' But, no. Actually, last night, she did go to the movies with Paul. I tried to hide my excitement."

Unfazed and unapologetic, Erica seems comfortable with who she is—and who she isn't. But she is quick to note, for the record, that she had been close to Molly and JV runner Kayli Carl when the three were younger, and she also mentions that she remains friendly with Davis High's top runner, Ada Naranjo, as the two have competed against each other fiercely since middle school.

"I was close with Molly, but then I just became so enveloped with my running," Erica says. "So we don't have that relationship to bond anymore. Now, me trying to figure out what I'm supposed to say and stuff, I end up getting frustrated at myself and them too. It's super-strained, and whenever we talk about the team, she'll say, 'But yeah, you don't really care about the team.' She's OK saying those very passive-aggressive things."

Molly, for her part, has mixed feelings about Erica. It shows in her pinched expression when pulled aside from a workout to talk.

"Yes, me and Erica, we used to, like, read each other's minds," Molly says. "I mean, really close. We're still buddy-buddy, but when it comes to the team, that's where the separate rules come in. Erica doesn't really care about the team. [But] they don't really look up to her. They think like, 'Oh, she's the No. 1 runner. She's really good.' But they don't really listen to her. And [Erica] knows that. Some of the girls wish she'd be more involved, but . . .'"

Part of the problem may just be Erica's inherent bluntness. She never has been one for game playing and passive-aggressiveness. She'll say what's on her mind. But part of it also may be her perfectionism, her high standards, her feeling that everyone needs to be as dedicated to running as she and, if they aren't, it's something of a failing, something she cannot slough off.

Occasionally, over the summer, Erica made efforts to at least run with her teammates. It turned out a little awkward.

"I was running with two of the girls, and they were talking with each other and then one had to go to the bathroom [and veered off], and I was just kind of running along and [the other girl] said to me, 'So you don't really talk much when you run, do you?' And I'm, like, 'Oh, yeah.' It just never comes across my mind that I should strike up a conversation while I'm running."

Another time, when Erica was a junior, Sophi Rodriquez approached Erica and unburdened herself concerning a personal problem. Erica freaked a little.

"I don't know," Erica says, recalling the encounter, "it was like I was on *Real Housewives*. I didn't know what to say. They [fellow runners] talk to each other about their emotions. I'm like, 'What's going on? What is this?'"

Erica has always just wanted to run. Then again, in the next breath, she will speak approvingly of how close the boys' team has become, how they have trained hard as a group and still find time to joke around, without an undue amount of teenage psychodrama. If the boys have a disagreement, she says, it is usually verbalized and settled right away. Erica admires that.

At many practices, after finishing the workout slightly behind the boys but well ahead of the girls, Erica would linger in a kind of no-woman's-land next to the water jugs, listening in to the boys' conversations about video games or the virtues of one barber over another. She would smile at their jokes but hardly ever said a word. And when the girls trotted up, Erica often would not join them. She, physically, was torn between the two groups.

"I don't know where I'm supposed to belong on this team," she says, dry-eyed and matter-of-factly. "I mean, I think [the girls] like me. I hope they do. But it's not the end of my life if they don't. That's kind of how I think of it."

The issue of Erica's role on the team reached a partial resolution at another Camp Ghormley meeting a few hours after the Bethel Ridge

Road run mercifully was behind the team. Mister announced that the coaches would have Erica do all drills and "routine" running with the girls, at the girls' pace, but that she would do targeted workouts with the JV boys. No more trying to keep up with the varsity boys for Erica, because soon the boys' pack would be striving for sub-five-minute miles in workouts, a pace that Erica, good as she is, simply cannot sustain.

So, by the time of Erica's one-on-one interview—the last runner interviewed at camp, coming on Sunday morning—little is left to hash out about the chasm between her and the girls. Instead, Mister breaks the ice asking about Erica's college scholarship thinking.

Mister: "One of the places that would fit that if you have an interest is WSU."

"Whaaaaat? Ew."

"Why, Erica?"

"I don't know. I never considered WSU or U-Dub [University of Washington]. They are just ginormous schools."

"Don't be putting artificial blocks on your talent."

"I figure the bigger the school, the more competitive the classes are."

Mister rubs his temples and then grumbles, "Oh, my goodness."

"I'm going to be doing more than running in college, you know."

"You'll be fine with the classes, Erica. You're a smart girl."

"OK, I'll think about WSU."

"This is a battle you and I are going to have to have. Just like the first few years of high school, you had a tendency to set the bar too low for running goals. Now you're doing the same thing going into college."

"OK."

"What's your greatest strength, Erica?"

"I'm able to push through some stuff, like pain."

"Weakness?"

"Mental, maybe. Like thinking, 'Oh, I'm not an elite runner.'"

"What's your biggest fear?"

"Not having the cross season be what I want it to be. I have way bigger goals than other years. One of the goals is to get top five at State."

"I think that's doable. The team can't be a handicap to you. I know that's a concern for you. But in the same vein, this is your *team*. There are days you'll need to run easy *with them*. It'll feel very easy to you, but that's your workout. It's not going to ruin your season."

"OK, Mister."

JONAS

The Price family home, on the corner of 32nd Avenue and West Chestnut Avenue on the fringe of Yakima's "historic neighborhood," was a grocery store back in the 1950s and, thus, was bifurcated between retail and residential space. The larger left side of the split-level ranch home is devoted to mom Lisa's ballet studio, where for more than two decades, aspiring dancers have worked on pliés and pirouettes before floor-to-ceiling windows in full view of traffic streaming by. The other side houses a typical domestic scene, a lived-in space housing two teenage boys, the older one just now away at college. A huge flat-screen television dominates the living room, and a fluffy futon serves as both coffee table and close-in viewing space. A virtual-reality helmet for videogame usage dangles over a table edge and, upstairs, in the kids' bedroom, bib numbers from races and inspirational running posters dominate, goals tacked to the walls. On the back porch, away from public view, discarded running shoes lay splayed like exhausted soldiers back from the front lines of an eternal war.

Order and disorder live harmoniously, mostly, at the Price residence. But during the cross-country season, Lisa, a former dancer with a Canadian ballet company who still maintains the lithe stature, regal bearing, and preternatural grace years after hanging up her slippers, could feel a little impinged upon, a little bit like running has invaded her (and her dancers') space. Such as on this day, when nearly every inch of the barre that runs along the mirrored back wall is draped with sweaty running

T-shirts, shorts, and socks. She looks at the hanging laundry and seems more amused than irritated.

"All that'll be gone by the time class starts," she assures. "It better be."

In the past few years, she has become accustomed to the encroachment of running in the family's life. Especially in the fall, when cross-country season is in full swing. But also in spring, during track season. And in summer, during heavy training. Winter? She catches a break then. Somewhat. But this is what she has come to expect—and embrace—being the wife of Robert Price, a former Olympic trials steeplechaser who now coaches his own sons in cross-country and track. She is outnumbered, three to two, by males bantering about mileage and time splits and which drills to do on which days. Lisa, emphatically not a runner, had only the family dog, Lola, a shaggy Yorkshire terrier, on her side. But, actually, she embraces her role as de facto runner support staff, the sensible one who occasionally can remind the guys that there is more to life than putting one foot in front of the other as swiftly as possible.

"No, it's not always running [discussed] at the dinner table," she says. "Well, I guess, it sort of is. It always has to come up. There's always going to be talk of running, but it's not all running."

Far from minding, Lisa (and, occasionally, Lola) always is there on cross-country meet Saturdays, cheering with the other parents. The 2016 season, when Ronan was a senior and Jonas a freshman, had been more nerve-racking for her, what with two kids running in the same races. But she's found it is no less fraught now that Ronan is at Eastern Washington University and Jonas is the sole focus here at home. Yet the stakes, in many respects, are even higher—mainly because Jonas and his lofty expectations have raised them.

Jonas has always been the driven, obsessive Price child. Ronan, two years older and blessed with natural talent, had been more laid-back and accepting of whatever result came from the hard work his dad and Mister had him log. But Jonas? Not so much. He takes training to an extreme, pumps himself full of self-motivation, and accepts nothing less than total victory and complete effort at all times, no exceptions. He's been, in some respects, just like the younger Robert Price was, the one whom Lisa saw around campus at Carroll High all those years ago, pushing himself beyond limits.

"A lot of people say I'm looking at myself in the mirror," Robert says. He smiles, ruefully but with a dash of pride. Nearing 50, his dark crew cut showing the first signs of speckled gray, Robert maintains the hard body and regimental bearing of his competitive years. Though a bum knee has curtailed his own running, Robert sees many of the qualities he brought to cross-country (drive, ambition, obsessiveness) displayed in his youngest son.

"I never thought of myself as being that much of a puissant," he says of Jonas, making sport of himself more than his son. "My dad had a saying that applied to Jonas—he's full of piss and vinegar. He's that raw. Just the past couple of weeks, he's driving us nuts. He has this way about him. Relentless. It can get tiring."

What his dad refers to is Jonas's occasional knack for crossing the line between expressing his lofty goals and oversharing said goals. The boy, just 15, spent part of the summer walking around the house arms upraised and hands cupped in a circle—the symbol of the University of Oregon athletic teams. Jonas's most ambitious goal, besides making the Olympic team, is to get a scholarship to run for Oregon, a college track and cross-country program rich in running lore, a place that has produced such Olympians as Steve Prefontaine and Galen Rupp and was once led by coach Bill Bowerman, the cofounder of Nike. Among the goals Jonas has written and hung in his room is to earn a scholarship to Oregon. That piece of paper gets top billing on his goal wall, above even the lofty goal of qualifying for NXN, the national championship of prep cross-country. Maybe—*maybe*—two or three of the nation's top distance runners each year earn a coveted Oregon scholarship, but Jonas has this goal in his sights, and he will not be dissuaded.

Just as Mister tries to rein in Jonas's need to run more miles, to run them harder and faster than he should, his father and mother try to quell Jonas's ambitious goals—or, at least, the public declaration of them. Granted, Jonas's times in the 1,600 and 3,200 meters as a freshman in track season were the best for his class in the state, and his fast summer training in cross-country did, indeed, bode well for success in November at the state meet. But Robert urges caution, especially because Jonas is only a sophomore and not even close to having to decide about college. Heck, the kid still hasn't finished his driver training courses. That's how young he is.

"I try to stay away, but I know Jonas is motivated and I try not to be 'the dad,' so it doesn't become the whole Lavar Ball scenario, saying, he's going to do this, do that," Robert says, referring to Ball, the notorious parent of top-notch collegiate and pro basketball players who openly boasted about his sons' exploits. "There's too many things that can get in the way. You never want to set your sons up for failure, saying, 'You're going to be this.' When I won my first state title, I said to myself, 'Don't be cocky about it. Don't be cocky.' And I was not vocal about it. I tell Jonas, 'If you're gonna be like this, if you're gonna talk like this, talk at *home*. Don't talk outside or online about what you're gonna do and how you're gonna do it.' That's why he drives us nuts at home; he'll start talking about how he's going to Oregon, compare that to Ronan running to Eastern."

Whenever Jonas invokes Oregon, which is often, Robert becomes the stern dad, not wanting to tamp down ambitions but also wanting to avoid inflating his son's already healthy ego.

"Prove it, little squirt," he'll tell Jonas with a sly smile. "Prove it on the course."

What really drives Jonas, even more than the prospect of a state title or a scholarship to Oregon, has everything to do with his complicated paternal feelings. He may have been too young to fully examine the deep-seated motives behind his striving, but there clearly were some Oedipal dynamics at work. Robert Price knows. He teaches psychology and history at Eisenhower. Jonas wants to not only equal but surpass his father's high-school and college running exploits. It would be hard to do, as Robert won eight state titles (three in cross-country, five in track and field) in his three years of running for Mister at Carroll in the mid-1980s. He later ran for Washington State, specializing in the steeplechase. He medaled in the competitive Pacific-10 conference and qualified for the 1992 Olympic trials.

"Jonas doesn't want to beat my records," Robert says. "He wants to obliterate them."

That would be a lofty perch for a kid to ascend, especially because Robert competed on the small school level (1A in Washington State), and Eisenhower is in the largest category (4A). And Robert, too, was a different type of runner than his two sons have been. He was solidly built and powerfully fast, like an 800-meter runner; Ronan and Jonas are lithe and rangy, better suited to much longer distances. In a way, Jonas had been blessed with a genetic mix to which any distance runner would aspire. His frame is rangy and agile, like his mother, but he also has a robust cardiovascular system that clearly came from his father and his sturdy, middle-distance body. What father and sons share, however, is what Mister calls "an ease of movement, a way of making running look very easy by being efficient. . . . Jonas may be lighter, but he's got Robert's big engine [lung capacity]. And mentally, Jonas is more on the Robert end of things." Meaning, mentally tough, willing to endure certain pain for potential glory.

This younger version of Robert Price, the one Mister and Lisa recall as intense to an extreme, is nothing if not driven. He possesses a get-tough attitude that extends beyond the track. In 1992, shortly after running in

Olympic trials for the steeplechase, Robert was diagnosed with testicular cancer, enduring nine months of chemotherapy and, later, surgery to remove 20 lymph glands in his torso. He has been cancer-free ever since and, even at 49, keeps his body in race condition. When he pulls up his T-shirt to expose the six-inch vertical scar that runs like a railroad track down his abdomen, you don't see the paunch most middle-aged men carry. You see a nasty gash that is testimony to Robert's toughness, what coaches well versed in cliché might call his intestinal fortitude.

"I've never seen a high-school runner so tough and so dedicated as Bobby," said Kris Vickers, a few years ahead of Price at Carroll and a state champion who ran for Mister. "He was putting in some huge mileage and refused to lose."

Originally, Robert only went out for the Carroll cross-country program as a sophomore to get in shape for basketball. His older brother, George, was a 400-meter runner and a sprinter, but "he did cross, so I did too," Robert recalls. "I was competitive but when it came to wanting to be good at something, I wanted to prove better than my brother. It was that sibling rivalry thing. My first workout I puked when I got home. But Mister, he called it the Ugly Duckling Syndrome. I was one of that storyline. He could take somebody raw and make me into a state champion from what ability I had."

Where English sees the most similarity between Robert and Jonas is in their demeanor, their relentless drive to be the best. Robert, not quite apologetically, admits to being obsessed with winning. Then again, he adds, most really successful people harbor some degree of obsession.

"I wanted to win," he says. "I'd get into a mind-set that you are not going to beat me. It wasn't cockiness, because I didn't say that to people. But in my mind, I'm thinking, 'You're gonna have to beat me and kill me if you're going to win this race.' It was part of my personality. Mister hated it when I'd get in a race and think I'd have to go to the front. Luckily, I was blessed with some speed, but once I finally figured out late in my sophomore year that you don't have to lead to win, that you can sit and kick at the end, that's the way to win. Yeah, I was one of those assholes who, if I'm sitting on your shoulder, your ass is mine. But early on, I would go so hard that it would hurt. The lungs would hurt. The head would hurt. In this day and age, a kid'll come up and say, 'I think this'll hurt.' I say, as a coach, 'It's OK, you're not gonna die, you just aren't in that great of shape, so let's try this.' In our day, we'd never complain like that, unless you were bleeding, or some bone was sticking out.'"

That Robert sees such passion in Jonas is heartening and a little troubling. Heartening in that his son is passionate about his sport. Troubling, perhaps, because such single-minded fervor potentially can lead to crushing disappointment if he falls short.

To Jonas, though, the main motivation is to top his father's exploits, like some sporting version of Oedipus sans the whole marry-your-mother thing. Hanging on a wall in his room is a blown-up photograph of 2016 Olympic 1,500-meter champion Matt Centrowitz, shirtless, bearing a chest-length tattoo with the inscription: "Like Father Like Son." It's a reference to Centrowitz's father, Matt Sr., who also was a champion distance runner in his day. Jonas has talked about getting a similar tattoo, in honor of Robert's influence, a prospect that makes the humble Robert wince.

Their relationship is at once close and guarded, at least around the team. Jonas is an affectionate, tactile teenager; and sometimes without notice, he sidles up to Robert during breaks in workouts and nestles his head into Robert's shoulder. On these occasions, Robert, perhaps trying to maintain a coach-runner distance, usually pats Jonas two or three times on the back and pulls away. Sometimes, though, Jonas persists, usually because he wants something from his dad. "Price," Jonas would say, using the family surname, which was what other runners call Robert, "can we get a new pair of Brooks [running shoes]?" It is the standard teenage gambit, something familiar to any parent—be all affectionate in hopes of getting something you want. And, yeah, occasionally, it works, and Robert softens and assents.

"My dad pushes me to be the best," Jonas says after one hot summer workout in the coolness of the track shed. "But I'm thinking, I want to be *better* than my dad because I always tell him, 'I want to impress you so much, I'll be better than you.' He's like, 'Let me see it then.' I'm like, 'OK, you'll see it.' You know, when I was younger, he talked about his college career, how he got third in the PAC-12 once. I was pretty amazed what he'd done, coming from Yakima and going to WSU. I was surprised he went to the Olympic trials. I've watch the trials now on TV, and I think, 'Wow, my dad was on TV once. My dad told me once, when I asked about his running, he said, 'You know, I was an eight-time state champ.' I was like, 'OK, Dad.' I wasn't impressed at all. But as I kept getting older and older, I was like, 'How can he do that?' It is mind-blowing to me now.

"I think of that, and I think I do want to run Division 1. I want to do what my dad didn't do . . . make the Olympic team. It's my biggest goal."

Jonas speaks with such bubbling enthusiasm, such lack of guile, that the declaration does not come off as braggadocio. He is, rather, dreaming big. He has the luminous smile, toothy with the slightest of overbites, of his mother; and the laserlike, slightly menacing stare of his father. His intensity, occasionally, veers off the charts.

Lisa has often heard such big talk from her youngest. She didn't encourage it and says Robert didn't either. Yet, in something of a parental conundrum, neither wanted to extinguish Jonas's competitive fire or kill his dreams. As she sits on the back porch one late July afternoon, while Robert is running errands and Jonas is at a driver's education class, she talks family dynamics.

"I don't think it's healthy in that, you know, I don't want Jonas to be disappointed in himself," she says of the comparisons between father and son. "Jonas takes things really hard. And we've talked about it. What if it doesn't happen? What if you aren't as good as your dad? With your dad, it was years ago, and it was a smaller school. Jonas said, 'I'll take that into consideration.' So we'll see. He hears it a lot around the team, like, 'Oh, your dad won this many state titles,' and that's hard to hear. I think Jonas is starting to learn [to keep his ambitions to himself]."

She pauses and then smiles.

"But he is one who will put his goals up on his wall."

Big brother Ronan, true to his laid-back demeanor, brushes off his brother's big talk.

"I think it's because after the success he's seen with me, he wants to be better than me—and my dad," Ronan says. "He's very competitive, and that's what drives him on that cocky edge, like, 'Oh, I'm better than you were as a freshman, and I'll be better than you all the other times.' I'm OK with it, but sometimes he takes it too far. He doesn't mean anyone any harm, and he's one of the nicest kids on this team. He just gets so into it, he takes everything seriously, and he says stuff like that."

Erica Simison, Ronan's girlfriend, has a different perspective.

"Jonas is becoming annoying," she says, bluntly. "Mister and Price, they are building a monster in that guy."

Of all of the Price men, Lisa says, Jonas is the most intense. *Ornery* is the word she uses.

"He wants to do it his way; very headstrong," she says. "Always has been."

When it came time for Jonas to start his education, to join his older brother at a Catholic school in downtown Yakima, Lisa seemed more excited than her second son was. Perhaps it was because now, for a large chunk of the day, she'd have time to devote fully to her ballet teaching. But when she pulled up the car at the school's front office on Jonas's first day of kindergarten, the little guy squirmed out of her arms and took off—running away from, not toward, school. Even then, Jonas was super-fast. Lisa gave chase and caught up with him. She asked what was wrong.

"I don't want to go," he told her.

This became a routine nearly every day at kindergarten: Jonas bolting, Lisa chasing.

"Other parents would look and say, 'Oh, there goes Jonas again,'" Lisa recalls.

The standoff extended to homework. One example: The kindergarten teacher had given students a packet of homework on Monday, and the students had to turn it in on Friday. Late-afternoon homework sessions were required at the Price household, both to instill in Ronan and Jonas an early academic discipline and to give Lisa a respite to teach afternoon dance classes without interruption.

Too many times to recall, though, Jonas would crack open the door to the studio and call over to his mom, such as on this particular Monday.

"Can I watch TV?"

"Have you finished your homework?"

"I'm done with it."

Later, after teaching dance class and before making dinner, Lisa asked to see Jonas's homework. Jonas responded by going to his room and returning with worksheets shredded, all torn up.

"What did you do?" she asked, exasperated.

"I'm *done* with it," Jonas responded. "I can't do it this way."

Lisa shook her head in wonderment at such a headstrong little boy.

"Robert and I used to think, 'Oh, my gosh, this is not [normal],'" Lisa says. "Because Ronan was just so easygoing. But somewhere in fourth grade, it changed. On our drive home from school one day, Jonas had his homework out and doing it. Ever since then, he's been a very good student, a straight-A student. He just made his mind up to do it. That's what I mean by stubborn. He decides something, and that's it."

It wasn't just running that fueled Jonas's competitiveness. As a preadolescent, he would form these obsessions and not let them go. Unlike kids with short attention spans, who pick up a hobby one day and discard it the next, Jonas rarely wavered when he found an interest. He would immerse himself and not relent until those around him would take his ambitions seriously.

When he was five years old, his passion was to be a fencer—not just any fencer, but a world-class youth fencer, a future Olympian. Dream big, kid.

"I think he saw this movie, *The Spiderwick Chronicles*, and there was a girl in it who was a fencer," Robert says. "So Jonas insisted on fencing. Why? Who knows?"

"The problem," Lisa recalls, smiling, "was that he was too young for fencing lessons. The instructor said, 'When your son is eight, if he's still interested, he can try it.'"

Jonas, not surprising, was still interested three years later. He had not moved on.

"The problem was, the instructor had quit, so we couldn't find anybody in Yakima who taught fencing," Lisa says. "So then, Jonas turned to basketball."

"Yeah," Robert says, picking up the story, "he comes up to me one day and says, 'Dad, I want to go to the NBA.' What could I say? It's not like I could say no, you're too short or something. He was in fifth grade and dead serious. So I told him he had to train every day, work on his ball handling and his shot, stuff like that."

Robert, in other words, spouted one of those parental platitudes that, by most kids, aren't taken to heart. But Jonas was not like most kids. He practiced basketball every day, for at least two years, dribbling the ball in the ballet studio, and actually became an expert ball handler. But, with Jonas measuring under five feet in height as an eighth grader, an NBA career seemed, literally and figuratively, way out of reach.

It was at about that time, though, that Ronan started running cross-country for Eisenhower.

"I think he saw me having success and got the idea in his head to run too," Ronan said.

Not so, according to Jonas.

"I always heard my dad talk about cross and the team," Jonas says. "I'd go to practice with my dad, every day. I wouldn't be doing the workouts, but I'd watch them and think, 'What are they doing out there?' And when [Ronan] started to run, I realized that's probably what I should be doing too."

What was unusual about Jonas's sudden interest in running was that he cared about more than just running. Even as a grade and middle schooler, he wanted to perform the drills that Mister imposed upon the team. And he *liked* the boring, repetitive regimen. By the time Jonas started high school, he had better form, thanks to those drills, than many of the varsity runners.

"He's asking me, his seventh-grade year, 'Hey Dad, should I run to school in the morning?' So he starts running from our house on 32nd

[Avenue] to St. Paul's on 12th [Avenue]. He started doing it a couple of times a week. Then more and more. Following fall, eighth grade, he starts running almost every day to school. Then track season rolls around, and I have people telling me they've seen little Jonas up at 40th and Summit-view [Road]. I asked him, 'What were you doing way up there?' He said, 'I thought I'd get more mileage in.' Then he says, 'Dad, should I run from St. Paul to Marquette Stadium?' This is from 12th to 56th after school, before his practice. I didn't discourage him. The kid's motivated, obviously. And while he's doing this, he's working on his form that he learned from Mister. He's asking me, 'Dad, does this look good? Can you videotape me to see how my form is?'"

Interesting—early on, Jonas was not quite the natural runner that Robert had been.

"In seventh-grade track, he got beat quite a bit," Robert says.

Robert was fine with it; Jonas was not.

"He would get beaten by this kid from Riverside Christian [Middle School], who was about a head taller than Jonas. The next year, the kid is still running. The first meet is up at Kittitas, and Jonas is super-motivated."

That upcoming race dominated the dinner table conversation the night before the meet.

"Dad. I'm going to beat this kid."

"OK, Jo-Jo."

"I'm ready, Dad. Really. I'm going to beat him."

"Great. Let's see it. But you realize if you go out too hard with him, you're going to die, possibly."

"I know, Dad. I'll give it a shot."

Jonas went out too fast in that race. Robert checked his watch—a 63-second first lap, insanely fast for an eighth-grade mile run.

"Holy crap," Robert muttered, watching Jonas nearly sprint around the oval.

But Jonas stuck with the Riverside Christian front-runner, mere steps behind him, as if tethered to the guy's right shoulder. On the backstretch of the second lap, the Riverside Christian runner slowed and then started really struggling.

"It was like Jonas was breaking a horse—the kid's broken at that point by the pressure Jonas put on him," Robert says.

Jonas kept moving at the same pace, hitting 800 meters at 2 minutes, 13 seconds—faster than any scrawny eighth-grade boy had the right to run. That second 800 meters, Jonas slowed but did not falter. He beat that

Riverside Christian runner and, in doing so, broke five minutes for the first time.

Was Jonas satisfied? No, he was not. He simply adjusted his goals upward.

Entering high school, Jonas was hell-bent on making the varsity as a freshman so that he could run with his older brother, a senior. Though he was barely 5-foot and weighed just 107 pounds after a heavy dinner, he was keeping up with the varsity during informal summer runs. Then he started doing extra work on the sly. When Mister cut a workout short because he sensed the team needed a break to recover physically and mentally, Jonas would go back later in the day or early the next morning to finish it, regardless.

Jonas's spot on the varsity his freshman year was never in doubt. What concerned English was that the kid was almost too gung ho, too motivated. These were the type of kids, overachievers, who could burn out early, and Mister certainly didn't want that.

"He wants to be good *right now*," Mister says. "Not next week; right now! But you've got to be careful with guys like that. You have to ask, where are they going to be as juniors and seniors? There always has to be a progression. You don't want too much too soon. We want our runners to be their fastest as seniors."

Jonas shakes his head when told his coaches believe he needs to make slow and steady progress. He is a year older now, he says. He is taller (5-foot-6) and heavier (116 pounds) and stronger. Jonas doesn't want to wait any longer. Bring it on.

"When they say that I need to be held back, I think they mean I'm doing too much mileage," Jonas says. "Last year, sometimes in the mornings when we didn't have morning practice, if I felt I hadn't done a good workout the day before, I'd go out and do the workout myself like at Franklin Park, I'd run there. I'd come home and have breakfast, and my brother would be awake and say, 'What are you doing?' I'd say, 'I'm finishing the workout.' He's like, 'Don't do that. You'll tire yourself out.' One day, Mister came over to my house. I asked him, 'Am I doing too much?' He said, 'Just stick to the workouts, Jonas.' I do think I'm smarter than that now."

Maybe. Maybe not. One afternoon, during summer conditioning, Ronan and Robert were standing on the edge of the grass watching the boys' varsity go through an interval workout when, suddenly, Jonas veered off and jogged, somewhat gingerly, toward the two.

"Dad, my calf's bothering me," he said.

Robert shot Jonas a squinty-eyed look of skepticism.

"What did you do to it?"

"I think I did too many calf raises yesterday?"

"How many did you do?"

"Six-times-30."

"*What?*"

Ronan laughed. "Duh, that was stupid. Why'd you do that?"

"Because Dad said he used to do five-times-100 calf raises, and I wanted to do that."

Robert cringed. Here was Jonas again, trying to top his old man. Perhaps, Robert thought, I never should've told him about doing calf raises. He sighed.

"Don't do that again, Jo-Jo."

"OK. But can you rub the knots out of my calves?"

When the anecdote was relayed to Mister, he smirked. Just like Jonas, he said. It was an interesting dynamic, when a coach had to deal with his child on a team. Mister had done it himself, with daughter Liza on the mid-1990s state championship team, and in the early 2000s with his son Michael. Both English offspring called their dad "Mister" everywhere except at home. The Prices had adopted a similar strategy. If even one runner is within earshot, Jonas does not use the D-word, instead calling out "Hey, Price," as would any other runner trying to get the coach's attention.

Jonas says he felt more comfortable approaching his dad for advice; Mister, after all, could be intimidating even to the son of a longtime assistant coach. "I'll go to my dad for day-to-day stuff," Jonas says. "But if there's a serious problem, like an injury, I'll go to Mister. If it's race strategy, I'll go to Mister too. But I also might ask my dad."

To Lisa, having Mister as a buffer helps separate home and cross-country life between father and son.

"Surprisingly, it's worked very well having Robert as their coach," Lisa says. "I don't know if I could have done it as well. With Robert, he's just really good at being coach and being dad in each situation. But he knows when to back off and let Phil make the final call. At the dinner table, Jonas might bring something up and ask why they did a certain workout, and Robert'll say, 'Go ask Mister.'"

At moments, however, when the lines between team and family blur, other runners get to see glimpses of the Price family dynamic play out. During a drill session at Camp Ghormley, Jonas talks a bit too much for

Robert's liking, and the dad overtakes the coach. Robert snaps at his son with a ferocity and tone he would not use with other runners. "Cut it out, Jonas," he yells. "The world does not revolve around you." Jonas bows his head and stops talking. Later, asked about that brief tiff and others like it periodically over the summer, Jonas shakes his head.

"Sometimes," he says, "my dad will say some stuff, and I can't handle that, because I get the same stuff [from him] at home. I just think in my head, 'Just do what he says. Don't make anything worse.'"

Such tense public moments between the two are not common. Jonas admits to being "in awe" of his father and wanting to emulate him. Occasionally, around the team, father and son drop their coach-athlete relationship and display a raucous kind of affection—roughhousing sublimating for tenderness.

One night at Camp Ghormley, during the epic Jenga game between the boys' and girls' teams, Jonas and Robert queued up the Floyd Mayweather-Conor McGregor fight on Robert's smartphone. While waiting for it to begin, Jonas playfully "attacked" his dad with mock punches to the midsection, and Robert, laughing, responded with playful, fake, open-handed slaps upside Jonas's head. At one point, the two were squared off in the lodge room, laughing madly, reduced to four arms flailing. The other boys cheered on Jonas, while most of the girls just eye-rolled. This went on for a good minute before Mister shook his head and barked, "OK, all right, that's enough!"

Mostly, though, Robert remains professional and nonpartisan around Jonas and the boys' team. When it comes time for Jonas's one-on-one interview at camp, Robert lets Mister handle the questioning. He sits with legs crossed and fiddles with his phone while Mister grills Jonas on goals and team dynamics. Jonas, for his part, seemingly has learned the right thing to say—all the clichés pro athletes spout by rote in interviews. He almost—almost—seems to have been programmed to answer, indoctrinated to say the right thing. So when Mister asks him to assess his freshman year of running, Jonas doesn't miss a beat.

"I thought I had a pretty good experience," he says, nodding. "It was real mind-changing. I had a fun time spending it with everyone who was part of the journey, and I like how I grew as a runner."

Mister: "OK. How about goals?"

Everyone at the table—Mister, Robin, Robert—knows what is coming, because they've heard the answer many times before. But Mister asks that question of all runners, so with Jonas it is no different.

"I kind of want to have more state titles than my dad. I gotta start now."

Mister: "As all of his [Robert's] contemporaries tell him, those were in the 1A division, not 4A."

Jonas makes an effort not to look at his dad, choosing to focus on the illuminated "HP" on the backside of Mister's laptop screen.

"No difference there, Mister. Eight is eight."

"So let me ask you, Jonas," Mister continues, "you had such an outstanding freshman year. If there's a little bit of a letdown this year, how will you deal with that?"

Jonas scrunches his face, as if asked to solve a quadratic equation without scratch paper.

"Letdown, as in *what?*" he asks.

"Well, Jonas, say your place at State isn't what you think or you don't get the times that you want. How will you react?"

He pauses for a moment. He bites his bottom lip, opens his mouth to speak and then closes it. It is as if Mister has asked him something unfathomable. Finally, he answers.

"Oh, uh, I'll just keep training harder."

"OK. How do you feel you can move the rest of the team toward elite performances?"

"Just with motivation, Mister. Because, like, if you keep talking to them, they'll start to realize what's at stake and focus on State."

"Do you feel intimidated at all, Jonas, because you're a sophomore telling a senior to keep up in workouts? Are you OK with it, or is it weird?"

"It is weird, Mister, because I'd expect them to stay up just as easily as I would be. But I guess people are different than me."

Mister smiles. There were many funny, slightly sarcastic comebacks the coach could have delivered at that moment. After all, Mister has known Jonas all of Jonas's 15 years. But Mister holds back. Better to let any further comment slide.

This kid is obviously the future of the program. A kid like this, obsessed and maybe even possessed with a love of running, perhaps comes around only a few times in a coach's career. Mister had the father, who was just such a case. Now here comes the son.

MISTER

The pep band, leaning heavy on the bass, plays the same song over and over as the students stream out of class on this first Friday of the school year and file into the Eisenhower High gym. The vibration from the drums, being flogged with impunity by four blue-and-red-clad percussionists whose bodies shake like bobblehead dolls, can be felt underfoot as the students fill the bleachers; the cheerleaders shake pom-poms and do dance moves that would make their parents cringe; and the student leadership team scrambles madly to set up for the activities on the floor.

Lining one wall, all with arms crossed, stand the coaches from the school's fall sports teams—football, of course, but also swimming, volley-ball, girls' soccer, and cross-country. Their role in this, the first assembly, is to say a few words about the prospects for the upcoming season, throw out a platitude or two, and then participate in some student-run hijinks to get everybody excited for the new school year.

Mister loves all spectacle and ritual, and he always looks forward to these autumnal rites in which he has participated for what, 37, no, 38 years now. He beams out at the mass of students in the bleachers, looking for his team. Always on the lookout for his team. And there they are, sitting en masse, in a section near the midcourt line, better to both mock him and cheer him on. The band strikes up the fight song, and the entire student body, numbering more than 2,000, claps along without apparent irony and with detectable gusto. When the shout "Go! Fight! Win! Ike!" rings out at song's end, no one is more vocal than the cross-country kids, who for all of their too-cool-to-care poses really do get into the school spirit. They wear Eisenhower on their chests at cross-country meets and, to them, that means something: success, commitment, dedication, camaraderie.

By the time the ceremony begins, Mister is wiping sweat off his brow windshield wiper-like, with the flick of his index finger. The gym had taken on an overheated, frenzied feel, smoke from the lingering wildfires mixing with the heady combination of teen sweat and Axe body spray. Mister speaks first—he always does; seniority, you know, and, at 63, he's the school's oldest teacher—and the team hoots as he begins.

"Another season, off and running," he says. No one laughs at the pun, one he's used lo these many years and one that usually at least gets a chuckle. Not this time. He soldiers on. "I've done this for 30-plus years . . ."

Once all of the coaches are finished introducing their squads, the games begin. Mister and the other coaches are led to center court, where chairs are placed in a circle for a game the student body president calls "Confession." Jesus and Rogelio whoop it up, and Izzy lets loose with a "Go, Mister" yell. The object of the game is for coaches and a select player from each team (the cross-country team selected Mo, a senior) to move over spots in the circle if they have been "guilty" of the "accusation" the student body president announces. Mister sits as primly as a schoolmaster, posture perfect, hands clasped in his lap, white hair shining in the bright lights.

"Move one chair to the right if you've ever snuck out of the house."

Mister stays put.

"Move three seats to the left if you've ever stolen something."

Mister grins when Anthony Stewart, the school's soccer coach who ran cross-country for him back in the day and whose eldest son ran for Mister only a few years ago, plops down in Mister's lap. Mister furrows his salt-and-pepper brows, in mock disapproval. Students laugh and clap.

"Move one chair to the left if you've ever gotten drunk."

With that, Jonas leaps out of his seat and points to Mister down on the floor. "Get up!" he yells and then turns to teammates: "I've seen it, at my house, with my dad!" Mister stands, moves over one chair. The cross-country team applauds.

"Move two seats to the right if you've ever gotten into a fight."

Mister shrugs his shoulders and moves over. In the stands, several of the boys, Jesus and Tony in particular, find it hilarious. They slap palms, but given the flaring of temper they sometimes see from their coach during practice, they do not seem entirely surprised.

"Move one seat to the left if you've ever done anything illegal."

The briefest hush comes over the gym, waiting for someone to rise. Only one coach stands—and it is Mister. The gym explodes in applause. In the cross-country team section, heads swivel and laughter erupts. Fonzi shouts, "Gansta! Old school." What the cross-country kids don't know is that Mister's crime really was the most minor of misdemeanors: stealing apples from the parish orchard as a lad in his native Ireland.

The team, frankly, looks a little shocked. Shocked and amused. They trade glances and break into laughter. Here is their upright, rules-enforcing coach, model of probity and moral rectitude, the man who preaches each day about making good choices on and off the cross-country course, admitting to the whole school that he once flouted the law.

Not shocked, as in disappointed or let down. Not shocked, as in perversely proud that their coach was a badass once upon a time. More like surprised that their leader, something of a surrogate dad to many, actually has a *past*, and, it seemed, a colorful one at that. When the runners think about it, for all of the stories and anecdotes Mister has told them during their time on the team, all those tales of past teams and the glorious successes, he has never really opened up about his own youth, his own cross-country and track career, his carefree days running wild on the emerald plains of Ireland.

★ ★ ★

Portrait of the coach as a young runner . . .
When Phil English starts talking about the old days, all of that pining for the Auld Sod of his native Ireland, a transformation takes hold. Decades of Americanization melt away. His accent, still strong after all these years but weakened a bit from his time in the States, thickens once more. He starts dropping consonants without "tinking" and gives listeners a quizzical look when "dey" strain to follow along, the letter "h" vanishing without a trace. His wry smirk, usually his default facial expression, morphs into a broad smile. His eyes shine as blue as the water of Lough Gur after the morning mist burns off.

English has stories to tell, and over the years, friends and family have heard most of them. Generations of runners, too, have heard edited versions of some, expurgated to leave out potentially embarrassing details, and mostly passed along to the "yutes" as object lessons about running and the virtues of hard work and perseverance, all of that in-my-day-we-had-it-tougher rhetoric that elicits eye-rolling in many kids but, for Mister's charges, is mostly absorbed as wisdom well taken.

To his runners, this version of Mister as a mere lad is almost that of a mythical figure—like that leprechaun on their cereal boxes. It doesn't seem real; to them, as it is with most kids, adult authority figures just spring forth from the womb fully formed as upstanding adults. To outsiders—and English, despite his garrulousness, is not one to confide, even with longtime friends—it seems incongruous that this graying Irish gent who can sometimes come off as more than a tad grumpy would dedicate his life to coaching generations of kids, many Hispanic and low-income. Why would he open his wallet, his home, his heart to teenagers so unlike himself? What's in it for him?

Delving into English's past can provide, if not definitive answers, at least some clues to his motivation. A parallel starts to make sense. Here you have a poor, rural Irish kid who grew up without a TV or a telephone, who worked the fields and ran track and cross-country with dreams of immigrating to the United States and getting a college education. And here you have kids from Yakima, some of whom have migrant parents and join their family picking crops in the summer, running toward a dream of a college education denied to their parents and siblings. Every day at practice, Mister brings the past with him and can see it repeated—not the actual circumstances, of course, but the spirit of his earlier, youthful self—in many of his runners. The striving. The willfulness. The sly playful nature of someone who, though he takes his sport seriously, can appreciate the elemental joy in the act of running itself. In Erica, English can see flashes of his own no-nonsense work ethic, his sometimes prickly habit of not suffering fools gladly. In Jonas, there resides the obsessiveness and single-minded focus on running, which took English far—a whole continent away, in fact. And in Fonzi, he can see another earlier version of himself, this one striving to be one of the first in his family to go to college thanks to his fleet feet and agile mind. In every kid, from the slowest to the swiftest, he can project a part of himself.

And besides, being around young people all day keeps him young—or, at least, young at heart. One day at practice, Mister commandeered a medical scooter being used by a runner who had just undergone Achilles tendon surgery and raced up and down the stadium walkway, nearly crashing the thing.

"When I was a kid in Ireland," he told the team when the laughing died down, "we used to race trollies down the dirt streets. Oh, boy, was that a good time."

"Did you win, Mister?" Rogelio asked.

That half grimace turned into all smile. "I did all right, don't you know."

The team waited for more, but Mister would not elaborate. Time for practice. Time to get serious.

Maybe he suppresses his born storyteller impulses because, if he started, the team might never get around to doing the workout. Get him away from the cross-country course, though, and listen to the stories pour forth. They flow like so much Guinness from the two pubs in English's hometown, the tiny village of Cullen (population 282), straddling the landlocked border of County Tipperary and County Limerick.

He came of age in the early 1960s. TV? Nope. Didn't own one. Kids made their own fun, mostly harmless mischief frolicking all day in the wheat fields, cows outnumbering townsfolk. And from an early age, the second youngest of Mickey and Lizzie English's brood of five kids was a handful. Too young back then to help his father, a cottier, akin to a tenant farmer in the United States, milk the cows and "save" the hay, and too rambunctious to stay at the modest house on the small plot of land the farm owner allotted to the Englishes, Philip made Cullen his playground, the dirt roads his running track, the fields his fortress.

Word quickly got out around the village that this youngest boy of Mickey and Lizzie was a headstrong little squirt. He was not made of the solid, sturdy stuff of his Da, a strapping figure with the largest, strongest hands folks had ever seen, hands that could coax milk out of the most stubborn of cows, hands that could encircle a pint or four of ale after the day was done, hands that could grab a misbehaving child—that means *you*, Philip—by the scruff of the neck and lay down the law. Nor was he anything like his brother, John, seven years his senior, whose work ethic on the farm, as well as his imposing physical stature, mirrored that of his dad. Philip, rather, was small for his age. Not weak; wiry. Oh, he did his chores, all right. He put in his share of long days of manual labor, which English now says gives him an appreciation for those of his runners who work as fruit pickers during the summers and, occasionally, early in the school year.

But young Philip's interests clearly seemed to lie elsewhere, out in the world beyond the farm, a world that first was limited to the village schoolhouse, pubs, and church parish but, in time, gradually would expand to the rest of the country, the British-controlled northern territory, and, ultimately, the bright shining promise of America.

Yeah, this tyke was going to be a handful. That much was evident early on. Those arresting blue eyes, which contrasted starkly with jet-black hair, suggested a devilish streak, a gentle pushing of boundaries in the milieu that revolved in equal measure around the church and pub.

For most of his childhood, being much younger than his siblings, Philip was free to be a kid and roam. And it was with this unfettered access to the land that seemed to him in retrospect as his personal cross-country course writ large, and with only his feet to get him where he wanted to go, that English first discovered the pleasure of running. Sure, he tried other sports that his Catholic parish Christian Brothers overseers offered: Gaelic football and hurling. But English, unlike his father and older brother, didn't have the build to excel in those rough-and-tumble endeavors. He was small for his age, hitting puberty at a mere 5-foot-3 and 100 pounds, so he gravitated toward running. At times, running was an act of self-preservation. Always an intense kid, young Philip got into his share of "skirmishes," most notably with his big brother.

At least once a week, sometimes more often, the English boys would have it out—the usual little brother getting on the big brother's nerves scenario. Blows would be exchanged, with little Philip sometimes delivering the first punch, and that meant Philip needed to run away, fast, lest his older, stronger, and occasionally meaner older brother would catch him and execute a pummeling. But Philip was ready for his own version of the running of the bulls, his brother playing the role of the rampaging bull and Phil the foolhardy runner fleeing the prospect of a goring. He had a running course well plotted. It was a quarter mile to the Riordan house down the dirt road and around a corner. Philip knew if he could get there before his lumbering brother could run him down, he would be safe, because the Riordans looked down on fisticuffs, and Philip's older brother knew that if he even touched the little brat, word would get back to his mother. The key to beating his brother, Philip knew, was the clever use of shortcuts that included hopping fences and cutting through pothole-saturated fields. Still, it took all of Philip's effort, those stick-figure legs churning up the boggy grass and thin arms pumping madly, to arrive at the finish safely.

"He'd be gaining on me," English remembers with a wide smile, "and just before he could reach me, I'd be up and over the stone wall. Ger's house was my safe zone. My brother never caught me. Never."

Phil and Ger were mischievous youths. Same age, same circumstances. Their older sisters, too, were best friends. Longstone Cross, the dirt street where they lived outside of Cullen, was a great place to be a kid in the early 1960s, with limitations. Economically, times were tough. Farmers worked the land but, in most cases, did not own it. Another massive wave of emigration had taken hold, the young and able taking off for London or the States. But for Phil and Ger, that rural milieu was a playground, a substitute for the ubiquity of television elsewhere. Kids there had to enter- tain themselves, and the two found inventive ways to do just that. When they weren't in church or in school, which took up a not inconsiderable amount of time, they simply roamed. And ran.

In fact, the boys enjoyed their morning mile-long walk to the gram- mar school in Cullen. A gaggle of children, and their parents and family members, would form a procession and saunter along. They would aug- ment their breakfast by raiding an apple orchard. They did, at least, until the morning Philip was caught by the parish priest in mid-bite.

"Philip, did you feck an apple from this orchard?" the priest asked, using the Gaelic word for *steal*.

He hesitated answering because it wasn't polite to talk with one's mouth full, especially if it was full of purloined apple.

And, in the fall, all of the kids in Cullen would stop along the roads to collect nuts (called conkers) from the horse chestnut trees. These hard, brown nuts would later be used by the kids for a game aptly called Conk- ers, a match of skill and hand-eye coordination that the Eisenhower kids play each October in a highly competitive tournament refereed by Mister.

"We were never in any hurry to reach the classroom," Riordan said.

The commute home in the afternoon was quite a different matter. Some of the kids who lived at Longstone Cross had bikes, and two broth- ers, several years older than Phil and Ger, went to school atop a gig, or a trap, pulled by a donkey. The parking lot for these vehicles was a field owned by the Cullen publican, not far from the schoolhouse. Not exactly jealous of the older students and their modes of transportation, but per- haps prideful of his own swiftness, Phil challenged the older boys to a race home. Ger was right there beside him. There was a series of races, each more competitive than the next. When the teacher dismissed class at 3 p.m., the pursuit was on.

"Phil and I would have the initial advantage and, by the time the trap and bicycles were on the road, we would have opened up a considerable lead, which would, however, continue to diminish as we neared the sharp bend at Longstone Cross," Riordan said. "We were both thin and scrawny kids, but our years of running through fields and meadows around our locality had built up the necessary strength and endurance which enabled us maintain a strong and unrelenting pace."

The boys had won every race, but the older kids were gaining ground each day, getting closer to reclaiming bragging rights. Then came the day of what would be, for reasons soon to be made obvious, the final race.

"That day, the brothers on the trap made a determined effort to defeat us," Ger said. "As we neared the finish line, they were right behind us, driving the jennet [female donkey] faster and harder than ever before. We were running flat out as we turned the bend, just glancing behind us to see the jennet unable to take the bend, mount a grass bank and take the trap into a neighbor's garden."

Phil and Ger retired undefeated from the endeavor. But even then, Ger knew Phil had more of a talent for running. When English was younger, the motivation for swiftness was obvious: to not get caught and to not face repercussions. Eventually, Phil and Ger and a few other kids his age from the county's three parishes were enlisted by one of the Christian Brothers, Father James Joyce, to join a cross-country and track club in Tipperary organized by the church. (Schools had no sports teams; in Ireland at the time, competition was centered solely around the church.) Always one of the fastest kids around, at age 13 Phil (he no longer wanted to be called the childish "Philip") was beating competitors as much as five years older. His biggest obstacle early on, though, came from home. "My mother was totally dead set against me running," English said. "Absolutely. I was very small and light, and she thought I was way, way out of it. That I was going to pass out or something. She was very protective of me."

And here came another standoff between mother and son. Phil wanted to run for the church team; Lizzie absolutely forbade it. He considered competing on the sly, behind his parents' backs; that's how much he loved the raw physicality of running and the sheer thrill of trying to beat the other guy in a race. Phil never lied, remember. But he considered it this time. The problem was that the club team needed a copy of Phil's birth certificate. Lizzie balked.

"Mom," he cajoled, "I need it to run. I want to do this. You've got no problem with me doing hurling or football. Why not?"

The idea of her slim boy, the baby of the family, running himself to exhaustion just didn't jibe with her motherly instincts. A stalemate ensued. Phil wanted to run, desperately. Lizzie was just as adamant to keep him safe at home. The Tipp Town running team would travel throughout Munster Province, sometimes in minibuses and sometimes by bicycle, to compete, and Phil was beyond eager to test himself against the kids in cities such as Limerick and equally as excited to see other parts of Ireland. Phil was hardly a homebody. He wanted to be part of the wider world beyond the farm. In this battle of wills, Phil was forced to take extreme measures, to make a declaration very serious, indeed, in a society where the Catholic Church ruled.

"I'm done with church unless you do this," he said, keeping the quaver out of his voice. "I'm not serving at mass anymore until you let me run."

Both stood there stunned. Was Lizzie hearing this right? This was her son, a devout Catholic who until about age 11 had considered entering the priesthood, actually threatening to leave his faith for something she thought so trivial, for hyperventilating in tank tops and tiny shorts all over the country for mere ribbons and maybe a mention in the local paper now and then?

Phil was adamant. But also maybe bluffing. Church had always been important to him. Church provided a moral center for him and the whole village; it taught him discipline, determination, and piety. Yet this running obsession of his lifted his spirits as well, gave him a feeling of freedom, a hope of seeing the wider world and perhaps even breaking away from a life that seemed preordained for Cullen kids: schooling when young, then farmwork and then raising a family of your own and continuing the cycle. In many ways, young Phil was not unlike some of the talented Hispanic runners under his tutelage at Eisenhower—seeing running as a means to a new life, striving for something different, if not necessarily better, out of life.

The rest of the English family gave mother and son a wide berth. Mickey, who had done a little boxing in his day and never backed down from competition, had no problem with Phil running. He knew the kid loved it, and it didn't hurt that he had some obvious talent lurking in his lanky limbs. His siblings, John and his three sisters, served as Switzerland in the standoff, not taking sides. None of them had any compulsion to run, but then again, Phil was always a little different from the rest. At last, Lizzie relented and handed over the birth certificate, but not without registering serious reservations about the whole enterprise. The very house itself seemed to exhale. Crisis averted.

Would Phil have carried through on the threat? Some 50 years later, recalling the dramatic scene as his Eisenhower runners dashed by in the blur, he smiles.

"I don't really know," he says, after a considerable pause. "I was hoping it wouldn't come to that."

Thus began the running life that would take English halfway around the world, that would provide him a college education in the United

States unavailable to any of his siblings and most anyone else in Cullen, that would lead him to meet a strawberry-blonde California girl whom he'd eventually marry and with whom he would have two children, that would see him get his green card and devote his professional life to teaching biology and coaching cross-country to a diverse group of students for more than three decades.

★ ★ ★

But that very first race, that first step into that bright future? It was a stumble. At least, though, it provided English with a story, a cautionary tale, he could impart to generations of runners.

The club traveled 25 miles northeast to Thurles, a town with a high triple-digit population and more than one pub. Thurles was celebrating a festival, and a highlight was the youth one-mile race called "Around the Houses." As its name implied, the race's course followed a simple square in which runners would literally run around the houses dotting the town square. Phil, who toed the starting line in a white singlet that hung on his scrawny frame and with his jet-black hair falling over his eyes, took off. He was leading. He was feeling strong. "I took a wrong turn," he says, still pulling an anguished face some 50 years after the fact. "Look, I knew nothing about the race or about racing. I knew no strategy, nothing about where to go. I grew up in the country. 'What kind of houses are you talking about?' I remember thinking. I ended up finishing sixth. I got a tongue-lashing from my brother for not knowing where to go. To me, the race was like organized chaos."

English got more savvy after age 13 and got much better, really fast, though the Thurles wrong-way incident was not an anomaly. "Two years later, I lost a national [junior] title that same way. There were various courses for various ages, you see. And so I followed another course, adjacent to the finish line. I had a substantial lead, and I went one way on another course and had to come back. This was 400 meters away from the finish, mind you. I think I got second in the damn race." He did, indeed. A photograph that appeared in the local newspaper the day after the Under-16 All-Ireland Cross-Country Championships at Tullamore, outside of Dublin, shows the top three runners from the race. The winner, Tony Ryan, and the third-place finisher, Gerry Deegan, were all smiles. On the left is English, glowering into the camera, dark brows scrunched, a ringlet of hair falling like an accusatory finger over his forehead. He was, to say the least, not a happy runner-up. To this day, English is chagrined by the outcome. More than once, his Eisenhower runners have heard the story as a warning to pay attention to turns and shifts in a course.

Once he stopped making wrong turns, English progressed quickly to being one of Ireland's top junior runners. He was known as a dogged competitor, persistent as hell, using strategic surges and moves to wear down opponents. He kept a detailed diary of every race he ran as a "junior," obsessively detailing everything from time splits to weather conditions to "transport" (how he arrived at the event) to "how I performed." Those diaries show that English eventually exacted revenge against Ryan and Deegan later that year at the Mini-Tipperary Olympics at Rockwell College. It was the under-17 "mini-marathon" (called the 5,000 meters in the United States), and English beat both rivals. In his diary recap of the race, English documented how he stayed in third place until the final 400 meters, biding his time, stalking his foes, before "increasing the tempo" with a feverish kick to win with a personal best.

That race typifies English's doggedness. He said his grit came from his father, his stubbornness from his mother. Anyone around County Tipperary who knew the Englishes wouldn't begrudge the family's hard-nosed nature. Ask any old-timer around the area, and they'll tell the story of Mickey English's boxing exploits. Phil still relishes a retelling. "This was back in the 1930s. My father's very, very young. He went to a town in the south part of Tipperary called Clonmel. These traveling shows would come along, right? And they'd do some scam or another. This time, they wanted to see if anyone could last three rounds with this professional boxer. You had to pay something, of course, to get in the ring with the boxer. That was the scam. I'm sure my father had been in some scrapes, but nothing like this. They offered prize money if you could last. Well, my father lasted the three rounds, and the outfit, they didn't have the money to pay him. The whole place erupted in a riot. These people got an incredible beating."

Running, for the painfully thin Phil, was a more genteel endeavor, yet he approached it with the fervor of a pugilist. Maybe that's why his mother fretted. His first major junior race was on the track, and it was held on June 17, 1971, in Dublin, the trials for the Irish National Team that would compete in the prestigious British Isles School Championships in Edinburgh, Scotland. His best chance of qualifying among runners that included future Olympians Eamonn Coghlan and the Treacy brothers, John and Ray, was the steeplechase, a challenging event contested on the track that includes multiple hurdles to clear as well as a water jump. Phil was considered a contender for the title, even though he trained with only one barrier to hurdle and no water jump. He liked his chances. His father and older brother made the trip to the big city to watch in person. His mother, as usual, stayed home, uncomfortable with her youngest son running all over the country, exhausting himself. But this was a big deal, the national championships. The meet was carried live on the radio, nationwide, with celebrity broadcaster Brendan O'Reilly making the call. The Englishes may not have had a telephone, but they had a radio. Lizzie English flipped on the knob at 1:15 p.m., just in time to hear the starting gun. One lap into the 2,000-meter race, the pack approached the first water jump. O'Reilly, in his distinctive baritone, told the listeners, "English is down in the water!" At which point, Lizzie leaped from her chair and flipped off the switch, perhaps muttering an I-told-you-so at the radio. Phil had, indeed, fallen, but what Lizzie didn't know was that he promptly bounced back up and rejoined the pack. He won that race, earning the right for the first of many times to represent Ireland in international competitions.

"She didn't know I'd won the race until I came home later that night and told her," Phil says. "She hated the idea of me competing. I don't think in all the years I ran that she ever saw me compete." He pauses, then hastens to add that in all other ways his mother was fully supportive of him, especially when it came to education. She just couldn't take the pressure of watching her son push his body to the limit and beyond. "It was a different time then, when it came to parental involvement," he adds softly, a touch of melancholy creeping in.

Despite Lizzie's qualms, she and Mickey never forbade Phil from competing abroad, such as in the European Cross Country Championships in Cambridge. They even let him travel with a group of standout athletes from Munster Province in a series of goodwill meets in Ulster, the section of Northern Ireland controlled by the Protestant British and the scene throughout the 1960s and '70s of what amounted to a civil war involving the Catholic-dominated Republican nationalists. The "Troubles," as they were euphemistically called, were a constant backdrop to Phil's youth, but he had never experienced anti-Catholic sentiment until he made this trip. His overseer, Father Joyce, hoped that athletics would foster cooperation between the Protestants in the north and the Catholics in the south, so he set up a trip to Ulster, during Easter week no less, for his top junior runners, girls and boys. It was a controversial proposal that had prompted many parishioners to try to get the trip canceled, concerned not only about the teenagers' safety but also the message of appeasement, or tacit approval, it would send to the Ulster government by having track meets in that disputed territory. It was 1969, the height of tensions, with IRA bombings happening in Great Britain and border skirmishes in Northern Ireland almost a daily occurrence. But Father Joyce, an ardent nationalist, wanted, in English's words, to try to "foster understanding" between the sides. An ardent competitor, too, Joyce also wanted his runners to dominate the Ulsterites on the track. A young teenager, Phil obviously was aware of the ongoing hostilities. In fact, the first shots fired in the 1919 Irish War of Independence, the Ambush at Soloheadbeg, happened about a mile and a half from the Englishes' home in Cullen. But it was not top of mind. Cullen was hardly a hot spot of uprisings, being overwhelmingly Catholic and solidly nationalist, but two of English's relatives in Ulster, both nationalists, had been involved in fighting. So Phil had no concerns about running in the north. A meet is a meet. He soon learned that life was not so placid the closer one got to Northern Ireland.

"Everyone there was armed to the teeth," he recalls. "There were British paratroopers installed on our bus, armed. There was one meet I remember on that trip, there was this popping sound going back and forth; you could hear it on the track. It was not the starter's gun. I asked one of the North kids, I said, 'What is that?' And he goes, 'Oh, that's just sniper fire.' It was part of life for those guys up there."

A subsequent trip north, under Father Joyce's auspices, more than a year later, showed a more impish, impetuous side of English. The team was staying in Strabane, an Ulster city that had seen considerable fighting. This time, the team stayed at a bed-and-breakfast lorded over by a morbidly obese landlady with a stern mien. And here is where Phil's wild side emerged, the side Lizzie often tried and failed to suppress.

"Brother Joyce told her these guys were not to leave under any circumstances because of the danger," he says. "But I was in a room by myself. I wanted to go visit my mates. John Treacy was on that trip. I'm up three stories. It's kind of an L-shaped building, and I'm by myself. This lady's absolutely not letting us out of our room. This thing is not going well at all. So I climb out the window. Looking back, it was really dangerous, three stories up and all. Another one of our guys was in a room across the way. So I jump from the ledge across onto the window and into his room. We were just hanging out. It may have been 11 o'clock at night. She does a bed check, and we hear her. She checks my room, and, of course, I'm not there. Oh, my God. She just went crazy. She's checking all the rooms now. By that time, I'd worked my way down to John Treacy's room—the last room on the corridor. Now, remember, she was a huge woman, huge. There was only one place to hide, and it was underneath the bed. So I'm thinking, she's carrying so much weight, she can't bend down. I figure this out. I tell Treacy before I slide under, 'Tell her you know nothing, you didn't see me.' I go under the bed, and she's shouting and screaming at him. I can hardly understand her because she has a really strong Northern accent. Then she turns around and all of a sudden, she sits down on the bed. Right on my chest. Oooph! I'm not expecting this at all, and I give a squeak out of me. She jumps up and says, 'What's that?' Treacy says, 'Mice.' She goes crazy, because now she's accused of having mice in her hotel. So I eventually work my way back. I had to go back the same way, through the window and leap the ledge. Crazy. I was not smart. I'm back in my room 10 minutes, and she comes barging in again. I calmly say, 'Hello, what do you need?' She screams, 'Where were you?' I say, 'I've been here all along.' I got away with it. I don't think Brother Joyce found out about it. But Brother Joyce, he was quite the guy himself. A tough customer. Many years later, he was up north visiting an IRA house that got attacked by the British army, and he got thrown out a glass window to save his life. I'm glad he didn't find out about my leaving the room."

It is understandable why, of all the Ireland stories English imparts to his Eisenhower runners, he never mentions the bed-and-breakfast shenanigans. English's wild streak and athletic prowess, however, never drew the attention of the IRA leaders looking for recruits. "It just wasn't part of life for us that far south, although there were a lot of Sinn Fein [the radical wing of the IRA] where I grew up, even though they didn't say they were Sinn Fein."

But options were limited for teenagers such as English after completing secondary school. Nearly all of the boys worked the farms, and the adventurous ones migrated toward bigger cities to find work. Families such as the Englishes couldn't afford college—"It wasn't even in people's thinking back then," he says. None of his older siblings considered the option; the family couldn't afford it. "Once you left school, you entered the workforce. That's just the way it was. Going to university? That was beyond the pale."

But this kid could flat-out run, and that opened doors for English, opportunities far beyond trips to Ulster or stopovers in the United Kingdom for international track meets. He had a chance, through his running and aided by his excellent grades, especially in science courses, to get a scholarship to an American university. Phil loved science, couldn't get enough of knowing how and why the human body worked, the biome-chanical principles that made it possible to run so fast. It was yet another dichotomy: English, the devout Catholic, who put his faith in science.

America was his goal, the place to run and study and maybe com-bine the two. Other Irishmen had emigrated before him. Coghlan, the champion miler, received a full ride to Villanova, and even though English had no idea where the university was located (Pennsylvania) and any-thing about it other than it was a Catholic school and fielded a great track team, he longed to go there. Villanova, however, wasn't interested in one of Ireland's top cross-country runners and steeplechasers; "They only wanted milers," English says. But another Irish runner, Dan Murphy, had signed with Washington State University the year before. He told the WSU coach, John Chaplin, about English. Chaplin, new to Washington State, was building the program on foreign athletes, most notably Kenyans such as former world record holder Henry Rono. So, sight unseen, but possessing English's results and his top times from international meets, he was ready to offer him a scholarship. The problem was communicating with English to make the offer.

"We didn't have a telephone," English says. "No one around us did."

The head of English's athletic club had a phone at home, but that was 15 miles away. English caught a ride in a car, waiting patiently for the call. The call, when it came, lasted all of 50 seconds. English's contribution to the conversation: "Yeah. OK. Sounds good." He had his heart set on getting a college education at an American university. Running, too, of course. But what sold him on Washington State was not its nationally ranked cross-country team, but the fact that the school had a major in exercise physiology. He explained all of that to his parents once he caught a ride back to Cullen. His father was losing a potential worker on the farm, but he was proud of his son's ambition. His mother, however, was wary and fretful at the prospect of her youngest son going to America. She sought the counsel of the local parish priest. Was she doing the right thing, letting Philip fly off to America? Would it be a sin, or just motherly prerogative, if she held firm and refused to give her blessing? The priest told her, "Lizzie, it's time to let go," that her son wasn't the first to want to leave the home-land and certainly wouldn't be the last. Still, she fretted.

Ireland, of course, has a long, storied history of its bright youth emi-grating to America. From the mid-1800s potato famine to the economic and social upheaval of the early 1900s fight for independence to the pres-ent day Celtic Tiger economic boom and bust, Ireland has lost many of its most promising native sons and daughters. They've headed "across the pond," to the United States, or leapfrogged to London. It's been a tradition and a sorrow both, and Lizzie feared a scenario in which Phil would arrive at this Washington State University, find a job; marry some American girl entranced by his brooding countenance, black-hair and blue-eyed looks, and enchanting brogue; and never come back. Assurances were made, promises sworn. Lizzie knew that, even if she wanted to stand in his way and forbid him from going, it would be of no use. The boy, driven and stubborn, had his mind set. She agreed to let him go, even though it seemed a world away, which, in a sense, it was.

But where, exactly, in the States was he going? None of the Englishes was sure.

"I got out an atlas and found a map of the United States," English said. "I remembered that Coach Chaplin told him on the phone that this [college] wasn't Washington, DC. He said it was in the other Washington. But I still didn't know where that was. I was aware of some of the states. Pennsylvania, where Villanova was. California and Oregon, because that's where a lot of the good runners came from. But not this Washington State. I started tracing my finger down the map, the East Coast first, along the South, up to the Midwest. I finally worked my way to Washington. And then I had to find Pullman, the town where the school is at. All of a sudden, it hit me: This is a long way from home. I did the calculations. It was 3,000 miles from [Cullen] to this East Coast, then another 3,000 to Washington. This was huge. I was 18. I'd done some traveling, competed in track in Germany, Wales, Scotland, and England. But this was beyond comprehension."

Phil's send-off was a big deal in Cullen and environs. The family had no money to pay for his airfare to the States, so the village pooled its resources and held a fund-raiser at a bigger pub, the Golden Thatch, in a larger nearby town, Emly. At the end of the night, Phil went home with a fat envelope full of money, and many of his well-wishers awoke the next morning with massive hangovers.

No second thoughts, though, even with that heartfelt bon voyage. In the late summer of 1973, Phil officially became yet another Irish expat, one of those innocents abroad who are such a part of the Irish and Irish-American literary history, from James Joyce to James T. Farrell, William Kennedy to Colm Toibin. English got his passport stamped in New York, and wound up in Spokane, where fellow Irishman and Washington State runner Dan Murphy met him. The plan was for English to spend a day or two with Murphy in Spokane, then English would take the bus by himself to Pullman for new-student orientation. The bus ride lasted only 80 minutes, but English will never forget it.

"I get to the Spokane bus station in the morning," he says, "and I see 'Greyhound' written on the side of the bus. Now, greyhound racing is huge in Ireland. So I'm thinking, are they are transporting dogs as well? I'm looking all around for the racing dogs, but all I see are people with their baggage, you know. I had relatives who raced greyhounds, so I was hoping they had dog racing maybe down in Pullman. In fact, I grew up catching rabbits to feed to greyhounds. Anyway, the fact I'm about to get on a bus that's supposed to be for dogs, this made no sense. I go to the conductor, the driver, and I ask, 'How many dogs you have?' He doesn't know what on Earth I'm saying. Probably couldn't understand my accent to begin with. It was quite thick in those days."

Assured no canines were on board, English settled into his seat. As Spokane, a big and impressive city to him at the time, receded into the distance, English was able to exhale. He stared out the window mile upon mile, and saw a sight at once familiar and foreign: wheat fields. Miles upon miles of them. But they were brown—OK, golden—not the verdant fields of his homeland. And the warm high desert wind coming in through his cracked bus window, so incredibly dry and scorching, certainly wasn't the damp, dank feel of home.

This culture clash only continued once the bus deposited him on the WSU campus. English thought it wouldn't be such a stark transition. After all, he spoke the same language as his American cohorts. At least, he thought he did. Turns out, people gave him blank stares when he'd pipe up and join a conversation. That accent, it was thick as an Irish bog. Barely understandable.

Chaplin knew what to expect from this new Irish runner. He'd had Murphy before him, after all, and he knew the Irish had just as much of an adjustment to Pullman as the Kenyan runners. "I remember the first thing I said to Phil, I said, 'For an Irishman with a name like English, I can certainly see why you'd want to leave the country,'" Chaplin said, "and Phil laughed. But it was somewhat true. Ireland back in those days had lots of problems with the English. But Phil settled in nicely."

Not so, English says. "My first class was Communications 101, Monday morning, my first full day there," he says. "It was a terrible class to put me in at the beginning. I mean, it was relatively easy, but the class was overflowing, and I get there late because I can't find the building on such a big campus. The instructor is taking roll and calls on me to talk, but he can't understand my accent and asks me to repeat myself. Then he still can't understand it. The first test in that class, he's asking things like, 'Who are the senators from Washington, and who are the congressmen, and what's the name of the newspaper in Spokane?' I mean, I'm just off the plane. I don't know anything about Washington State. The only thing that saved me in the class is that I could write fairly well."

It was all so disorienting. English felt completely out of place and without a clue. It is a feeling he tries to remember now, when encountering a young runner from a migrant family. He'll recall how unnervingly alienated he felt in Pullman as a minority back then, which is why he reaches out to Eisenhower's Hispanic kids—a majority among the school's population, true, but exceedingly underrepresented in the state in cross-country and track and field.

Early on in Pullman, English survived by embracing his strengths and working on weaknesses, which is what he imparts to students to this day. He aced all of his college science courses, and he eventually settled in and felt almost at home on a campus with more population than County Tipperary. Of course, there was his running. Always the running. That's what he was there to do, at least in the coaches' eyes.

English set a few school records in the steeplechase—at least until Rono came to WSU in English's senior year and broke not only the school record but world records. In cross-country, English proved a solid scoring member all four years on Cougar teams that never finished lower than fourth in the NCAA national meet. His best finish was in 1975, when Washington State placed second in the nation. English finished 47th out of 250 runners in that race. He was 26 places behind his former Irish teammate John Treacy, who was competing for Providence College.

Make no mistake: English was a good runner on the collegiate level. But not great—not like the Kenyans whom Chaplin had recruited. But English was known for his work ethic and his camaraderie with his Kenyan and American teammates, though many still had problems deciphering what he was saying through his thick accent. His senior year, English considered his options. He wanted to move up to the marathon and train for the 1980 Irish Olympic team, but that was still three years hence. The professional running circuit, at that nascent period, was developed only to the point to nurture the very top runners, and English, good as he was, wasn't there. He leaned toward graduate school, wanted to pursue a master's in exercise physiology in order to marry his love of running with love of science. He wasn't sure what he was going to do, exactly, with a graduate degree—or where. His student visa, after all, eventually would expire, and English, confirming part of his mother's fears, had come to enjoy the States and wanted to stay. The spring before graduation, at a party on campus thrown by some of English's track teammates, he began the process of confirming the other part of his mother's fears. Namely, he met a girl, Darcy Brown, a strawberry-blonde Southern Californian who was drawn to English's wavy, shoulder-length black hair and piercing blue eyes but for the life of her couldn't understand much of what the guy was saying.

"He tried to charm me into free beer, but I was in a bad mood and wouldn't budge," Darcy said. "We started talking, and he won me over. He had an Irish wit—if you could understand what he was saying. I'm serious. We used to have phone conversations, and I'd ask him to repeat himself. That's how thick it was. When my parents first met him, my mom used to say, over and over, 'What did you say?'"

The two dated, then graduated, and then parted. But they both decided to pursue graduate degrees at WSU, Darcy's in business communications. They married—Lizzie back in Cullen did, in fact, give her blessing to the union—and while both were finishing their master's theses (Phil's was on the physiology of the foot), Darcy got pregnant with Liza. This changed Phil's plans. He had wanted to pursue a doctorate at the University of Oregon while training for the 1980 Olympics. Instead, with a burgeoning family, he needed a steady income. He decided to teach school and train for a berth on the Irish Olympic marathon team before and after teaching class. This gig would be just for a year, maybe two. He didn't think of becoming a coach either. He needed time to train. None of this fell into Phil and Darcy's long-term plan. When he cast about for teaching jobs, only two schools showed interest: an elementary school in Spokane and a Catholic high school, Carroll, in Yakima.

He had never been to Yakima, half a state away from Pullman, before he showed up in 1979 for the job interview. But by now he was accustomed to new situations, new challenges. After Phil accepted the position, the Carroll High principal just happened to mention in passing, "By the way, we need a cross-country and track coach."

Several years later, when Carroll closed, the public school Eisenhower beckoned.

The Irishman had found a home in rural Washington State. He could now find it on a map.

SEASON

TIME TRIAL

Eisenhower's cross-country team is all about tradition. From Dwight the gnome, the "mascot" they bring to every meet, to the taping of wrists before heading to the starting line, to the T-shirts with funny slogans they design, to the camps at White Pass and Ghormley, traditions must be upheld lest the program descend into utter chaos and three decades of Mister's carefully cultivated work be all for naught. Well, that might be putting it a little dramatically, but, truly, they honor their rituals.

The annual season kickoff Time Trial, uppercase letters required because of its importance to the runners, is one of the latter. The Time Trial is talked about, on and off, all summer. It will be the first real test of the team's fitness before the real meets began. It is a way for the top runners to compare themselves to stars of seasons past and for those currently on the cusp of making the varsity team to solidify a place in the top seven going into the first invitational. And because it is held annually on a Saturday morning at a local park, Chesterley, it will be the first chance since the end of track season that parents will get to see their kids race. It is always a big deal. Runners wear their uniforms. Professional timers are brought in. The local newspaper photographer sometimes drops by to snap pics. Kids pit themselves against each other as much as against the clock.

You can always tell when the Time Trial is approaching. In the days leading up, workouts become more intense. Absent is the jocular camaraderie of camp. There is a seriousness, a sense of urgency, not felt earlier in the summer. The Tuesday before the TT, with the temperature pushing

100 degrees and a slight whiff of smoke in the air from two uncontained wildfires on the eastern slopes of the Cascade Range, Mister brings the boys out to the orchards bordering the Yakama Nation reservation for a 12-mile run, with five at tempo pace. This is a punishing workout, especially in the heat with little shade lining the dirt-and-gravel fire road, but the boys are running well on this day, hitting all time goals. By the time they reach Mister's truck at the six-mile mark, their shirtless torsos are glazed with sweat, but they are pumped up. Rogelio picks up a water cooler from the bed of the truck, raises it over his head, and points the spigot directly over Fonzi's head. The icy water streams down Fonzi's head, neck, and back.

"Ah, I like that feeling," Fonzi says. "Feels like *season*."

Next afternoon, the day before the first day of school, the smoke hovering over the Yakima Valley becomes more pronounced but still has not reached the "unhealthy air-quality reading" (150 particulates) that would prompt the Yakima School District to cancel practice and send runners indoors to the treadmills, stationary bikes, and elliptical machines in the school's fitness center. The runners take off for Randall Park for interval work on a triple-digit afternoon. The workout slays several runners, who cannot complete it due to fatigue or asthma-induced breathing problems. The most surprising, and troubling, casualty is Angel, who never, ever, begs off a workout early. But he is utterly spent. He has, in running parlance, "bonked." He is dehydrated, and his blood sugar is low. He is feeling a little woozy and sits slumped at a picnic table, sipping water. Mister hands him a glucose tablet, but by this point it won't perk him up enough to let him finish the workout. But later at the team shed, Mister takes Angel aside, quiet and uncomplaining Angel, and tries to draw him out.

"Are you still working the orchards, Angel?"

"Just for a few more days."

"OK. What have you eaten today?"

"Just some bread."

"That's it. Just a slice of bread. Breakfast? Lunch?"

"No, Mister."

"Do you need something to eat?"

"Yes, Mister."

He leads Angel to the fridge and takes out a can of Progresso Chicken Noodle Soup. It is over 100 degrees outside, and Mister is offering him *soup*?

"Is that OK, Angel? I'll microwave it for you."

He nods.

Other runners mill about, not paying much mind to the scene transpiring. Mister raises his voice. More than a few of them have raided the fridge and freezer to add to their food intake when they haven't eaten enough at home. "Guys, we've got all sorts of stuff to eat in the fridge. You don't need to ask, none of you. You need the calories."

By the next day, two days before the TT, Angel is back training strongly. The team goes to Gilbert Park for fartlek intervals—30-second bursts of sprinting in the middle of a steady run—but Mister almost has to take the kids inside because of the air quality, a gray haze like a quilt covering the valley. Fonzi has some shin "issues," and a few girls lag behind, but everyone seems ready for the TT two days hence. But the smoke rolls even heavier by the next morning, the wildfires 30 miles away burning out of control and the wind dumping smoke into the bowl of the valley. State department of ecology maps show a dark red dot at Yakima: "unhealthy." The football team's home game is moved 30 miles south to Richland, where the air is better. Mister warns the runners, who are doing just a light workout, that the TT might be moved to Monday, Labor Day, if the air quality is too smoky on Saturday morning. The runners are to text him in the morning for the verdict.

Molly, in a team-bonding gesture, has each girl pick a name from a plastic storage baggie she is holding. "Secret Sister time," she says, meaning each girl will handwrite an inspirational letter to whichever runner's name she selects.

TT day dawns, and no one really needs to text Mister. Smoke has blotted out the sun. The dot next to Yakima on the ecology department website is purple ("very unhealthy"). The team meets at the fitness center, looking glum. Not only is the TT postponed but the treadmill workout Mister has drawn up for them (12 sets of three-minute hard running on Level 12 with a 5-percent uphill grade) is daunting.

Jonas is particularly bummed. He has been studying the TT records that Mister had printed out and posted in the shed earlier in the week. He is gunning for the record on the 3.4-mile course, 17:42, set by Santos Vargas six years earlier, in 2011. Jonas feels in shape to at least—*at least*—break 18 minutes, and now he'll have to wait a day or two.

"We'll try again Monday, but if the smoke's still bad we may have to do the Time Trial on the treadmills," Mister says.

Jonas, who has been grousing to teammates about the smoke, raises his hand.

"How can you time us all on treadmills?"

"We'll deal with it, Jonas."

In the meantime, the runners slog through a 110-minute treadmill workout that taxes even their advanced fitness levels. The school has turned off the air conditioning for the weekend, and the fitness center quickly becomes nearly as muggy as a sauna. Fonzi and Jonas, who never complain about a workout, complain. "This isn't a workout; it's torture," Jonas mutters. Jesus has sweated so much that, at one point, he peels off his shirt and wrings it out over a trash can. They know why Mister is putting them through their paces. The team's first race, the Ash Creek Festival in Monmouth, Oregon, is only a week away. No time to let up now.

"It's a hard question to answer," Mister says, when asked whether fitness is lost running indoors. "There's always a drop when you come in here. They're still running under five-minute pace, but . . ."

He moves off and walks down the line, shouting above the drone of the treadmills and bikes, "Good pace, push, push. Heads up. Don't watch the monitor. Heart rates over 150, you on the bikes. Dantzel, you're moving your shoulders. Arms straight back. Tony, heels up, especially that left heel."

The runners adopt that thousand-yard stare as they peer into the distance. But all they see out the plate-glass window is the hazy outline of the backstop and light poles of the school's baseball field and the roofs of the surrounding neighborhood. Anything beyond is just gray haze. The tawny foothills that usually bracket the valley are erased, Etch A Sketch–like, by the smoke. Afterward, most kids are as drenched in sweat as if they'd plunged in a pool. No one likes the treadmill, but Fonzi confides, "It's actually a little easier than running outside. Doing 4:40s [miles] in here is not like doing 4:40s outside. You get pushed along [by the treadmill]."

Any hope of a Monday TT is dashed. The fires worsen over the long weekend, and by Labor Day, the dot next to Yakima is black ("hazardous"). Mister changes his mind about doing a treadmill version of the TT. "There may be a chance the smoke will clear a bit on Wednesday, and we'll try to get it in then," he tells the team. "Anything after Wednesday, and it's too close to the first race to do us any good."

Jonas groans. Mister, internally, groans as well, but he keeps a stoic exterior so that the kids won't descend into negativity. His TT tradition has come to an end. His record book dating back three decades will be blank for the year 2017. But more important, he is worried about the team's conditioning going into the Oregon meet.

By Wednesday the smoke still has not cleared enough for the school district to allow outdoor activities. It now has been a week since Eisenhower's team has run out of doors. Ike runners will go into the season having spent their last week like health-club hamsters atop spinning treadmills. Teams west of the Cascades, or even in Spokane, don't have to deal with the smoke for as long as those in the Yakima Valley, where an inversion layer traps the sooty air like a lid over a boiling pot on the stove.

Just another obstacle for the kids to overcome. They'll deal with it. They always do.

SMOKE AND ASH CREEK

The charter bus's belching of diesel fumes, as it idles outside Eisenhower's stadium, only adds to the miasmic smoke that has blanketed Yakima and most of central Washington for going on a month now, thanks to the fires. This toxic bouillabaisse, the sky nothing but a gray canopy, does little to brighten Mister's mood as he stands, arms crossed, supervising the loading of the bus, the team tents, first-aid equipment, water jugs, tarps, massage equipment such as foam rollers, and the bags for 25 kids making the trip southwest to Monmouth, Oregon.

In nearly four decades of coaching, Mister has never seen smoke this bad, has never seen it hovering over the valley for this long a period. Five years ago, sure, he had been forced to cancel the Sunfair Invitational, the huge race Eisenhower puts on annually the last Saturday in September, because of smoke wafting over from northern wildfires. But, even then, the haze wasn't like this. "If this goes on another week or two, it's going to affect our training for the whole season," Mister muses. "You just can't substitute actual running outdoors." Then he purses his lips, as if to ward off negativity and says, "The kids are resilient, though. They are tough kids."

They also are slightly hyper, some downright giddy, as they gambol onto the bus. It has been a long 10 days of indoor workouts on the treadmill—or "dreadmill," as some put it—and soon they will be making their escape to Western Oregon University, 50 miles south of Portland, for the season-opening Ash Creek Cross-Country Festival, in which nearly 1,000 runners from 40 schools, most from Oregon or western Washington, will compete on a fast, relatively flat 5K course. No team will travel as far as Eisenhower. On a good traffic day, it takes four and a half hours on Interstate 84 along the Columbia River gorge to make the trip. But yet another wildfire, this one in the foothills right along the gorge, has closed I-84, which means the bus will have to negotiate the winding, two-lane Highway 14 and then cut over into Oregon just before Portland right in the middle of the Friday afternoon commute. It will take five hours, Mister estimates, to arrive in the rural enclave of Monmouth, where Ike runners then will have to hustle to get in a quick workout on the course before evening descends.

All that matters to the kids now, though, is that they are leaving Yakima, leaving the air that could be seen and smelled and, if you ran a finger along the body of the bus, felt in a sort of brown soot that collected there. "Have you guys noticed the name of the meet?" Molly asks her teammates as she joins the girls' team in the middle section of the bus (the boys having commandeered the back). "We run inside for two weeks in the smoke and then we go to a meet called *Ash* Creek." Izzy laughs. "Guess that means we're ready for it." It certainly seems that way. All of the runners are seated and surprisingly quiet as assistant coach Ivan Alfaro comes aboard cradling the team good-luck tchotchke, the gnome, as one would carry a newborn. "Gnome!" A cheer rises from the back. "Gnome!"

At last, Mister boards, putting on his trademark Donegal hat for the first time this season. They are ready to go. He chats briefly with the bus driver, Rick Glenn, who isn't just any bus driver but the father of three former Eisenhower runners. In this program, and in this small a town, the degrees of separation number far fewer than six. The bus has traveled all of seven miles, to a fruit-packing facility in Wapato, when Glenn pulls over. A light indicates that the bus is overheating. A phone call to the dispatcher, a few minutes to let the engine cool, and then they are back on the road, bus temperature holding steady. The runners have ordered sack lunches from the school cafeteria, which explains why the first hour of the trip passes in near silence. The only commotion, it turns out, comes from Mister himself. One of his students told him that morning about a viral video that was shown on *Jimmy Kimmel Live!*, some Irish guy battling a bat that had alighted in his house. Anything having to do with Ireland is automatically passed on to Mister, because he wears his Irish pride like he wears that jaunty hat. Now, on the bus, he takes out his iPad and plays the video, volume at full blast. The runners, accustomed to Mister telling them to keep the noise down, shout at him.

"What are you watching, Mister?"

"This is hilarious," the coach says.

He plays it again. And again. Then the runners get bored, and the dull murmur of conversation takes hold once more. By the time the bus reaches the Columbia River, the sky has darkened even more than it had in Yakima. Across the Columbia, billows of smoke and occasional licks of flame emanate from the hillside. Even with the air conditioning blasting inside the bus, the smell of smoke is evident. As the bus chugs along the winding road with steep drop-offs to the gorge, the girls play that game in which passengers hold their breath as they pass through tunnels. Just outside the town of Lyle, Dantzel ambles to the front and takes the trash can from where it sits near the driver's right leg and carries it back with her. Suddenly, several voices rise.

"Mister, Nayeli's sick."

"Pull over, will ya, Rick?" Mister orders.

For 10 minutes, the bus idles on the side of a road while the coaching staff and sophomore Nayeli Barron walk around, trying to settle her car sickness. The smoke and the curves have gotten to her, she says. What no one knows is that, in the back of the bus, Fonzi is feeling poorly as well. Nauseated. He feels a head cold coming on. That, plus the motion sickness, is weighing on him. He keeps it quiet, though. When they finally come back aboard, Nayeli sits in Mister's spot up front, and Mister takes her seat amid the girls. Having their coach next to them doesn't silence the girls; in fact, his presence perks them up.

"Hey, Mister," Kayli Carl asks. "What are some words in the Irish language you can tell us?"

He beams and turns pedagogical.

"There actually are some words in Gaelic that are acceptable as proper English now, like the word 'smithereens.'"

"Isn't that a bad word?" Sophi Rodriquez asks.

"Whattya mean, bad word? It's a perfectly fine word."

By the time the bus reaches Salem, 30 miles from the destination, Molly takes a selfie of her seatmates and posts it on the girls' team's Instagram account. Several of the boys grumble. They have been blocked because they had made mean comments about some of the girls' postings. Eventually, a truce is reached right there on the bus. "OK, congratulations, Tony and Jonas, you're unblocked now," Molly says. Several runners whip out their smartphones when the bus makes a wrong turn and is stuck in bumper-to-bumper traffic in West Salem. The kids have a clear view of an unconventional picnic taking place, a large aggregation of neo-hippies and quasi-homeless milling around a park abutting the Willamette River. Several runners snap pictures of a couple sprawled on the grass, making out. Some boys in the back whoop it up. A picnicker who appears to be wearing an eye mask, a la Zorro or the Lone Ranger, sways and stumbles on the sidewalk, but then Jesus observes that it isn't a mask, it is a *tattoo* of a mask. "Look, I swear," Jesus says. "Mannnn!"

"What is this," Erica observes wryly, "a typical Friday night in Oregon?"

By the time the bus gets moving again, the kids can see the banner, "Hugs Not Drugs: Recovery Celebration," draped between two trees in the park. Only a few of the kids laugh, perhaps because Yakima, itself, certainly is not untouched by drug use.

"Now it makes sense," Erica says.

Six hours after they had left Yakima, the runners finally reach the course. The sky's color is a blissful baby blue, with wisps of clouds adding just a hint of a chill. No smoky gray gloom. The team quickly puts on shoes for a 30-minute run, course maps for the next day's race in hand. Fonzi lags behind and then stops altogether, bent double. Mister ambles over.

"My stomach's upset, Mister. I think it's the ride. But I've got a cold too."

"Pack it in, Fonzi. Just go back to the bus. We'll get you some cold medicine before we go to dinner."

At the Italian restaurant the coaches have found via Google search, Mister announces to the team, "Get dressed. Don't go into the restaurant with running gear on."

A shout of rebellion: "What?"

"I just mean, put a shirt on. And wear shoes."

"OK, Mister."

"And if you don't have any money, come see me. We don't want you not eating."

★ ★ ★

Just after 10 p.m., right around lights-out time according to the itinerary Mister has printed out for each runner, the boys' team gathers in Room 207 of the Comfort Inn, Mister's room, for the prerace meeting.

"The things we're looking for tomorrow: Are you competing, and what does your technique look like," Mister begins. Some boys lean against the wall, others sprawl prone on the bed, a few sit cross-legged on the floor.

"If you're competing, we don't really care what your time is or where you finish. We've been working very hard on this, and we see you're all over the place with technique, the first thing we wonder is, What happened to the Emotional Intelligence that we've talked about?"

For several weeks now, Mister has made use of the psychological concept of Emotional Intelligence, based on the principles of self-awareness and empathy, tweaked to pertain to running. Mister's definition holds that if runners have presence of mind and stoutness of heart to recognize moments during races when pain will descend, they can mentally override it by telling themselves to "hang on for six seconds." He has given the concept the shorthand "EI-6."

"Sometime tomorrow, you're going to be running hard. It might be at the end of the race, the middle of the race, but when discomfort sets in, you've got to be able to use that Emotional Intelligence to know your body and consciously push through that discomfort for six seconds. If we ask you [afterward], 'Did you run with Emotional Intelligence?' and you say, 'No,' that means right at the first difficulty of the race, you collapsed. You let go emotionally. Some of you are capable of pushing through more than once. Remember what the whole basis of this Emotional Intelligence is: If you push through it once, your body will recalibrate, and you can continue. But if you never reach that point, you're going to be shutting down and waiting for the finish line to come. Your racing is over. You'll know it. We'll know it. And the video will show it. Any questions?"

Silence.

"Now, get to sleep. We'll wake you for breakfast."

The girls then hear the same Emotional Intelligence speech, the same spiel on technique. Most of the girls' team will be competing in the junior varsity race because Mister feels their training isn't strong enough yet this early in the season for a big varsity meet; thus only Erica and Molly will run varsity. When Mister asks if there are questions, Erica raises her hand.

"What's Jesuit's fastest girl?" she asks.

"Girl named Kelsey, I think," Bryson-Driver says.

"Anyone run under 19 [minutes]?"

Bryson-Driver shakes her head.

Mister smiles.

"It's not like you're *not* going to have somebody to run with, Erica," he says.

* * *

The varsity boys and girls have more than a three-hour wait for their races, and they hunker down under the tent, swaddled in sweats. Fonzi and Rogelio have earbuds in, Fonzi sniffling and coughing. Jonas stares at the grass. Erica rests on her back, staring at the underside of the tent. They all rustle themselves once the races started. Everyone is curious to see how Diego Vargas, a senior who has just taken up cross-country this past summer, will fare in his first race ever. He's shown talent, but Mister has entered him in the Novice division (on a shorter 3K course) to ease him into it.

Diego transferred to Eisenhower the previous spring. Originally from Rialto, California, in East Los Angeles, he had spent the previous two years in Mexico because his grandfather had suffered from a rare brain disease and needed experimental treatment. He has never run formally. And when he ran while playing in the street or at school, it was always as sprinter, a fast one. He feels he lacks endurance, but decided to give cross-country a shot over the summer. After a few workouts, Mister pulled him aside, told him that by the end of the season, he could perhaps make the varsity. "I didn't believe him," Diego says.

Now, at the start line, Mister pulls him aside again.

"Don't go out too fast, Diego. But move on through. Keep passing people."

Mister moves off then, jogging down the course to set up at about the half-mile mark. He has no idea what to expect from Diego. The kid might pull it off, or he might crash and burn. His training has been good, but he's never run in anything but a workout. Who knows?

A mile in, Diego holds steady in second place. When he passes Mister, he hears the bellowing command, "Arms, Diego!" At a mile and a half, before a series of four rolling berms (mini-hills), Diego has taken the lead. Mister has run over just in time to see him go by. The question at this point is, Can Diego hold on? When the lead pack, with Diego laboring in front, reaches the final triangle of a turn before a 200-meter uphill finishing straightaway, Diego's lead is three meters. His teammates, boys and girls, line the fencing to cheer him on. Suddenly, he takes off, arms pumping, feet a blur, leaving the three others on his tail far, far behind. He wins going away, by more than six seconds. A few minutes later, after getting a slap on the back by Mister, Diego returns to the tent, still breathing hard. Jesus and Jonathan, the Nos. 6 and 7 varsity runners, ask him what the course was like, specifically, how tough the berms were.

"They seemed hella long," he says. "I was dying even before that."

Before every race, the PA announcer makes a point of mentioning that "Eisenhower has come all the way from Yakima and hasn't run outdoors in two weeks!"

The runners aren't certain whether the pronouncement takes the pressure off of them or adds on more. In any event, Dantzel doesn't need more pressure going into the girls' JV race, a 5K. She isn't thrilled about being bumped down in status after being the No. 2 varsity runner last year, but her summer of training went poorly: She was unable to finish some workouts and was feeling weak in others. Her blood test for ferritin came back at a solid 44; she is not anemic, but, as Mister and her parents have mentioned, she needs to consume more calories to keep up her strength. Mister knows it peeves Dantzel not to run varsity at Ash Creek, but he feels she needs a confidence booster, and a high finish will be a good way to slowly build her confidence and stamina for later on.

Three-quarters of the way through the first lap, Dantzel has settled into third and is feeling strong. On the long back straightaway, she hears Mister bark, "Hands closed, Dan. Use the arms." At the sound of his voice, she picks up the pace. By the time she reaches the berms for the first of two laps, she has moved up to second place. Mister cups his hands to his mouth and shouts, "Lower the arms, big swing. You're going to win this race, Dantzel! Win it!" When she hears Mister's command to win, she almost turns her head to say, "What?" Hadn't Mister told her before the start to just run at 85 percent for this race, just to use this season opener to work on her form? Now he's yelling at her to win? In any event, she follows orders. Dantzel always follows orders, and she takes off. The second time over the berms, Dantzel has, indeed, taken the lead. Mister yells, "Chin down on the hill. You're going to win this race with technique!"

Win, she does, in 20 minutes, 44 seconds. Mister beams. This is precisely what he had in mind for Dantzel, a good race to jump-start the season. Dantzel, however, is not so thrilled. To her thinking, she shouldn't have been in this race. Yeah, some of those Jesuit High JV girls could make the varsity on other teams, but come on, she didn't belong in that race. As she would say later, "I didn't talk to him, but I was a little upset. I think what got me through it was saying to myself, 'I'm a varsity runner, and I shouldn't be running in this race, but I better win it.'"

It will not be so easy for the boys' varsity team. Two of the top 20 ranked teams in the nation, Jesuit High of Beaverton and Crater High of Central Point, Oregon, are racing. Jesuit's program has been strong for decades, and it is huge. Mister gazes at the five tents erected on a swath of grass and cracks, "Looks like a Catholic revival meeting." Even though Jesuit plans to rest its top runner, Josh Schumacher, son of Nike Bowerman Project professional coach Jerry Schumacher (who trains Olympic medalists Evan Jager and Shalane Flanagan, among others), it still is the team to beat.

In the final half hour before the boys are to be called to the starting line, Jonas seems like a thoroughbred kicking at the stalls before the Kentucky Derby. He is raring to run. The smoke has prevented him from getting that school Time Trial record, but now the sky is clear, the sun beating down, and a light breeze picking up. Rogelio, too, seems antsy. He calls over Mister to get out the pungent Tiger Balm ointment and rub some of it into his sore left calf. Other varsity runners—Mo, Angel, and Jesus—are in line for the porta potties, breathing in another type of pungent odor. Fonzi stands off to the side, still in sweats, head down, earbuds in. Eisenhower has drawn the far left starting line box—a prime spot, considering that the course makes a sharp right turn less than 200 meters after the start, so Eisenhower will not be cut off by merging runners. Cross-country's scoring system is opposite of most sports; lowest score wins here. Runners earn a point for the place they finish in the race, and the top five of the seven runners on each time are "scoring members." So the lowest score a team could earn would be 15, that is, if the team captured the top five places in the race.

Good as Jesuit is rumored to be, it's doubtful that the school will score 15 on this day. Eisenhower is hoping for a top three—podium—finish. From the gun, the race is not going at all as Eisenhower planned. Mister has set himself up along the long backstretch at the half-mile mark while Price, videotaping the race, plants himself on the berms. The lead pack of seven runners passes Mister—with no Eisenhower blue singlet in sight. They come three abreast—Jonas, Fonzi, and Rogelio—shortly thereafter in the chase pack. Mister grumbles. Sure, he wants them not to go out too fast, but hell, not too slow either. Cripes, they need to get going. "Move along! You gotta go now and get to that lead group." As he watches the trio pass, he calls behind them, "Arms, Fonzi!" Over at the berms, Price waits with camera poised. Still no Ike runners when the lead pack emerges, though Jonas has moved up slightly. Fonzi and Rogelio are five meters behind him. "Get to the back of the front pack," Price yells to his son. "Rogelio, eyes up. Fonzi, apply force to the ground." Mo and Angel move up, at least, now about 10 to 15 seconds behind Rogelio and Fonzi.

Another lap around, and Mister is feeling better. Jonas has moved to fifth in the lead pack. Rogelio has settled into the chase pack, but Fonzi is struggling to keep up with that pack. As the runners' heads emerge climbing the final set of berms, Price lowers his camera for a minute, peers ahead. "Yesss!" he hisses, excitedly. Jonas has moved into third place and is challenging the leaders, Jesuit's Grant Summers and Evan Holland of Ashland, Oregon's top sophomore runner. "Chin, down, chin, chin, Jo Jo," Price yells, voice a hoarse wheeze by this point. "You got this!"

As the trio hits the final straightaway, Holland passes Summers, but Jonas cannot gain much ground on either. It isn't for lack of effort. Jonas's face is scrunched, teeth bared like a predator animal. He finishes a strong third, four seconds behind Holland and three behind Summers. From there, Jesuit dominates. Its five scoring runners cross among the first 10 individuals, a dominant display of pack running. The race now is for second place, teamwise, between Eisenhower, Summit High from Bend, and South Eugene. Forty seconds behind Jonas comes Rogelio in 15th place. It is the first time in cross-country Rogelio has ever beaten his best friend, Fonzi. Up the course a way, Fonzi is flagging. He has been struggling the entire last mile. He tries to make surges but feels spent. His chest seems tight from the head cold, but that is no excuse. The leg turnover just isn't there. Just before the final straightaway, Angel passes him—the first time since freshman year that that has happened. Angel finishes as Ike's third runner, 31st in team scoring, Fonzi close behind in 37th place. But if Eisenhower had any hope of making the podium (top three), it needs its fifth and final scoring runner to show up—and soon. At the turn, the fifth runners from South Eugene (Liam Monroe) and Summit (Cole Rene) are battling with each other, stride for stride. Neither knows the scoring situation, but the runner who prevails will catapult his team to second place, overall. Looming behind them, closing fast, comes Mo, all 6-foot-2 of him, eating up the grass with those long legs. With a hundred meters to go, Mo passes Summit's Rene, and then he passes another runner and is bearing down on Monroe. The rest of the Eisenhower team lines the final straightaway, shouting encouragement to Mo. Twenty meters from the finish, Mo shows his 800-meter track speed and passes Monroe. He leans into the nonexistent tape—habit from track, perhaps—and nearly collapses.

Mo's ability to pick off those two runners has given Eisenhower 126 points and the second-place finish, one point ahead of Summit and three ahead of South Eugene. With Jonas finishing third overall, and the boys' varsity second, Mister has much to like. But, except for a quick smile, he has no time to savor it before the girls' varsity race. Fonzi, on the other hand, has plenty of time to brood. He has torn off his bib number in disgust, leaving behind the safety pins on his singlet, and he plops down, coughing, under the team tent. No one approaches him. They know better. In times like this, Fonzi could turn dark and inward. Jonas, who often turns puppy-doggish playful after a good race, is uncharacteristically subdued afterward. He has run a smart, at times cautious, race. His mile splits are consistent: 5:05; 5:05; 5:14. "I probably could've won if my strategy was different," he says. "Honestly, that front pack wasn't going out as fast as I thought it was going to. Because, like, when I finally got right up behind [the pack], I started passing people."

As the boys' team, sans Fonzi, trots the perimeter of the course for a cooldown jog, the girls' race is heating up right from the gun. Erica, shortest girl in the field, learned long ago, as is cross-country etiquette, to place her hand gently on the back of a runner who drifts over and is threatening to cut her off. There can be a lot of jostling in races, especially at the start. Here, just before that first sharp right-hand turn, a runner at least six inches taller and considerably stockier cuts off Erica. Her stride momentarily broken, Erica reaches out with both hands to touch the back of the offending runner. Maybe it is adrenaline, or maybe she is moving too fast, but Erica's touch is more like a shove—a soft shove, but a shove nonetheless. The girl goes down. Erica instinctively hurdles the fallen runner and keeps going. But a panic thought strikes her, over and over, for the next half mile: *I'm going to get DQed, I'm going to get DQed.* Eventually, she pushes thoughts about disqualification away: *If it happens, it happens. Just run your best race.* And she does for that first mile. She settles into the lead pack with three other runners, wondering why the pace feels so easy. No one is pushing it. By the time the three hit the berms for the first time, Erica has pulled away into the lead by a few meters. Mister, on the berms, shakes his head, thinking it too soon for such a decisive move. Even Erica's dad, Eric, jogging up to the berms, is surprised. "Seems early," he says. By the time they come around to the berms a second time, Erica has slipped to third. Her body is starting to "lock up," meaning her form is breaking down due to something, either fatigue or impending injury. All Erica knows is that her knee lift is failing her, and her hips, a chronic weakness she's learned to live with, feel tired. She holds on to finish fifth, her dad and grandpa and aunt who have come down from Yakima cheering wildly near the finishing chute. But Erica isn't pleased. She pronounces her race "crappy" and laments, "It wasn't what I imagined it to be, because I thought I had a strong summer." Molly, Eisenhower's other varsity runner, finishes 26th out of 190. Her time, 20:46, is two seconds slower than Dantzel's winning JV time. So, going into Thursday's league meet and the first showdown with rival Davis High, the girls have three solid times on which to build, setting Mister's mind, temporarily at least, at ease.

Then there is Fonzi, still brooding by himself long after his race is finished. Mister makes it a point to pull him aside. He tells him not to worry. He tells him it is just one race. He tells him that the head cold and getting used to the orthotics put into his shoes to correct his pronation problem could explain his poor race. He tells him that he has full confidence in him. All the while, Fonzi stands with his arms crossed. He is looking at Mister, though, looking at him dead in the eye. A good sign. Mister sees some fire and frustration in those eyes. Fonzi cares, cares deeply. He wants to be the best. Even two days postrace, Fonzi is down. It doesn't help that he can't shake the head cold, and he hopes it will subside before the league meet late in the week or the giant Fort Steilacoom Invitational the coming weekend.

"I haven't had a good race since last cross season," Fonzi says. "I mean, all of track. Even this summer wasn't good getting used to the orthotics. So your confidence does get affected."

Mister has noticed—noticed and backed off, giving Fonzi room to brood. Part of the trick of being a good coach, Mister says, is knowing when not to push. "Guys like Fonzi, you don't need to be hard on," he says. "They are hard enough on themselves. His times will be there by the end of the season. Everything's in place."

Speaking of times, the bus ride back to Yakima takes an hour less than the ride to the meet. The team stops at a mall food court in Salem, where many runners buy enough food for several meals. Angel pulls Mister aside outside the bus, saying he is running a little short cashwise, and Mister pulls out a roll of bills and peels off a couple. No big deal. Hyped up on sugar, the runners have the festive chattiness on the ride back of a team that performed, on the whole, pretty well. At one point, the din reaches such a pitch that Mister rises from his seat and bellows, "Guys, keep it down back there. You sound like rats on steroids."

Once darkness descends, most on the bus nod off, including Price sitting across from Mister up front. The driver, Rick Glenn, turns to Mister and says, "Hey, Jonas had a pretty good race, huh?"

"Let me tell you," Mister says, leaning in to the driver and speaking in a whisper, "If he had gone out with that lead group a little earlier, he would've won the whole dang race."

"You guys did pretty well, though, right?"

"Guess so. The boys were on the podium again."

Indeed, they were. At the awards ceremony, the runner-up Eisenhower boys stood sandwiched between first-place Jesuit High of Beaverton, Oregon, and third-place Summit of Bend, Oregon.

Ike's boys were the only nonwhite runners on the podium, something that Eisenhower has long grown accustomed to. And taken pride in.

RACING AND LA RAZA

Ask Mister, the Irishman whose formative years were spent in what amounted to a racial monoculture, what it is like coaching teams comprised mostly of Hispanic runners, and he doesn't answer directly. Instead, he reverts to storyteller mode. He speaks in anecdotes. Two, specifically:

- The only time Jesus Medina's father, an undocumented migrant farm worker, saw his son run.
- The 2010 season, in which two plucky bands of self-described "brown kids" conquered the state meet in unprecedented fashion.

★ ★ ★

He cannot remember the year, precisely. It was either 2012 or '13. The years all run together for Mister now. But the incident, he will never forget. He had driven the boys' team out to the Rez—the apple and pear orchards south of Yakima, bordering Yakama Nation tribal lands—for a 16-mile, out-and-back workout, and he had parked his truck at the eight-mile turnaround, about a half mile beyond where the migrant pickers were bringing in the last of the apple crop. When the runners made it to English's truck for a water break before the eight miles back to the trail-head, Drew Schreiber and Jesus Medina as always leading the pack, Mister overheard snippets of conversation. The runners were gathered around Medina, but the coach couldn't quite make out what they were saying. He thought little of it and sent them back on their way, this time following behind the pack in his truck.

A mile back down the road, Mister figured out what the buzz had been about.

"All the pickers—I mean every single one of them—had left the trees and their bins, and they lined the edge of the orchard. As the guys ran past, the pickers stood there and clapped, just applauded. I'd never seen something like that before. When we got back, I asked the kids, 'What was that about? Did you say something to those workers back on the Rez?' And Jesus just said, 'No, it was my dad and other guys.' I left it there. I didn't press him. I knew there was some conflict between them. Jesus's father wanted him to work picking. Jesus wanted to run.

"The next day, Jesus comes up to me and told me what happened. He said the pickers saw them run by on the way out, and that was the first time Jesus's dad had ever seen him run. He told me, 'My dad didn't know how good I was. When I went home that night, my dad was blown away that his son could run that fast but also run with that white kid [Schreiber].'"

Schreiber remembered it as one of the high points of the season for the team.

"The workers, they lined both sides of the road like a tunnel," Schreiber said. "It was incredible. We were really moving as we passed them on our tempo run, but Jesus's dad shouted something to him in Spanish. I turned and looked at Jesus, and he smiled and said something back in Spanish. We ended up finishing second at State that year, and Jesus was our second runner, pretty close to me."

Medina, for his part, breaks into a grin when reminded of the anecdote.

"I was really proud of what happened out there," he says. "It wasn't like [my father] didn't want me to run; he just never got the chance to see me do it. But he'd drop me off at practice in the morning before he went to work. I think he liked it when he saw I was good at it."

A dark coda, however, attached itself to the story. Medina, whose parents were undocumented workers and brought him illegally to the United States as a child, had a history of grade trouble in school. Midway through his senior year, just before track season, he dropped out of Eisenhower.

"I think part of the reason I dropped out was that I knew, because of my [undocumented] status, I would have trouble going to college," he says. "Mister tried to help me out, but I guess I just wanted to drop out."

Medina's life went into a downward spiral for a time thereafter. He was arrested for a DUI and possession of 40 grams of marijuana in August 2016 and, because he was an undocumented immigrant, was sent to an Immigration and Customs Enforcement detention center in Tacoma, awaiting deportation.

"I spent seven months there," Medina says, sitting on the leather sofa in the mobile home he shares with his wife, Jax, and his parents, in Union Gap. "It was really tough. But I'm out now, and we're in the process of clearing up the whole [immigration] situation."

Medina recently married Jax, his American-born girlfriend, and he works at a warehouse for the Hanson Fruit Company. Once his legal problems are resolved, he says he wants to train to become a barber. Only 21, Medina still runs regularly and sometimes daydreams about whether he could have run in college, like Schreiber and Miguel Vargas, another former teammate.

"I still really like to go out and just run, especially the hills just outside of town," Medina says, pointing to the Ahtanum Ridge abutting Yakama Tribal Land, about 10 miles from the old Rez run he and his teammates ran.

Mister was happy to hear it. To him, it meant that Medina was in the process of rebuilding his life, step-by-step.

"Running," Mister adds, frowning, "probably kept him in school longer than he would've stayed otherwise."

★ ★ ★

And then there was the magical 2010 season, happy endings sprouting all around. At Eisenhower, the mention of 2010 brings on chest-swelling reminiscences. . . .

Low clouds hovered over Pasco on the morning of November 6, 2010, making the site of the 4A state cross-country championships, Sun Willows Golf Course, something of a misnomer. You might say it was perfect running weather, 43 degrees for the first races and topping out in the late afternoon at 49—conditions ripe for a record-setting day. But the Eisenhower girls' and boys' teams that day looked swaddled for a big chill, wearing layer upon layer, only to be shed right before the starting gun fired. These runners, nearly all Hispanic kids from the valley accustomed to the heat, would have preferred those long, hot days of summer, going shirtless and running into a purplish sunset under a backdrop of orchards thick with cherries and apples to be plucked.

In the dog days of summer, the boys' team works on running drills. From left: Antonio Heredia, Alfonso (Fonzi) Cuevas, Rogelio Mares. Back row, from left: Angel Cuevas, Diego Vargas.
Sam McManis

After a hot summer workout, the boys and girls teams enjoyed ice baths. From Left: Antonio Heredia (sitting), Alfonso (Fonzi) Cuevas, Jonas Price (sitting), John Campos and Jesus Gonzalez (standing in back). Girls' bath: Izzy Guttierez (sitting in front), Madi Oliva, Dantzel Peterson and Julia Johnson (standing in back).
Sam McManis

Coach Phil (Mister) English takes a walk before the action starts at Richland.
Beth McManis

A portrait of Fonzi, his mother Sonya and sister Caris.
Beth McManis

The start of the boys race at Ash Creek Invitational.
Beth McManis

The Boys' start at the first league meet.
Sam McManis

Phil (Mister) English shares a laugh with runners from another school at the Fort Steilacoom Invitational.
Beth McManis

Fonzi en route to a third-place finish at the Bellevue Invitational.
Beth McManis

Jonas and his dad Robert celebrating Jonas's win at Bellevue.
Beth McManis

Erica Simison wears a surgical mask in her science class to ward off germs from classmates that might cause her to get a cold. In the final two weeks before the state meet, all runners were required to wear masks at school.
Sam McManis

Erica Simison shares a laugh with Angel Cuevas and Nayeli Barron after the District meet.
Beth McManis

Erica Simison furtively pets her new dog, which was smuggled into the state meet.
Beth McManis

Nothing if not adaptable, the Eisenhower team took whatever conditions were handed to them. They were too focused on the task at hand, too driven to let something so minor as a dank day deter them. Their goal was nothing less than winning both the girls' and boys' 4A state championship in the same year, something no large-division Washington school had ever accomplished. The fact that the top 10 Eisenhower runners—the scoring five from each team—were Hispanic was not lost either on the crowd or the athletes themselves. Ike, by this time, was accustomed to being the token "minority" team in a state and a sport dominated by whites, but this year, the team was almost entirely Hispanic. And they were good, crushingly good. Especially the boys' team, whose depth made it so that runners one through five were almost interchangeable. The boys reveled in their favorite status, secure that they could easily handle the guys from Lewis and Clark High in Spokane. But Eisenhower's girls' team, led by the potent one-two punch of Mayra Chavez and Berenice Penaloza, was far from the prohibitive favorite. Those white girls from the west side, Tahoma and Eastlake, could easily spoil Ike's party.

The girls' race went off first, and Eisenhower held back and let the race unfold, which was Mister's strategy all season. With about a mile to go, the girls made their move, getting encouragement from a chorus of voices along the course. It was the boys' team, and coaches, cheering them on.

"They were yelling at me, 'You guys are doing this. You guys are doing this,'" Chavez recalled. "I thought to myself, my goodness, we are. I just gave it all, and I could feel Berenice right behind me and thinking, we have to do this. That helped me immensely and created a chain reaction on the team. Some of us weren't feeling their best. One runner had bronchitis, I think. But Mister pulled me to the side [before the start], and he was telling me how Berenice and I had to work together, and the rest of the girls would follow. He believed we could win and should win. He told me if you want something, you'll have to work for it. It won't be easy, but you'll have to persevere."

Eventually, Chavez and Penaloza weaved in and out of bodies and approached the lead pack, holding steady to the end, finishing 11th and 15th, ahead of all runners from rival schools except for Eastlake's top girl. And there came Ike's No. 3 runner, tiny freshman Elise Tello, running the race of her life and finishing just three-tenths of a second behind Tahoma's third runner. A gaggle of runners started passing through the chute, and Penaloza was frantically looking for the familiar blue Eisenhower singlet. There she was, Katherine Bravo in 48th. But Tahoma and Eastlake runners were crossing the line, and Eisenhower's fifth and final scorer, Alyssa Pena, another freshman, had yet to finish. Wait finally over, Pena crossed in 96th place.

But now came the longer wait—the numbers crunching as scores were tallied and recounted. Which team would finish with the fewest points? Which would win? This was taking five, 10 minutes. Still, no word. The boys' team could wait no longer. Mister and Price herded the boys over to a secluded patch of grass, far from the hubbub of activity, to warm up. The boys were all business; they seemingly had forgotten all about the pending girls' outcome.

"After we finished, people are saying, oh, you guys got fifth or sixth, and all the parents told us too," Chavez said. "We were waiting for the official score. . . . It was the longest wait of my life. Ugh. It was terrible. At that time, we kept overhearing comments from other coaches, and there were actually teams that thought they'd won, and they were yelling. So, we thought, 'Oh, I guess we didn't win.'"

Minutes later, Mister's cell phone rang. What he heard in his ear were squeals of delight, shouts of exultation, exclamations of "We won, Mister! We actually won!" Final score: Eisenhower 110, Tahoma and Eastlake 116, a second-place tie.

"All of us are crying, because none of us thought we could actually win," Penaloza recalls. "The focus was all on the boys. But Mister was the only one telling us we could actually do it. Mister was right."

Eisenhower boys, running strides to burn off extra adrenaline, took the girls' victory as a challenge. More pressure, but more incentive.

"We didn't want to let the girls have all the glory on the bus ride home," Jaziel Rodriguez says. "We kept telling each other, 'We gotta win.'"

Win they did, in impressive fashion. Eisenhower's top four runners came in No. 7, 8, 9, and 11, respectively. But it was the order of finish that surprised many. Rodriguez, at best the fourth fastest among the boys, ran the race of his life to be the team's top finisher, something Ike desperately needed because German Silva and Tim Cummings had off-days.

"It was my first state meet," Rodriguez recalls. "I had no idea what to expect. I just decided to run with Santos and run our race. The gun goes off, and I got stuck in back with Santos for a while, and I'm like, 'Dude, we gotta move forward. We gotta catch up.' We started slowly moving to the front. I was supposed to be the fourth person on our team—I'm not supposed to be up there with the rest of them—but for some reason, I felt so good. Maybe I was running a little scared. Santos and I worked our way up, and we saw German dying, and I said, 'Let's catch up to German.' We just kept going. Strong and comfortable. We had a lot left. We tried telling German, 'C'mon, man, let's go.' He's like, 'I'm just going to try to hold on.' He went out too fast, I guess. There's like, 800 meters left, and we're closing in on Timothy. We tried to catch him. Santos and I were going as fast as we could, and we couldn't believe we caught up to Tim. He's like, 'Keep going.' We finish, and I say to Santos, 'How'd we do that?' Then the rest of the guys came in."

When the fifth runner, Delfino Dominguez, crossed in 38th place, the boys knew they had won—no recount, no fingernail biting, needed. Perhaps it wasn't as dominant a performance as they had anticipated, but they would take it. Later, after all of the races concluded and the awards ceremony wrapped up, the two victorious teams gathered with trophies in hand and medals around necks for a group photo.

"Almost all the brown faces at the meet were in that one photo," says Nieves Negrete, Cummings's mother. "There was a lot of pride in that."

"Yeah, almost like that Disney movie, *McFarland, USA*," says Santos Vargas, referring to the 2015 movie about a Hispanic prep team from California farm country that beat the odds to win a title in the late 1980s. "An article was even written in a Seattle paper about how we were largely Hispanic."

Chavez has tried to downplay the fact that all 10 scoring runners from the 2010 teams were Hispanic. That's just the way it worked out, she says. But she does admit that, speaking among themselves, the runners showed considerable ethnic pride.

"I'm not trying to say it was better, us being Hispanic, but it was very special and cool," she says. "We were all coming from similar backgrounds. Our parents were farm workers in Yakima. To have the community involved was great."

In fact, Cummings, whose mother, Nieves Negrete, is Latina and whose father is African American, didn't really think of the racial aspect of the achievement until he arrived at the University of Washington the next fall for the start of cross-country practice.

"When I got to college, the other runners said to me, 'Oh, yeah, you went to Eisenhower. That's the team full of Hispanics.' I mean, they were right, but you never really think about it living in Yakima. That's just the way things are. A lot of the kids in school are children of migrants, and a lot come from families where the father is not in the picture. That was my situation. You don't think it's anything special until you go away and find out it's not like that everywhere."

★ ★ ★

Before that historic 2010 team, Eisenhower had a smattering of quality Hispanic runners, most notably Tim Cummings's older brother, Charles, in the early 2000s. But since 2010, the teams, particularly on the boys' side, have been overwhelmingly Hispanic. Granted, there still have been quality white runners, including Schreiber in 2013, and, more recently, the Price brothers, but Mister says the team's strong Hispanic bond has become a permanent part of the program. No longer were Yakima's Hispanic youth sticking with soccer; running had become ingrained in the culture.

Take the Chavez-Silva-Penaloza-Vargas connection on the 2010 squad. Penaloza, who went on to run college Division I cross-country first at New Mexico State and later Eastern Washington, says she had no compulsion to run until her close friends, Chavez and Silva, kept pestering her to try out. She showed up the first day in Converse high tops but eventually came to love the sport. She passed on that love to her cousin, Santos Vargas, who had always thought of himself as a soccer player, then a tennis player. "Berenice was like, just try conditioning for a week. I was hooked," says Vargas, who ran collegiately at the University of Idaho. "Then I got Miguel into it." That would be Santos's kid brother, Miguel, who graduated in 2015 and now runs at Eastern Washington University.

"There's a strong work ethic in the Hispanic community," Price says. "That comes from family, I guess. Many of our kids, our runners, are cousins, family members, or so close that they might as well be family members. It's hard to keep track sometimes. Mister is really good in cultivating that segment of the population."

The changing demographics of the cross-country teams have mirrored that of the school itself. Eisenhower is 65 percent Hispanic, so it's in Mister's best interest to recruit Hispanic runners, trying to steal the best athletes from Eisenhower's so-so soccer program.

Mister is blunt about one motivation for nurturing Hispanic runners.

"Quite frankly," he says, "the reality is that unless we get Hispanic kids competing, we aren't going to be very successful anymore. That said, it's a great way forward for these kids as well. It's one of the best things that ever happened to this program."

For much of the early years of Mister's tenure at Eisenhower—at Carroll in the 1980s, he rarely had Hispanic runners—the teams were almost exclusively white simply because whites dominated the student body. As late as the early 1990s, Eisenhower's Hispanic student body hovered around mid–double digits. But the city demographics evolved steadily. More Hispanic families moved into the area for agricultural jobs; some white families moved to the West Valley school district. And because the Yakima school district allowed students to choose between Eisenhower and rival high school Davis, which was more than 90 percent Hispanic at the time, more Hispanics began opting for Eisenhower, even though it meant a longer bus ride from the east side. By the 2010s, the demographic shift among students was almost complete. Now Davis and Eisenhower both are predominantly Hispanic.

Jose Garcia, the Davis High School coach who came to Yakima at age 9 from Mexico and was a star runner at Davis in the late 1980s, says he did not begrudge many of the top Hispanic runners choosing Eisenhower, even though their residences may be, in many cases, extremely close to Davis's campus.

"Davis, for many years, has been seen as lower income among the two schools," Garcia says. "Since the 1950s, when they built Eisenhower, they had unspoken barriers. It was always understood if you were Hispanic, you'd go to Davis High, because that's where it is—in the Hispanic area. After a while, it was de facto. When I was growing up, if you were east of 16th Avenue, you went to Davis. That was the dividing line. What started in the 1990s was what they call white flight. You saw white families move out to West Valley [an unincorporated area with a separate school district, located just west of Yakima].

"Now, because Phil has built up such a program, the thinking is, if you are serious about running, that's where you go. That's the way it's been. You work with the kids who come through the door."

Only rarely has a cross-country runner transferred from Davis to Eisenhower, but it has happened. "We had a kid, one signed up to go to Davis, and then in the middle of the summer after his eighth-grade year, he ended up transferring," Garcia says, wryly. "And he ended up really good. It was Robbie Barany."

Barany turned out to be one of Eisenhower's all-time great runners. He finished second in the state cross-country meet in 2004 and still holds the third-fastest time in Eisenhower history on the state-meet course. Barany ran collegiately at Notre Dame and died in 2012, at age 25, from complications after a stroke. Another transfer: Jaziel Rodriguez, the unlikely star of the 2010 state meet. He ran his sophomore year at Davis before moving to Eisenhower as a junior and helping the team win the title. Rodriguez says he was not "recruited" by Eisenhower; in fact, Mister didn't know who he was when he first arrived at practice. "I'd been a random 18-minute guy at Davis," Rodriguez says. "I don't really think Davis cared that I left because my times were so slow."

Regardless of where in Yakima runners live, most now have chosen Eisenhower almost by default, except, Garcia says, if they want to study in Davis's academically rigorous International Baccalaureate program. "A lot of our good runners are in IB," he says. "It's our big draw. Running is not our big draw. Davis does get better soccer and basketball players than Ike, though. But give Phil credit; he does great things with his runners."

Mister, for his part, recognized early on that Yakima was a changing community, with Hispanics playing a much more visible role in community life. A 2014 ACLU lawsuit has brought a measure of balance to the city council—three of the six council members, as of 2017, were Hispanic—and, Mister observes, "you see a lot more Hispanic-owned businesses here than before. That's going to continue to develop, and I think that's reflected in the school too. When I first got here, Eisenhower was pretty much all white."

But then Mister met a kid named Juan Zavala, and everything changed.

★ ★ ★

When he turned the corner and saw a sea of white faces huddled near the Eisenhower track, Juan Zavala almost bolted, almost turned on the heels of his running shoes and took off back to his locker and back to his home on Yakima's east side.

It was one thing for Zavala, as a sophomore in the fall of 1991, to make the bold decision to attend Eisenhower High when nearly all of his friends chose Davis. Growing up in a low-income neighborhood abutting the Yakima Fairgrounds, Zavala wanted to "try something different" and break away from sketchy neighborhood influences by attending Eisenhower. That meant getting up by 6 a.m. to catch a city bus, and that meant enduring the subtle (and sometimes not-so-subtle) racism in the school hallways and classrooms.

"You've got to remember, Eisenhower was different then," Zavala says. "At the time, I was one of maybe 10 people in the entire school who was Hispanic. There may have been another handful of African American students, too, but that was it. I asked for it. I wanted to go there. I wanted to experience something different than the people I grew up with. And I did. In school, I experienced some tension with some of the teachers, just because of my, you know, difference."

So being the only brown face in a crowd was something Zavala was forced to accept, but he wasn't sure he wanted to become further alienated by joining the cross-country team. He wasn't even sure what type of sport cross-country was. But the previous spring, a friend of his at school, a white kid named Ivan Haas, saw how fast Zavala ran the mile in PE class and pulled him aside.

"Juan, you gotta come out for cross."

"I don't know anyone on the team. I'm not comfortable with that."

"You'll know me."

"Are there any other Hispanics out there?"

"No, but you'd be the first. You'd be great at it."

Over the summer, Zavala ran on his own. And mulled. And ran some more. He decided to give it a try. That is, until he arrived for that first practice and was confronted by all white faces, including the white-haired coach, whom everyone called "Mister," barking out orders.

"It was very intimidating, all those white people there," Zavala recalls. "I was like, 'Is this really for me?' I was about to turn around and go back when Ivan spotted me, brought me in, and introduced everybody to me. Immediately, it was an atmosphere of acceptance and community, and I ended up sharing that with Mister later. It was an atmosphere of friendliness and openness. It was so much different than in school. With Mister, it was like, 'Whatever you need, call me, let me know.' I never had another teacher say that to me, ever. He just accepted me, and all the runners, for who they are."

So now that Zavala was a cross-country member, he had to wake up at 5 a.m. to catch the bus for morning practice and then catch a late city bus home. That made for a long day at school, but Zavala thrived on being busy. And he thrived on Mister's discipline and toughness.

"That's what I liked about him," Zavala says. "I came from a tough background, but him having those high expectations made us rise to the challenge and do better."

By his senior year, Zavala was one of Eisenhower's top three runners. But he said Mister treated him the same as when he was a scared sophomore just learning the sport. That is, with respect and caring.

"We didn't have medical or dental insurance growing up," Zavala says. "There was this time I had an infection in my tooth, and I couldn't afford to go to the dentist, and the infection was spreading to my jaw. One day, in between cross-country and track seasons, he saw me in the hallway and he asked me what was going on. My face was swelling, and it really hurt. I don't know how he did it, but Mister gave me the name of an orthodontist and told me to go there, and he'd 'take care of everything else.' Sure enough, there was a tooth that got abscessed and really infected. My mom was really concerned how we were going to pay for this, and so she went and talked to Mister. He said, 'We took care of it. Don't worry about it. We just wanted to make sure Juan was going to be OK.' I never found out who 'we' were. I guess Mister paid for it. That just increased my respect for him."

One day at practice, in his senior year, Zavala was approached by Mister. The coach looked him dead in the eyes.

"How can I get more Hispanics out for the team?" he asked.

Zavala was slightly taken aback. Mister, the expert running coach and mentor, was asking *him* for advice.

"It's all about family," Zavala answered. "You've got to make that connection. With Hispanics, it's all about community."

Mister nodded.

Late that spring, Zavala graduated and received a full academic scholarship to Washington State University. For a long time, years really, he really didn't think much about his conversation with Mister about increasing Hispanic participation. But he kept track, through friends and via social media, of Eisenhower's running results. In the fall of 2010, Zavala, who now is associate vice president of university development and director of technology for the Washington State University Foundation, went on the Web to check for scores of the Washington state meet. He saw that Eisenhower had won both the boys' and girls' titles. He saw, too, that all 10 of the scoring runners were Hispanic, with names like Rodriguez, Chavez, Vargas, and Dominguez.

"To see how that team was comprised at Eisenhower, just a few years after I ran there," he says, "well, it was joyful to me knowing that maybe I had a part in that."

★ ★ ★

One time, a few years ago, Mister and Nieves Negrete got in an argument at cross-country practice. Negrete cannot remember, exactly, the nature of the argument or even any of the details, though she vaguely recalls it had something to do with an Eisenhower parent who had said something degrading about women. Or, no, maybe that was another of their arguments. This one may have had something to do with booster club fund-raising. Whatever. Negrete, the cross-country team's booster club president from 2000, when her older son, Charles, joined, to 2014, well after her younger son, Timothy, graduated, was always arguing with Mister about something. The two were close and shared the same goals—to field the best team they could and provide support for every single member of that team—but both were headstrong and occasionally unyielding.

"I'm not by any means a shrinking violet," Negrete says. "I'll go toe-to-toe with whoever. People'd laugh because Phil and I would clash like that. I was his faithful servant. I respected the man. But people would walk away whenever he and I went at it.

"Oh, I remember now what the argument was about. It was about sexism. A parent was completely disrespectful to me and other women around the team. I told Phil he needed to rein that guy in. Phil took sides. We had a heated argument. It pissed me off. I said, 'How dare you side with him?' It was knock-down-drag-out, I tell you. But our relationship survived. People around the teams used to say, 'Stay away when the Irish-man and the Latina get in an argument.'

"But I tell you this, just like I told the parents back then: OK, maybe it's hyperbole, but I think this is one of the best [cross-country programs] in the country, given the town we're in and the funds available. Because there is no other program that I'm aware of with a coach who devotes so much time to the program. Mister can be hard on people. You either like him or you don't. But to my boys, he is like a surrogate father. I always tell people, if Phil English and I were drowning, my sons would probably save Phil first."

Mister laughs when told of Negrete's account of their battles.

"We had a few good ones, all right," he says. "But you have to remember this was a woman who cared so much about the runners. She'd do anything to help us. We wouldn't have built up the program without Nieves Negrete."

Negrete's admiration of Mister was hard-won. She was always a bit skeptical about the Irish coach with the funny accent who held an almost cult-like sway over runners. Negrete, through years of experience in the fields and later as an activist for farm workers, didn't automatically trust any white man in power. She'd been disappointed—and betrayed—too many times.

Her first exposure was in the fall of 2001, picking up Charles after his first cross-country practice, with Timothy bouncing around animatedly in the backseat.

"My brother," Timothy recalled, "gets in the front and is saying, 'Mis-ter wants me to get new shoes.' It was all, Mister wants us to do this, Mister wants us to do that. My mom says, sharply, 'Who is this Mister? Mister who?'"

Negrete remembers the conversation slightly differently.

"What I actually said, and excuse my language, but what I said was, 'Who the *fuck* is this Mister?' And Charles says, 'I don't know, Mom. That's what people call him. Anyway, he said I need shoes.' So we buy him shoes that night. He came back the next day and in the car he said, 'Mister says these are the wrong shoes.' Wrong shoes? So I decided I've got to meet this *Mister*. He's intimidating to a lot of people, but fortunately or unfortunately, I am a Latina woman. I'm a single mother and have two boys. So I wasn't going to back down. I rule in my house."

Just as Mister ruled on the cross-country course. The two clashed, initially, but then something strange happened: They clicked. Negrete learned of Mister's rural Irish background, how his father was essentially an Irish version of a Southern tenant farmer, how his family was poor but able to make ends meet through hard work. And Mister learned a similar story about Negrete, how she worked for decades as a migrant farm worker on the circuit, moving from Texas, to California, to Oregon, and then Washington each year as harvest time came, and how, eventually, she settled in Yakima in the 1990s and helped found the Valley's first Hispanic radio station.

"So, if you ask when did I drink the Kool-Aid, it had to be at the end of cross-country that first year," she says. "I saw how he treated the kids, including my son. I'd later tell parents, 'This man and these coaches probably care more about your kids than you do. They are willing to spend time to find out about their homework, and you're not.' It was true across the board. And it was not because they [the parents] were Latino. I had Caucasian parents who weren't involved, as well. Phil and his coaches would pick up that slack. They are amazing humans. They are raising these kids. Summers. Early mornings. The coaches were always there. Phil genuinely cared. You could sense it."

Santos Vargas says Mister was tough on him, exacting both about his running form and his studies, but fair.

"He never outcasted anyone or gave special attention," Vargas says. "To many of us that were there during my years running, he was like a second father. He believed in me when I didn't believe in myself."

Vargas says he was the first person in his immediate family to "do anything in sports." His mother, Carolina, was rearing four kids by herself, and "we didn't have the means to explore many options." After Santos's promising sophomore year, he wanted to participate fully in Eisenhower's summer conditioning program, which included twice-daily workouts. But his mother needed him to work, to help with expenses and to save money for college.

"I'd tell my mom, 'These guys on the team get out of high school as a senior, and they are going to college because of running, getting their [tuition] paid for,'" he says. "She didn't believe I had a chance to do this. She couldn't see any of my meets my first year because she had to work. So she knew nothing of this. She still insisted I work in the summer. It wasn't until after my sophomore year, at a parents' meeting, that Mister brought it up with my mom. After that meeting—I don't know what Mister said—she changed. It helped that I started bringing home medals, and she saw how I treated it [like a job]. She saw that I came home so tired. I'd just eat, do my homework, and go to sleep. Maybe she liked that. By the end of my junior year, the recruiting letters started coming in. Then, she paid attention."

What Vargas perhaps didn't know was that Mister had an advocate on retainer to sway reluctant Hispanic parents. Negrete agreed to serve as something of a liaison between Mister and Hispanic parents, many of whom did not speak English fluently. (Mister does not speak Spanish.)

"My mom was crucial in bridge building," Cummings says. "It was easy for my mom to serve as kind of surrogate to some of the parents. First, she speaks the language, and Mister doesn't. And the way a lot of people are, they are skeptical of Mister. To them, he's just another white guy, another con man, telling them what to do. But to hear from someone like my mom, someone who's lived it and who saw their kids go to college, it made them realize that they can get out of that perpetual cycle. Having someone like my mom talking to them means more. Mister never was a farm worker. They don't think he knows what their issues are."

Negrete says that, at first, she was little more than a glorified translator for Mister, a conduit to impart his strict team rules to Hispanic parents. Later, she was a calming influence to parents who look askance at the imposing man with the snow-white hair and piercing eyes. Still later, she became an unofficial assistant coach in charge of, among other things such as fund-raising, the parents.

"I would meet with parents and, face it, some of the kids had family issues," Negrete says. "Some were on the verge of going into gangs. They were at-risk kids. The parent meetings were mandatory. If parents didn't show up, the kids couldn't run. But a lot of the parents didn't get why

Phil was so involved in what their kids ate, how many hours they would sleep, how you couldn't even eat [French] fries. No candy either. And God forbid if Phil ever saw you drinking a soda in front of him. You did not break that rule. And he wanted parents to understand and agree with that.

"If a kid missed a homework assignment or two, Phil made them show up with the homework and sit in the bat cave (the west-facing shed under the stadium) and study. Then he'd want to speak with the parents. That's where I came in. I was the translator. But toward the end, he'd just say, 'Talk to her for me, Nieves.'"

Negrete developed her own spiel. "I'd tell them, you have to make sure your son attends school and is doing homework. If not, Mister won't let him run. If he can't run, he might get in trouble. Then, I'd tell them my story, how I was skeptical, but then how my two kids went to college, got scholarships, because of running. I'd say, 'You need to focus on your kids.' That was the kind of Mutt-and-Jeff thing Phil and I had going. It seemed to work."

One of the biggest success stories was German Silva, one of the top runners from the 2010 championship team. Today, Silva is married with two young daughters and works as a machine operator in Yakima. He occasionally comes to team workouts to say hello and maybe run a few laps. But back in the day, in middle school, Silva hung around with the Nortenos, a gang in Yakima. He wasn't officially a member, but "I was hanging around with the wrong crowd, if you know what I mean." But once he started hanging with Eisenhower's cross-country team, Silva found a peer group that was dedicated to a common purpose. Throughout his three years on the team, Silva backslid, often, failing to show up for class, blowing off homework assignments, that sort of at-risk but not over-the-top activity. But a harbinger of bad things, in Mister's mind. So, Mister came down hard, disciplinewise, on Silva. And Negrete worked the parental angle.

"If it wasn't for Mister and them, I don't know where I'd be today, probably dead," Silva says. "I'm serious. Guys I hung with in middle school, most of them are now in county jail or in prison. Some still have years and years to do until they get out. What Mister did, it put you on track, keeps your head on straight. I consider him like my second father. He was always behind me. There were times I'd still get into trouble. I was failing some classes, and he'd be on me. I probably would've dropped out of high school as a freshman if it wasn't for cross. I don't know if Mister still tells this to the young guys on this year's team, but he used to say that I was the reason for all his gray hair. He still talks to me, though. I really like Mister. He's not a friend now. He'll always be, like, the authority figure."

But an authority figure the athletes listen to.

Mister doesn't like to analyze why he can relate to Hispanic runners so well. He just does. When pressed, however, he points to his own background.

"Maybe they think, 'Well, he's not American,' so they'll give me more leeway or more trust to begin with," he says. "I can be tough on them, but I also think they can relate to me. I try to let them know a little about me—growing up in Ireland, running with the Kenyans at WSU, stuff like that."

And occasionally, Mister lets his sense of humor show. Cummings relates an anecdote about Mister that some might consider quasi-racist, but the team considered absolutely hilarious.

"I remember when I won the Sunfair [Invitational in Yakima], and someone asked Mister afterward where they had recruited me," Cummings says. "He looked the guy straight on and he said I was Kenyan. Mister called me Kipchoge, which is the classic Kenyan runner name. He thought it was funny. We all did. Here I am this half-black, half-Mexican kid, and now Mister's pretending I'm Kenyan? He kept it up too. It kind of became a thing for us. One time at the state meet, I was rounding a corner on the course, really working, and there was Mister yelling, 'Go, Kipchoge, go.'"

Mister, however, has never been one of those coaches who bends over backward to try to "relate" to his runners. He is not their friend; he is their coach, their mentor, their scold.

"Our guys have enough friends," he says. "I think they realize we coaches are committed to them. We've worked hard to set a standard here. When kids make that commitment and really buy into the program, you, as the coach, have got to be able to deliver as well. We have a long history of doing just that. Getting kids into college, whether by scholarship or not, is super-important to me. That's the pathway for these kids. It's a great way forward for them. Look at Berenice Penaloza."

Penaloza is one of the so-called Dreamers, children of undocumented workers brought to the United States by their parents at a young age and protected under President Obama's DACA executive order. Given her circumstances, Penaloza says she did not consider college an option until Mister kept broaching the subject.

"It was a tough situation [being undocumented], but I got lucky, I think, picking a school in Washington [Eastern Washington University]," she says. "I know this is something some people in Yakima still are facing. It is scary, not knowing what's going to happen. But in my case, Mister believed I could do this."

Mister said that, at one point, New Mexico State was interested in offering a scholarship to Penaloza. The coaches even talked about inviting her on a recruiting trip to the campus in Las Cruces. Two other Eisenhower athletes had run there, Erica Simison's older brother Bryan and Mayra Chavez. But, knowing Penaloza's immigration status, Mister talked to Penaloza and decided the school wasn't right for her.

"The problem was, we heard the cross-country team vans would get pulled over by immigration agents on their way back from runs or meets," Mister says. "We were worried this would be an issue, that she'd get caught up in a sweep. So she backed off New Mexico State. It wasn't right. This is a kid who hadn't been to Mexico since she was a year old. Fortunately, we were able to place her at Eastern."

Because of his collegiate running career at Washington State and his years of giving clinics on running mechanics to both high-school and college coaches, Mister holds some sway with college coaches. At the end of each track season, at the closing banquet, English updates an Excel spreadsheet that lists all of the runners, from 1979 to the present, who have gone on to compete in college. The current tally: 154.

* * *

By now Eisenhower should be well accustomed to being labeled, in Mister's words, "a minority school." At most meets, it is the only team with more than one or two Hispanics running.

Joe Clark, longtime coach at Lakes High School, in Lakewood, a suburb of Tacoma, tells the story of a Hispanic runner he recently coached. All season, the boy had been the only brown-skinned competitor he'd encountered. Then the team traveled to Yakima for the Sunfair Invitational.

"The kid runs up to me, all excited," Clark says. "I said, 'What's going on?' He says, 'Coach, coach, there are other *Mexicans* running.' Then he points over to Eisenhower's tent. He says, 'I've never seen any Mexicans running distance, outside of me.' Phil made a concerted effort to build his program with Hispanic runners. Phil did a talk here at camp once about the Kenyans and East Africans and their lifestyle growing up, and about how their ability to work, their work ethic, helps them to be successful. Then he said, in America, we have an untapped potential, and that is the migrant workers, the Hispanic population. Their families are so often working in the fields. Kids are working in the morning, coming to school, working after school. Phil says that's the equivalent to the East African population here in the US. Shortly after that talk, you started seeing more and more Hispanic runners at Eisenhower. But you wouldn't see that at other schools with that demographic."

Even east of the Cascades, Eisenhower's ethnic makeup was something of an anomaly when it faced big-school rivals—except, of course, for crosstown rival Davis and down-valley Sunnyside High. At the May 2017 district track and field championships, held in Wenatchee, the first seven runners in the 1,600 meters were from Eisenhower. A posse of kids from Wenatchee High School stood next to Lisa Price, mother of Ronan and Jonas, Eisenhower's only two white runners that spring. The Wenatchee kids marveled at Eisenhower's dominance.

"Oh, my God, that Ike team is so good! Those Hispanic kids are fast!" Lisa Price chuckled and made a friendly correction.

"Excuse me," she told the Wenatchee runners. "The first two kids who finished (Ronan and Jonas) aren't Hispanic."

Without missing a beat, the Wenatchee kids responded, "Gosh, they might as well be."

Now, in 2017, Jonas was the only white runner on the boys' cross-country team, a consistent source of amusement to the others. At the White Pass summer camp, Fonzi, Rogelio, and Jonathan would take Jonas by the arm and go up to random runners from other schools in attendance and ask them, "Is this kid Mexican or not?"

"About half thought I was Mexican," says Jonas, who is olive-complexioned and has brown hair.

"More than half," Fonzi corrects him.

Midway through the season, a few of the runners decided to do a bit of good-natured cultural appropriation. Some started calling their token white teammate "Yonas," the hard *j* replaced by the Spanish *y* sound.

FORT STEILACOOM
INVITATIONAL

66 "Here, Price. Drink this."

Molly thrusts out a shot-glass-sized container of hot sauce as assistant coach Robert Price walks down the bus aisle, counting heads before Eisenhower's trip over the Cascades to the Tacoma area for the second big meet of the season, the Fort Steilacoom Invitational.

He ignores her. Then he scowls.

"Give ya 10 bucks if you do it. C'mon, Price."

Price stops dead in his tracks, smiling now.

"You give me 10 bucks, sure."

Molly hits up the girls encircling her in the front part of the bus, as Price wanders to the back to check on the boys. Mister has yet to board. He is fetching a box of surgical masks from the shed. Some of the runners have colds, and others want to avoid getting colds, so a common practice for the team is to don the masks. At times, late in the season, near State, when many kids wear the masks all day at school and take them off only to run, the team looked like a traveling TB ward. Nothing worse, though, than a chest cold to ruin a race. Mister, as with most things, takes a case of the sniffles or a cough quite seriously.

But the mood on the bus is unexpectedly buoyant and lighthearted on this Friday afternoon. For one thing, the kids are getting out of school three hours early for the trip, and they also are leaving behind the gray

146

scrim of smoke. For another, their league meet two days before had been canceled due to the smoky sky, so getting out of Yakima is a relief. There will be time enough to be serious the next day, when Eisenhower's boys' team will face its first test of the season. The state's top 4A schools—Central Valley and Lewis and Clark, both from the Spokane area; Tahoma from Kent; and Camas from down south near Portland—will converge on Fort Steilacoom State Park for the race, and Eisenhower will try to justify its third ranking in the preseason poll despite being forced by the wildfires to train indoors on many days. As for the girls' team, it has no delusions of contending for the title; it just wants a solid opening effort after not even fielding a varsity squad at Ash Creek the week before. Erica, however, is the 2016 Fort Steilacoom individual champion, and if she is nervous about defending her title, her usual stoic demeanor masks it well.

It takes a while, but the girls manage to scrounge up ten dollars. Molly calls out to Price, "Here ya go, Price. Dare ya."

He takes the proffered cup, eyes it warily.

"This," Molly says, "is gonna be even better than when the boys got him to eat a whole cup of butter last year."

Then, in one fluid motion, Price tilts his head back and pours the hot sauce down his throat, to the hoots and laughter of the bus. Almost cartoonlike, Price's face and neck redden. Only momentarily affected, he gives the cup back and, voice only a little strained, asks Molly, "Where's the money?" He pockets it just as Mister walks up the bus steps and hears the commotion.

"What's going on here? Everybody ready to go?"

Price takes his seat up front, across the aisle from Mister. The roar is reduced to a murmur as the team members tuck into their lunches, Molly eating her burrito sans hot sauce. She turns to Erica and Sophi and muses, "Guys, if we each pitch in five bucks, do you think we can get Price to eat a box of tampons?"

She has no takers. Maybe the runners are saving their money for the trip to the Tacoma Mall, 10 minutes away from the team's hotel and the race site. That is another prerace highlight, the unleashing of 30 teenagers at a real, honest-to-goodness mall, not the sorry excuse of a few sad department stores and boutiques not even in Yakima but in neighboring Union Gap. The food court alone is the talk among the boys, who have Googled the options and are nearly unanimous in a selection. "Flaming Wok!" come the shouts from the rear of the bus as Rick, the driver, pulls into the parking lot and tries to find a parking spot. "Gonna get me some Flaming Wok," Jesus says, slapping palms with teammates.

But Diego Vargas, the newcomer who won the novice race the week before at Ash Creek and who will be among the favorites in the next day's JV race, has other ideas. He grabs a quick bite and then disappears down the corridor to check the mall directory. He is a man on a mission. He emerges 20 minutes later carrying a large box bearing the insignia "Build a Bear Workshop." Peeking out from holes cut in the cardboard are the nose and ears of a teddy bear. His turns his gaze downward as he walks to the back of the bus, a few of the girls saying, "Ah, Diego!" and "That's so cute!" But the boys do not hassle him, not a single comment. They respect Diego's mission. The dude has game when it comes to the ladies. The backstory is that, at the summer camp at White Pass, Diego hooked up with a girl from the Cedarcrest High team, and it turned into more than just a camp fling. The object of Diego's affection will be at Fort Steilacoom. Hence the teddy bear gift.

While the boys devour bowls of Flaming Wok teriyaki—some with extra cash reserves also hit up Mod Pizza for a snack later at the hotel—the girls eat quickly and mall-shop. Erica hangs out with Molly—the two have gotten chummier in recent weeks, at least when it comes to nonrunning activities—but Erica really just wants to get back on the bus and prepare for the meet. When Molly goes to the food court bathroom, Erica tags along. But Molly is taking so long that Erica starts getting bored, sipping her Smoothie at the sink. As she regales everyone within earshot later, back on the bus, "I wanted to get Molly going so I walked over to her stall and took off one of my flip flops and put my foot under the stall door, right? And I wagged it back and forth. I wiggled my toes. But I'm not getting any reaction out of Molly. So I'm like, 'Molly, is that you?' and I hear nothing. I'm like, 'Oh shit,' and then I hear Molly from another stall say, 'Erica?' I got out of there real fast, and I, like, loitered in the food court hoping whoever had been in that stall didn't notice my feet. God, I'm such an idiot."

The frivolity only goes so far, though. The team never loses sight of its purpose for being in Tacoma, and the bus rumbles to the course so that the runners can engage in a tradition among cross-country teams—walking the course. Though, in Eisenhower's case, of course, it is more like running the course.

★ ★ ★

Price takes off with the boys' team, Mister and Bryson-Driver with the girls. The course is already marked the day before the meet, and at least a dozen teams are in the process of doing the same thing—getting the lay of the land, navigating turns, checking out the elevation gain of the hills and changing terrain on the flats and downhills—by the time Eisenhower arrives.

"We want to get our starting spot on the right-hand side—there's no assignment starting boxes, guys—because you're going to make a sharp left up there," Price tells the boys. "Stay wide on that turn. Don't go out too fast. And watch that little rise about 20 meters after the start."

With that, Price starts loping. The team follows. They make a series of turns, left, then right, and another right before a sharp right at the dog park that leads back close to the starting line, where the runners make a left at a road that marks one mile.

"You're going to make wide turns. Round off those corners, and then make shallow cuts back into it. Otherwise, at this point in the race, you're going to get cut off by the crowd."

They saunter by more open fields, yellow with drought, and then reach the first of two hills, this one coming at about one and a half miles. Finally, some shade is provided by oak trees lining the path. Price stops them at the base of the hill.

"The map says it gains about 50 feet, but it's deceptive," he says. "Remember, chin down, the arms pull you up. This is where you guys start making a move. Jonas, you should be on the back of that lead pack. Fonzi and Rogelio, this is where you make your move. The rest of you need to push it. Let's go."

The team jogs up the hill, Jonas and Mo pointing out some roots and loose soil that might hinder them. Price stops abruptly near a bend on the climb.

"This is a false top," he says. "It keeps going for a little while. What do we always say? 'Run through the crest.' Don't ease up."

They resume.

"Now, coming off this hill, you've got the dirt and gravel path on the left here and the asphalt on the right. They've got cones blocking the asphalt, so don't get caught behind guys here or you'll get trapped. You need to pick guys off before this left turn heading to two miles."

Trudge on they do, past the two-mile mark, where a clock is set up to give runners their splits. Price jogs right through that mark for another quarter mile before stopping at a sharp left turn across from the placid expanse of Waughop Lake. The runners peer up at a steep, woodchip-laden path that gains 60 feet in three-tenths of a mile.

"You know what to do here. You need to be passing guys by this point. It's kind of narrow, so you might have to go on the grass on the edges, but you need to get by."

At the crest of the hill, just before a left-hand turn, Price stops them again. The group stares at a significant packed-dirt downhill, canopied by trees and wide enough for maybe two runners.

"It's only about 1,000 meters to the finish from here, and you've got to be flying. It's pretty much all downhill to the finish. If you get behind someone, you've got to find a way to get around them. This is also where you can see where Central Valley and Tahoma is. If you see a CV Bear on their back, you need to get up there now and pass them, because when you get to the dog park, there are too many turns, and it's hard."

They jog on, reaching the intersection with the dog park, less than 400 meters from the finish.

"No, you can't see the finish line from here, but it's deceptive. It's right around that corner. And you need to start sprinting now, before then. You need to pick up the pace. You know what I always say, 'Run like the devil's behind you with a very sharp pitchfork.'"

"OK, jog it in, guys, and then we'll practice the start a few times and call it a day."

With Jonas leading the charge, the boys take off and run toward the blue banner that proclaims, "FINISH." But just before Jonas reaches the chalk-marked finish line, he stops abruptly. The team settles around him.

"We can't go over!" he squeaks. "Bad luck."

Angel steps forward from outside of Jonas's peripheral view and grabs him in a bear hug. Jonas squirms like a caught salmon, as Angel, about the same height but maybe 20 pounds heavier, lifts him off his feet and carries him forward. Jonas kicks his legs and tried to escape. Angel drops him over the finish line with the same nonchalance he drops bins of cherries he picked over the summer.

"Darn it, Angel," Jonas says, scrambling back over the line.

Mister and the girls return from their walk-through a few minutes later, and he gathers everyone for a talk.

"Boys, you put as a goal a top-five finish here," Mister says. "I think that's a little soft. You can finish top three. That's reasonable. This is a precursor to State. We can get a gauge to our fitness. We've been inside with the smoke, but we can compete. You just can't get caught up in the early pace. Jonas needs to latch on to the back of the pack. Rogelio needs to go out slow but not too slow. Fonzi, you're right with him. Fonzi, your last mile needs to be fast. You need to negative split. The rest of you, you need to close the gap. If you're back 60th or 70th, that's too far to catch up in the last mile, CV and Lewis and Clark and all them, they don't have huge gaps between runners.

"Girls, you can't worry about the top teams. You're not there yet. You just need to *race*, not run. You can't start slow and stay slow. You need to work on your Emotional Intelligence, what we've been talking about. Push through the pain for six seconds and see what happens. Erica, you know what to do, make your move at the right time."

He asks for questions, gets none. Runners start picking up their spike bags, putting on sweatshirts, figuring they'd get back on the bus and go to the hotel. But Mister has other plans. He has almost forgotten another Eisenhower tradition.

"Conkers, guys," he says, clapping his hands and pointing to a looming horse chestnut tree behind the starting line. "Let's gather some, though it looks like there are none on the ground. We're gonna have to try to grab some off. Be careful. The shells are prickly."

Each year, sometime before State, Eisenhower runners gather horse chest-nuts for the traditional Irish children's game called Conkers, in which the hard-shelled seed of the horse chestnut is impaled on a string. Two players, each with a string threaded through a conker, then strike one another with the conker until the first chestnut falls apart. Rogelio cradles a few conkers, still encased in their green, spiky outer rind, in the crook of his arm and shows Mister the pads of his fingertips. There are pricks of blood seeping out.

"Be careful, guys," he says, laughing. "We can get some more nuts after the run too."

★ ★ ★

The boys' race unfolds just as planned—for Jonas.

At the one-mile mark, Jonas clings like a barnacle to the back of the lead pack, though Lincoln High of Tacoma's James Mwaura, defending 3A state champion and 18th at the nationals, already has opened a lead on the lead pack. Fonzi and Rogelio run side by side near the back of the second pack. Both feel strong and are running effortlessly at that point. But already, a major time gap, at least 30 seconds has opened between Fonzi and Eisenhower's fourth and fifth runners, Angel and Mo.

Up front, Jonas reaches the first hill and sees a white-and-blue jersey with a bear logo in front of him. It is Gabe Romney, CV's top runner. Jonas passes him on the uphill, but Romney regains the lead on the downhill and cruises to the two-mile mark three seconds ahead of Jonas. Jonas tells himself, "I can get him on the second hill. I *will* get him." He doesn't get Romney, but he does pass Tahoma's top runner, Dawson Besst. Nearing the crest, Jonas finds himself in fifth, stride for stride with Camas's Daniel Maton. He settles in behind Maton. Then, starting on the long downhill toward the finish, Jonas turns to Maton.

"C'mon, we can catch these guys."

Maton, perhaps too tired to speak, just nods.

Jonas keeps his head down and arms churning. Near the end of the tree-lined downhill, but before the dog park, he hears a familiar accented voice.

"These people are dying, Jonas," Mister yells, hands cupped around his mouth. "You've got to go *now*."

He passes Maton.

Then he passes Romney.

Making the turn home, he sees the third-place runner, Joe Waskom, the top returning finisher from 2016's state 4A race, faltering. With 30 meters to go, Jonas pulls within five meters, but, at that point, Waskom turns and shoots a glance at Jonas and picks up the pace. Meanwhile, runners are bearing down on Jonas, vying for fourth place. Amid the din, Jonas can distinctly hear shouts of "Go, Daniel." As he leans in and crosses the finish line, Jonas feels Maton's breath on his neck; that's how close he is, two-tenths of a second. Richland's Riley Moore is nearly as close, five-tenths behind Jonas, and Romney a second back.

Later, Jonas will say, "I was thinking, 'I'm not getting beaten by Daniel. No way.'" Richland's Moore, friends with both Jonas and Fonzi, tells Mister, "I didn't think I'd have to worry about Jonas this year, because he's still pretty small. I guess I was wrong."

Meanwhile, back up the course, Eisenhower isn't having great success. Central Valley has all five scoring runners past the two-mile mark before Rogelio and Fonzi make it. Part of the problem is, just as Price had warned in the walk-through, the pair get caught up in a traffic jam on the descent after the first hill. Fonzi scolds himself, thinking he and Rogelio should've been farther up to avoid the jam. Rogelio, however, gains strength on the second hill. He leaves Fonzi behind at that point and sets his sights on the green jerseys of three Tahoma runners ahead of him. He passes two on the long downhill but figures he's run out of room to pick off Tahoma's second runner, Brian Martinez, who earlier in the race was nearly

30 seconds ahead of Rogelio. "He was sprinting over by the dog park and I was thinking, 'I'm not going to go with him that early,'" Rogelio says later. "But then I saw him die and I'm like, 'OK, I can get this guy.'" He beats Martinez by half a second. But the fact that Tahoma has its second, third, and fourth runners finish within four seconds of each other in the top 20 does not bode well for Eisenhower. Fonzi struggles on the second hill and cannot not find the speed he possessed the year before on the downhill. Still, he keeps it together enough for a respectable 34th-place finish. The big problem is that Eisenhower has to wait another 30 seconds before its fourth runner, Angel, finishes and another 17 seconds after that for its fifth and final scoring runner, Mo, to finish. That gap is too big for Eisenhower to finish any higher than fifth.

Large as the boys' time split may have been, it pales before the wide gap in the girls' varsity race. Erica finishes third overall, averaging just under six minutes per mile and moving up from sixth at the two-mile mark. It is more than a two-minute wait at the finish line for Molly and Dantzel to cross the line in 37th and 40th place, respectively, and then another two minutes before Sophi finishes as the team's fourth runner. In all, there is a four-minute, 25-second split between Eisenhower's first and fifth runners.

Afterward, the boys are just about to start an hour-long, steady state workout—mandated because Mister isn't certain when, or if, the smoke will clear enough back in Yakima for them to run outside. Mister instead calls them over, where he is reading off the final boys' scores to them. Nobody talks for several awkward moments. Then Mister speaks.

"Don't worry too much about it," he says. "You can see there the gap between runners is holding you back. We just need to get more outdoor workouts in, some intervals. Hopefully, the weather can improve. We aren't where we normally are at this point. OK, guys, get running. You need to use every minute of good weather."

The girls' team has already taken off on a postrace run, except for Molly, who felt a pain "and a bump" on the top of her right foot during the race. She sits slumped on the ground, an ice bag perched on top of her foot. "Not a good day," she says.

Not everything is as gloomy as Yakima's smoky weather. Earlier in the day, Diego not only finished third overall in the JV race but he saw that his girlfriend from Cedarcrest loved the teddy bear gift. She gives him a chaste hug near the Eisenhower tent while the boys try hard to look as if they aren't looking. Once Diego's girlfriend departs, he wanders back into the tent and gets a hand-slap from Jesus.

Other than that, the team is chastened by the poor performance. No one remembers to pick up additional horse chestnuts, and Mister seems too preoccupied to notice. He sits at the front of the bus, his laptop open to the results, bifocals sliding down the bridge of his nose. Before him lay the statistics, harsh and unwelcoming. All five Central Valley runners crossed before Eisenhower's third runner.

"Geez, CV," he mutters.

"I thought we had a better chance than *fifth*," Price says.

"Yeah."

"Some damn good teams."

"Yeah."

. . .

"Where are we eating, Phil?"

"Mall."

THE MORMONS
AND THE HIPPIES

R anger is yapping. Ranger is nipping. Ranger is circling. Ranger is rearing back on his hind legs and
then taking off as fast as his little poodle paws can
take him toward any shorts-clad body he can find. Most runners reach
down and scratch him behind a curly ear, but others are still too groggy
this early in the morning to pay much attention. Yet Ranger persists, scurrying in something akin to interval training for dogs between the Central
Valley High track shack and lush grass of the football field. Occasionally,
Kieran Mahoney, Central Valley's boys' cross-country coach and Ranger's
human companion, tries to rein him in—"Ranger! Get back here! No,
Ranger!"—but who is there to rein in Mahoney?

On a hot, hazy Wednesday morning in the Spokane Valley, the sun is
mostly obscured by smoke from lingering forest fires that have scarred the
landscape in Eastern Washington and blown in from as far away as British
Columbia and Montana. Yet Mahoney himself is a ray of brilliant sunshine,
cutting through any gloom or morning torpor his runners might feel. On
tap for today for his team, top-ranked in the state and the overwhelming
favorite to win what would be its first championship since 2012, is a
routine day of interval training, bracketed around warm-up and cooldown
miles and a little core work thrown in at the end. But to Mahoney, hyped
up on caffeine and adrenaline, this workout is the most important because

it is the one his Bears will be doing now; anything past or future is of little immediate consequence.

So there he is, a few feet behind the ever-present Ranger, greeting each of his 72 runners as they file into the track shack for daily attendance. He is almost puppyish in his affection. He bear-hugs a slight kid named Troy, nearly crushing the runner's birdlike solar plexus. He high-fives Ryan Kline, his top runner; then he daps with a freshman and raises both arms and his voice and exclaims to a gaggle of runners shuffling along, heads hung and shoulders laden with backpacks, "Come on, boys! Buck up!" He points to two stragglers. "Yeah, baby, we're gonna do this." He puts his arm around one runner's shoulder and then stage-whispers, "Get on in here. You're late."

Observing a Central Valley practice, after several months' observing Eisenhower, is akin to entering some comic book bizarro world. Everything is upside down. Black is white, down is up, behavioral norms are flipped. It all begins with the coaches. Whereas Mister is stern and Irish pale and all business during practice, Mahoney, nearly two decades younger, is tanned, tattooed, and playful. Whereas the Eisenhower runners call their coach "Mister" and rarely engage in witty or sophomoric banter with him, the Central Valley runners are more jocular. They may call Mahoney "Coach," but they aren't above playing little pranks on him, such as furtively changing some of the words in the workout he has written on the dry erase board.

Another difference, and a big one: At a Central Valley practice, unlike at Eisenhower, runners do not perform a series of drills to improve form. In fact, there is little auxiliary work at all besides a little static and active stretching beforehand and sit-ups and core exercises using a medicine ball afterward. No exhortations about arm swing, no admonitions about proper foot plant or knee raising or the position of the head. After the morning meeting, they literally just go run, with Mahoney and his two assistant coaches, Dave Durand and J. J. Giachetti, perched at different spots on the track's infield to observe the intervals, and with Ranger roaming the area chasing after the two para-athletes doing laps around the track in their wheelchairs. Mahoney, unlike Mister, rarely shouts specifics to the packs of runners, even his top-seven varsity team, though occasionally he shouts encouragement such as, "You're killing it!" or "Way to grind!"

And that's another difference: the sheer numbers of runners. Mahoney is only responsible for the boys' team, but there are 72 of them. (The CV girls, about 40 strong, are coached separately, by Dennis McGuire, and work out at a different time. That team, too, is no slouch, having finished fourth in the state in 2016, with senior Kearn Nelson earning an individual spot at the Foot Locker Nationals.) At Eisenhower, the combined number, boys and girls, is 34, and Mister and staff are responsible for both teams.

Whereas Eisenhower's team is overwhelmingly Hispanic and low-income, Central Valley's boys' varsity is all white and solidly middle-class. Central Valley's sprawling campus is smack in the middle of suburbia several miles east of downtown Spokane, hugging the Idaho border. Roughly half of the team belongs to the Mormon faith and, according to Mahoney, the other half is "hippieish." One of the Bears' top runners, junior Joey Nicholls, is blond and lanky, with an angular face and flowing, beyond shoulder-length hair that, when he puts it in a bun, makes him look a lot like US steeplechase champion Evan Jager.

Mahoney, 45, self-identifies as a neo-hippie, and he certainly looks the part. Though he keeps his hair short and covered by an omnipresent USA ball cap, Mahoney has a right-arm sleeve tattoo, wrist to shoulder, and various other tattoos dotting his ankles and calves. He sports wooden, beaded bracelets to go with his GPS watch as well. But mostly he exudes what the original hippies called positive vibes and wears his emotions on his tattooed sleeves. His junior son, Sheamus, also has adopted the hippie aesthetic, his curly light-brown hair bursting out in all directions from his white, 1970s-style headband. Mahoney, too, is known for naming his team's workouts. A favorite is a nine-mile, steady state run he dubs "Temple of the Dawg," because, as Mahoney explains, "it runs by our Mormon temple, plus there was a '90s Seattle grunge band named that, and it gives me a chance to tell the kids about that." The team's traditional Saturday long run, a 10-mile out-and-back on the Centennial Trail, always ends with a gorge session at the local Krispy Kreme doughnut shop.

On this morning, one of Central Valley's seniors brings an old-school-style 1970s speaker out on the field to blast some music during the 30 minutes of interval training. Music is forbidden at Eisenhower's practices; Mister believes music detracts from concentration on technique and training. But Mahoney, initially surprised by this new wrinkle to practice, nods and goes with it. In fact, he shouts out requests. "I feel a little bit of the Doors coming on," he tells the runners. "You know the Doors? We're going to 'break on through to the other side' this morning."

Mahoney acknowledges that he is diametrically opposed, philosophically and sartorially, to Mister, but he says that only proves that there is no one right way to coach cross-country.

"That's Phil's personality, and I have tremendous respect for what he's done at Eisenhower," Mahoney says. "When I saw that movie, *McFarland*, I was thinking, 'Hell, Phil English has done that very thing for 20-something years. That's nothing new. . . . But me, I like a little bit of hippieism. I think coaching a team is a reflection of your personality. But you need to relate to everybody. You can see the Mormon boys, all clean-cut. That's about half the kids. And then there's my hippie boys. I like that. I like the hippieism because it's good for the Mormon boys to rub elbows with someone different. For a long time, the knock on CV was that we were soft and cliquish with all the Mormon kids. When I got here in 2009, I didn't see that at all. I told them, 'I don't care where you go to church on Sunday; we're a team.' The parents love it. They [parents of Mormon runners] may see this guy with tattoos and think, 'Who is this guy?' But they know I ultimately care about their sons. As a society, we've lost our collective minds with sports. What is the true meaning of high-school sports? To help these young men learn experiences they can't learn in the classroom. It's not winning or losing. As Coach Tyson often tells me, that shit takes care of itself."

Coach Tyson. That would be Pat Tyson, a coaching legend in Washington cross-country circles, who in his decades as coach at Mead High School in Spokane built powerhouse boys' teams from 1986 to 2003 that won 12 state titles—one more than Mister has won with the boys and girls at Eisenhower and Carroll. Now the men's coach at Gonzaga University, Tyson continues to influence prep coaches statewide, especially in the Spokane area. And one protégé is Mahoney, who grew up in the area and ran for Cheney High School while Tyson was at Mead. He later served as a student teacher/assistant coach at Mead under Tyson before leaving to start his coaching career at Port Angeles High, eventually landing at Central Valley in 2009. Even now, Mahoney will sound out Tyson for advice, and his mentor occasionally pays a visit.

Longtime cross-country observers in Washington remember the fierce rivalry that existed between Tyson and Mister, two strong personalities who found success in divergent ways. The two actually go back to college, when Tyson ran for Oregon and Mister for Washington State—though they never met because Tyson was several years older than Mister. (Tyson gained a measure of notoriety for being the college roommate of Olympian and running legend Steve Prefontaine, who died young in a car accident.) For many years, Tyson and Mister worked together building the White Pass summer cross-country camp, until, one summer, the two had a disagreement over what type of punishment to mete out to several campers from Tyson's own Mead High after they were caught shoplifting food from the Cracker Barrel store off Highway 12. Mister wanted the campers either sent home or, in Mister's words, "forced to make amends." Tyson sought leniency. Tyson pulled his teams from the camp after that. But the two coaches have long since patched up their differences and remain on speaking terms.

"Tyson was already on his way out of the camp even before that incident," English recalls. "He really didn't want to do the paperwork involved in running the camp. But after that incident, Mead never came back. But I'd say our relationship was always good. We were competitive against them, and we had some royal battles in regionals and the state meet."

Tyson says he long ago put aside any differences with Mister over the White Pass incident. "I don't know if 'falling out' is the word," Tyson says. "I didn't feel the whole situation was handled very well. It wasn't very professional. Phil wasn't the guy who directed that issue and made the decision, but I don't think I got backed up by Phil. It wasn't so much a conflict between he and I. It was a falling out of the camp. I felt our kids deserved better treatment."

He pauses, seemingly mulling his words carefully and then adds, "There was always mutual respect. Phil and I can go sit in a bar and have a beer and have a blast. We don't have many opportunities to do that anymore."

They always were an odd couple, Tyson and English. Whereas Mister's personality is no-nonsense and data-driven—emotion and spontaneity have their time and place in his carefully scripted workouts—Tyson's approach is more free-form and footloose.

"He was all about motivation, but on the emotional part," Mister says. "He may have picked up a thing or two I taught over the years about drills and technique, but that's not his approach."

"Not at all," Tyson rebuts. "There's more than one way to be very successful on the high-school level, and that's Phil's style. He's in the sciences, and I was more English- and history-oriented. That becomes part of your DNA. I grew up as a runner in a more organic style, and his style is more data-driven and perfecting form. Phil would probably be more like (former Olympian and now pro coach) Alberto Salazar is [as a coach], and I'm more like Bill Dellinger [legendary Oregon coach]. Alberto's a perfectionist about trying to create really good form because his was so terrible, and Phil is the same way. Phil thinks more science; I think more Woodstock, I guess."

Even though Tyson is now coaching a Division 1 college team, it could be argued that he is competing, by proxy, with English in the form of Central Valley. Mahoney says he has built his entire program based on Tyson's teachings. He invokes Tyson's name often, sometimes comically often.

Asked, for instance, why he eschews form drills and doesn't worry about technique, Mahoney says, "I understand where Phil is coming from. But I'm from the Tyson school. If there is a glaring form problem, I'll address it, and we'll make corrections. But if a guy's running well, I'm not going to change him. I'm more into teaching about racing on a course, how to run differently on a hill or downhill or turns. That's what Coach Tyson stresses. Phil comes at it from a different angle, and that's because he was trained differently. He's more science-based. It really works for him."

Mahoney, like Tyson, is a motivator, trying to reach runners through their hearts as much as their heads. English, too, has his moments of inspiring runners, but it's not an everyday occurrence as it was for Tyson and is for Mahoney. On this morning, after he and Ranger round up the runners and squeeze all 72 into the track shack, Mahoney spends 10 minutes lecturing the team on something right out of the Tyson playbook: "RKG." That stands for "right kind of guy," meaning that runners should strive to be, among other attributes, coachable, positive, hard-working, and "buy into the program." It takes less than a minute for Mahoney to invoke Tyson in the speech.

"When I was at Mead," Mahoney says, referring to his assistant coaching tenure in the 1990s, "we went down to Yakima and raced the Sunfair [Invitational], a great meet. They have flights—seventh man races the seventh, then sixth races the sixth, and on down. It's a cool format. The year I was student teaching with coach Tyson, we scored seven points. Seven! We won every single race. The *Spokesman* [Spokane newspaper] did an article. When the meet was over—and, as a young coach, I was watching coach Tyson intensely—as they were cooling down, Coach Tyson told the kids, 'We're cleaning up any trash we find. We're helping clean up before we leave.' So the next day, the *Spokesman* headline was something like 'Mead Cleans Up.' . . . As a young coach, I watched because Tyson was teaching his men not only to compete well but to be a class act. Imagine the other schools after getting a butt-kicking like that from Mead and then getting on their bus and see us picking up trash. That, guys, is an RKG."

Just as Eisenhower and pretty much every successful school have their traditions, so, too, does Central Valley. But many of the Bears' motivational triggers come from Mahoney via Tyson. The track shack walls are lined with motivational sayings: "100 Percent Positive," "Our Mission: Building a Distance Dynasty," and, by the door leading to the field, "I'm in, CVXC." Dangling overhead are at least a dozen gold spray-painted running shoes, left by seniors as a legacy and inspiration for the younger guys. Yes, another Tyson touch.

Central Valley's team has swelled so much in Mahoney's eight years that he divides the team into five groups for workouts, each according to their 5K personal records. These groups, with one notable exception, are named after great runners associated with Spokane's heyday as a distance-running Mecca in the late 1960s and '70s. There is the Tyson group, the Don Kardong group, the Rick Riley group, and the Gerry Lindgren group. Kardong was a standout marathoner who finished fourth in the 1976 Olympics and was the prime mover in the creation of one of the country's top road races, the Bloomsday, in Spokane. Lindgren, from Rogers High School, was quite possibly the greatest distance runner Spokane ever produced. Known for running as many as 200 miles a week, he set numerous national prep cross-country records that stood for decades, competed in the 1964 Olympics as a teenager, and, while at Washington State, won 11 NCAA individual titles, beating the legendary Prefontaine for the 1969 NCAA cross-country title. Riley, though not as accomplished, set a national two-mile record (8:48) while at Ferris High and ran with Lindgren at Washington State before injuries curtailed his career. The fifth and fastest of Mahoney's groups, the one reserved for the top seven varsity runners, is named for Prefontaine.

"We have a lot of history in our sport," Mahoney tells the assembled runners, who are getting a little antsy to start the workout. "I like to tap into it. Guys, not only are you running in these groups named for great Spokane runners, but you will be reporting back to us about those runners. You will find out about them and tell us."

The group with the easiest research project, no doubt, will be the Tyson boys, as not a practice goes by without Mahoney mentioning him about 14 times. Out on the track, as the groups lope along on the one-mile warm-up, Mahoney explains his coaching philosophy thus: "The most mileage per week my kids will do is 60 because I believe, like Coach Tyson said, 'Hard, easy, hard, easy.' If you go 'Hard, medium, hard, medium,' you're asking for injuries. As Tyson said, the big thing is to keep the kids healthy. . . . Now, the workout we're doing today is called 'Oregon Drills.' I got it from Coach Tyson, who got it from [Bill] Bowerman [former Oregon coach and cofounder of Nike]. This Oregon drill is Tyson's favorite. The first set of cones, go easy; then jog to the next set of cones in the middle and go race pace. Then at the last set of cones is a buildup to a full sprint. It's 30 minutes of up down, up down. It's fun because it keeps them together and off the hard surfaces. As Coach Tyson says, it's harder than they realize."

As Mahoney's top runners breeze through the cones, they seem to meld into a big blond bob of heads and tanned legs moving in tandem. It resembles nothing so much as a team of wild horses sprinting across pastureland. This is the key to Central Valley's success: a group of fast runners—perhaps not the state's fastest individuals, but collectively the fastest—working together. And for all of the team building and motivation and lack of the hard sell on performance, Mahoney admits, almost sotto voce, that he really, really wants to win too. Given the collective strength of his top seven varsity runners, there's a good chance they'll do just that. Mahoney fears Spokane rival Lewis and Clark High but also says he never overlooks Eisenhower.

At the head of the pack, a kid whose blond bangs fall on his white-rimmed sunglasses, is junior Ryan Kline, who finished 14th at State last year. Right behind is Gabe Romney (distant nephew of former presidential candidate Mitt), another blond whose baby-faced cheeks glow crimson with exertion. Evan Peters, Nicholls, Mahoney—all sandy-haired and rocking the hippie aesthetic—follow, as does the lone brown-haired runner, Fielding Demars, the senior class president who'll be attending BYU after his Mormon mission. Just as easily, the placing during the interval could've been inverted; that's how close the group runs together.

"I show the guys the legendary Mead team under Coach Tyson in 1993, where they scored 31 points to win State. How'd they do that? They cut down the gap, the time between when each runner finishes. I try to tell them that cross-country is the purest fundamental team sport there is. How you win a cross-country race is by closing the gap. If we focus on closing the gap between one and seven, we're guaranteed to have success on race day. That's all that matters. Right now our gap is probably 45 seconds. By the season's end, our goal is to get that under 20. Now Gabe and Ryan, their goal is to finish one and two at State. I try not to encourage that, because when you attach performance to an outcome, you run tight. Tyson told me that. When they are loosey-goosey and thinking of the team and running together, that's where you see success."

Mahoney has made it a point of personal pride over the summer not to utter the word "State" in front of his team. Too much pressure. Too many expectations . . . though, being as competitive as he is, he instead will sometimes substitute the word Pasco—site of the state meet—as a little extra motivation.

But as—you guessed it—Coach Tyson has often told Mahoney, "I don't care about the score, I care about the effort, and we'll add up the points at the end and see what happens."

BELLEVUE AND BEYOND

The week begins with Jonas, neck veins bulging and teeth bared, yelling at his teammates during a brutal set of mile-repeat intervals during a cold, windy afternoon workout, criticism accepted with mostly bowed heads and curt nods. The week ends with Jonas, mouth agape and chest heaving, accepting high fives and fist bumps from his teammates, the headiness of victory on a brisk fall afternoon perhaps making any lingering resentment fade.

It is a week in which Eisenhower runners "cleared the air" and in which the real air had finally, gloriously cleared after weeks of lingering smoke from the persistent wildfires. It is a week in which Mister puts his boys' team through some brutal workouts, both to purge the disappointment of the Fort Steilacoom race and to prepare them for three invitationals in as many weeks, not to mention the rescheduled midweek Columbia Basin Big 9 league meet. It is a week in which the girls' team, challenged by flagging confidence and nagging injuries, is seriously pressed to maintain a nine-year league winning streak, an oppressive burden that has weighed heavily on the girls all week.

It is a week of stocktaking, of soul-searching, of redemption. And, for at least one runner, a week of ascending to a new level of performance.

Monday

They all know what's coming when, during routine drills at Chesterley Park, Mister goes to his truck to take out the measuring wheel and the orange construction cones.

Intervals.

Harsh, painful speed work, near-maximum effort meant to simulate race conditions and get runners used to pushing themselves beyond "discomfort." No one, perhaps save Jonas, actively looks forward to interval sessions; but the members of the boys' team—and Erica—consider the workouts necessary if they harbor any hope of doing well at State. They actually are two weeks behind on interval work, thanks to being forced inside because the Yakima School District deemed the air quality too poor for outdoor activity. So Mister is chomping at the bit—almost literally, chomping down on his molars—as he strides across the grassy expanse of Chesterley with the measuring wheel out in front, clicking off yard after yard until he reaches 1,760. Ivan Alfaro, with his own measuring wheel, marks out a half-mile loop for the girls' intervals.

It seems to take Mister the longest time and then even longer for Price and Ivan to set down the construction cones marking the turns. Bryson-Driver keeps the runners on task during drills and strides. They've already done a two-mile warm-up, running to the park from the high school, and most are still sore from a partial tempo run they logged at six o'clock that morning. In a 10-minute wait that seems to them much longer, the weather is turning. The sun, no longer a hazy, smoke-obscured orange orb, has been blotted out now by dark gray clouds. The wind, too, has picked up. A few of the boys, who almost always run bare-chested, scramble to put on shirts.

At last, Mister calls the boys and Erica, who will do two mile repeats with the boys before rejoining the girls, to the starting cones. Robert Price leads the girls to their cones across the field. There is silence among the boys, none of the joshing with Mister or talk of their latest video-game obsession, *Clash Royale*. Angel and Tony have missed the workout with chest colds, the latest casualty of a bug that has spread for more than a week. Two weeks after the Ash Creek meet, Fonzi still has a lingering cough, and Jesus is hacking and spitting. Some on the team have taken to wearing the masks more often now.

"All right, now, OK," Mister says. "You're doing six of these mile repeats. I want the top boys, Jonas, Fonzi, and Rogelio to shoot for five minutes. The four through seven runners, you'll run 5:20. You'll get a four-minute recovery and then go again. OK? This is not tempo running. This is not steady effort. This is as close to race pace as we can get. Everybody hurts on these. It's supposed to. You need to push through it. It's what we've been saying. You need Emotional Intelligence."

Then Ivan holds up a stopwatch, and Mister barks, "Go."

They lean into a gathering head wind and take off—Jonas, Fonzi, and Rogelio immediately pulling away. Mister trots to various points on the course as the gap between the top three and the rest widens. When the runners make two sharp rights at the halfway point, Mister grumbles to them, "You need to pick it up." Jonas, Rogelio, and Fonzi finish at 5:20, way slower than expectations. Mo and Jesus follow at 5:30, Jonathan and younger brother Nathan at 5:50. Erica, who was supposed to do the repeat in 6 minutes, clocks 6:07.

Mister is not pleased.

"So much of this is you letting up mentally and just going through the motions," he says, that distinctive overbite exaggerating his frown. "What have I told you about Emotional Intelligence?"

For several weeks, Mister has been harping on Emotional Intelligence, that new catchphrase, defined as the mental ability to push back pain and endure. The concept isn't new to the runners, but the term is.

"At various times during a race, especially a high-level race, you're going to experience that time, especially if you've been running right on the edge of fatigue, whether you're going to be able to push through that breaking point," he says. "All you got to do is endure six seconds, and then the body will recalibrate that [pain threshold]. Can you push through for six seconds? That takes training, and it takes heart. Only you will know whether you did it or not. We can't get inside your head. One of the things I'm trying to connect it to is how big a drop-off you have in the last mile of a race. That's when you'll be able to use this Emotional Intelligence."

Mister speaks for almost the entire recovery period.

Off they go again, and, this time, Jonas quickly sprints ahead. Rogelio and Fonzi give chase, and eventually Rogelio puts some distance on Fonzi, who turns his head to throw up without breaking stride. The results: Jonas, 5:06; Rogelio, 5:14; Fonzi, 5:27; and Mo, 5:36. The rest come in slower than 5:45. Erica comes close to hitting her mark: 6:03. Most boys stand bent at the waist, hands on knees. When they gather near the starting cones for the third interval, Jonas suddenly takes two steps forward and turns to face his teammates.

"We've got to do better," he yells. His voice, already the high-pitched squeak of a young teen in the throes of puberty, rises in pitch with every word.

"I don't care about the friggin' smoke or anything else. We've gotta do this. No excuses. Dig deep."

By this point, Jonas's saucer-like brown eyes bulge, and his voice just keeps rising. Fonzi is the only runner to make eye contact with him. Way in the back, Erica, who has made no secret of her annoyance at Jonas, kid brother to her boyfriend, rolls her eyes in almost a parody of a teenage girl. But Jonas isn't finished.

"Aren't you guys tired of losing to Central Valley and the same people every friggin' year? I mean, c'mon. Let's do this."

Silence. If Jonas is expecting a rousing cheer from his pep talk, he doesn't get it. He may be the team's fastest runner, but he still is only a sophomore.

Fonzi, finally, speaks, softly but firmly.

"OK, boys."

Mister, off to the side, lets the tirade play itself out. Then he sends them on their way for the third interval. Once they are out of sight, he grins madly.

"His voice just kept getting higher and higher," he says of Jonas. "I had to bite my tongue to keep from laughing."

Then he adds, "You know, I don't expect them to hit [their marks] this first time out, so I'm not disappointed. I expected this. We've just got to get out here consistently now and get quality workouts in. We've been inside way too long."

The tongue-lashing by the team's smallest—but fastest—runner works, to a point. Jonas runs the third interval at 5:10; Fonzi, 5:14; Rogelio, 5:22. The rest of the boys, however, come in closer to 6 minutes than 5:30. Erica, eye roll notwithstanding, clocks an impressive 6:01, then trots over to complete her workout with the girls, half of whom have already begged off after only four of the half-mile repeats. The final three mile repeats pretty much play out the same, the boys getting only two to five seconds slower. Jonas refrains from any further motivational speeches; and as they lay sprawled on the grass, changing out of their racing spikes and back into their trainers, Fonzi and Rogelio review the session.

"I really felt that, really tough," Rogelio says.

"It's been a while since we had a good workout," Fonzi says.

Regarding the heated moment between intervals, Fonzi looks behind him to where Jonas is changing shoes and says, softly, "We can say anything to each other. It's just between the team. And everything he said was right. We all, or maybe most of us, will go off like that at some point in the season. I'm fine with it."

Mister, meanwhile, is going off a bit himself at the girls' performance during intervals.

"That last set," he says to the girls, brow furrowed, "a lot of you were close to jogging it. That's how much effort you put into it. You performed very poorly at Steilacoom. Now, granted, our league is weak, but the other teams in the league will see that and start coming after us."

Erica breaks an awkward silence.

"Well, at least Davis is struggling pretty bad. Did you see their score from their meet in Seattle? Pretty bad. I think Ada is coming back from an injury," she says, referring to Davis's top runner, Ada Naranjo, as close to a rival as Erica has had in the league and district.

"Still," Mister counters, "you can't be overconfident. Running 22s [22 minutes for a 5K] is OK at the start of the season, but not by now. We have the most difficult part of the team down—we've got a good No. 1 runner. Now we need to reduce the gap between Erica and the rest of you."

Tuesday

One day after mile repeats, the boys mill about the shed before the afternoon practice. Half of their attention is focused on speculating what type of workout Mister will have in store on this day. He usually prints out the workout and puts copies in a cubby next to the door. He is tardy doing that today.

But, really, the boys' attention is focused on their phones. Half a dozen guys have their heads buried on their screens, whooping and shouting occasionally and talking trash to each other. They have downloaded the app to *Clash Royale* and have been playing it every spare moment. They are joking with and teasing each other, Jonas taking his turn along with everybody else when he fails at the game.

Is there lingering resentment from the previous day's drama? It seems to be totally forgotten.

"That's the thing with the boys," observes Erica, off by herself near the shed. "They get things out in the open and then move on. Unlike the girls."

The boys end up going to the Rez—the dirt roads in the orchards bordering the Yakama Tribal Lands—for a 12-mile run, five miles of which will be at tempo pace. This will be three hard workouts in a row; Mister, obviously, is not messing around. But no one utters a syllable of complaint. They pile into either Mister's truck or Price's truck for the 10-minute drive to the trailhead, sipping water and talking *Clash Royale* on the way.

Most feel fairly strong heading into the six-mile turnaround, where Mister has parked his truck beside three rows of apple trees, two jugs of water in the bed for the runners. Everyone looks strong except, shockingly, Jonas.

"Mister, you got any toilet paper?"

"In the back."

Jonas grabs a roll and disappears into the trees. The varsity boys wait for him to return. A good five minutes elapse before Jonas comes trotting out, and the team resumes the workout. Mister drives back to the trailhead and waits for them. Eventually, the pack turns the final corner, a quarter mile from Mister's truck. Even from a distance, he can see that Jonas, several inches shorter than the rest, isn't in the pack.

"Aren't you missing someone?" he asks when the boys have finished and are starting to munch on Gala apples Mister has swiped from a few trees.

The boys seem amused.

"Yeah, Jonas!" Jesus says, laughing.

"He had to stop," Tony says.

"He wasn't feeling well—stomach," Fonzi says.

This is a first. Jonas has never failed to complete a workout. Now, a day after he'd chewed out his teammates for lack of effort, the pack has dropped him.

"Well, where is he now?" Mister asks.

"Somewhere back there."

Mister frowns, squints down the road.

"It could be," Jonathan says, "that he ate the mac-and-cheese chili for lunch."

"Oh Christ," Mister exclaims.

What follows is a good five minutes' worth of reviews of the lunchroom's dining options. The consensus: Never get the pizza because the cheese slides right off. The mac-and-cheese chili, avoid at all costs. Burritos? A dicey bet.

"I always get the chicken sandwich," Mister puts in. "It actually is quite good."

A few minutes later, Jonas lopes in. No one comments on his getting dropped from the workout. In fact, a few guys offer him water and ask, "You OK, bro?" About as heartfelt as the boys get, emotionwise.

Wednesday

This being a day before the first of two league meets that will determine the champion, an easy workout is planned at nearby Randall Park, easy running on the grass with a few hill repeats thrown in.

"But first, I want you to follow me into the gym," Mister says.

Quizzical looks spread across the team.

"What are we doing, Mister?" asks Izzy, never shy in speaking up.

"We're going to take a look at the record board. You'll see."

Cross-country and track records stretch across a 30-foot length of wall in a hallway outside the gym. But Mister huddles the team underneath the farthest board to the right, under the heading "School Team Records." Under league titles, it shows nine in a row for the girls' team, eight for the boys' team.

Mister directs his comments to the girls.

"You need to know what's gone before," he says. "A defeat in the league meet tomorrow will not go over well. How old were you the last time one of our teams lost a league meet? Grade school, right? There's very little explanation needed. You girls need to step up. It's called tradition."

As is customary when Mister lectures, no one dares speak. Not even Erica.

"OK, I think I made my point. Go on to Randall for the workout. Molly, stay behind with me."

A few girls give Molly puzzled looks, but they move on.

Back at the shed, which doubles as a trainer's room, Mister has Molly jump up on a padded table, her bare feet dangling off the edge.

"How long has this been going on?"

"Since Ash Creek."

"Ash Creek? Holy . . . Molly, why didn't you tell us about this before?"

"I thought it would go away, Mister," she says, voice quavering.

"Ah, Molly, really? You should know better. OK, which foot is it again?"

She reaches down and points to the tendon separating the first and second metatarsals on her left foot. After a few minutes of Q-and-A, Mister learns the whole story. Molly has been experiencing foot pain, sometimes sharp, sometimes dull, since stepping on a jutting rock on a downhill segment of the Ash Creek course, just after the series of berms. The pain originally was on the bottom of the foot, near the ball. Thinking it just a bruise, Molly kept training. But since the Fort Steilacoom race, the pain now has migrated to the top of her foot. It hurts whenever her foot either lands or pushes off. It took a few more days after that to come clean to Mister. There is no secret as to her hesitation. Molly really, really wants to compete in the league meet. Without her, the girls really might lose the title for the first time in a decade. So telling Mister about it, most likely, would mean not running. Molly already missed the latter half of her junior season after suffering a stress fracture in her right leg, so she frets about a repeat in her senior season.

Mister presses hard with his thumb on the large tendon connecting Molly's big toe.

"This hurt?"

"No."

"Well, that might be a good sign. You say you feel it landing and pushing off. Do you feel it just walking around?"

"Yeah."

"Not a good sign. Let's try a few things here."

He rummages through a large black medical bag, taking out several rolls of white tape and gauzy under-wrap, a pair of scissors, and a thin foam pad. He cuts out a circle shape, cuts a hole within the circle, and then tapes the pad to the ball of Molly's foot. After that, he performs an elaborate taping job on most of Molly's foot.

"OK, put your shoes on and jog on the grass to the fence and back."

Minutes later, Molly returns, not limping.

"I can still feel it."

"Between one and 10, Molly, painwise?"

"Four."

"You made a mistake, Molly, not telling us about it earlier. I'd rather lose the league meet than make this injury worse."

Molly eyes fill with tears, but she does not cry. She holds it together and lobbies her case.

"Can't I just run tomorrow and then take time off?"

"No, we can't risk it. It's got to be rested."

The two stare at each other, eyes locked. Mister's lips purse resolutely. Eventually, he speaks.

"I could try a thicker pad. Let's tape you up again."

She tests the second tape job on the grass and reports back that she felt little pain, especially if she put pressure on the outside of her foot.

"Obviously," Mister says, "the pronation is adding to it. It could well be just a bone bruise. We'll see."

In Mister's truck heading to Randall Park, Molly asks if she can run at leagues. Mister says, "Yes, but I'll pull you off the starting line if it isn't doing better."

At Randall, the girls huddle around Molly, asking about her foot.

"Hey, I know," says Erica, trying to lighten the mood, "we should run her tomorrow in league, then rest her until District finals. See, look at me. I'm thinking about the *team* for once."

Then, pausing for effect, Erica adds with a smile, "Really, I just don't want to be part of the team that lost a league meet."

Thursday

Molly runs, and runs well, at league, finishing a solid third on the team behind Erica, who wins going away, and Dantzel, who runs her best race of the season, placing second. The Eisenhower girls easily defeat all six teams in dual-meet matchup and take the overall team title (combining all runners) with 34 points, West Valley second at 85, and Davis at 90. Davis has three of the top seven runners—Naranjo sixth, coming back from a knee injury—but its fourth and fifth scorer place 36th and 37th. Eisenhower's fourth and fifth scorers, Sophi and Madi Oliva, finish 11th and 14th, respectively.

Afterward, Molly gingerly steps out of her racing spikes.

"It hurt," she says. "Every step. I hope Mister will let me run at Bellevue. It's my favorite course."

It will take less than 24 hours for Mister to make his decision: Molly will not be running at Bellevue—and may not be running for a while, until the pain subsides.

Molly's injury notwithstanding, Mister is pleased with the girls. He doesn't say much after the race but takes to his laptop later at home and, in his standard spreadsheet analysis of times and splits, writes of the girls: "A very strong team performance. All seven runners were running for the team and not themselves, and that made all the difference! Tradition played a role in the win . . ."

As for the boys, the league meet is a glorified workout. They dominate. Jonas cruises to a 16:07 win on a hilly 5K course, beating second-place Rogelio by 29 seconds and third-place Fonzi by 40. "I didn't feel it at all. I'm ready for Saturday," says Jonas afterward, referring to the stiff competition at the Bellevue Invite.

Fonzi isn't displeased with his performance, but an elderly man in a hoodie, propping himself up with a gnarled wooden cane, gets so emotional watching Fonzi pass the finish line that he tears up.

"Oh, that's just Fonzi's grandfather," Sonya Cuevas says, laughing. "He always does that."

Despite Chuck's history, there's one thing he knows for sure: Alfonso is a special kid. "It's good that one of my grandkids is being recognized for something positive," he says, referring to Fonzi's older sister, who found trouble with gangs and drugs. "He's a good runner, but forget about that. He's done good things with his life so far, and it's great to see a kid do that. He makes good decisions. The way the world is going, it's great to see a kid come up and try to do something with himself. It's not easy in that full house. But he's a good example for the other kids growing up there."

Then Chuck pauses, eyes welling.

"I just hope when Alfonso does make a bad choice, you know, if he makes one, it's nothing serious enough to hurt his future," he says. "I've seen enough of that in my life."

Friday

Not even Mister would work the team hard the afternoon before a major invitational. This practice features only drills (always the drills) and 20 minutes of easy running. Mister has arranged for a group of eighth graders from nearby Wilson Middle School's cross-country team to stop by and check out the program, a subtle way of keeping the program healthy in coming years. As an enticement, Mister calls up some friends at Brooks, the Seattle-based running shoe manufacturer, and asks for some "swag" to give the kids—Brooks sunglasses and shoelaces and posters with "Run _____ Run." Fonzi and Jonas host the middle-school boys; Dantzel and Molly, the girls ("Erica is on record as not liking kids," Molly says, smiling).

Jonas and Fonzi quiz the kids about their mile times, and Jonas even grabs a Magic Marker and fills out his own poster. He keeps it hidden from view until he is done; then he raises it over his head and runs around the field, showing it off to teammates.

It read: "Run, Lil' Pre, Run." Apparently, Jonas has given himself a lofty nickname, that of the legendary Oregon distance runner Steve Prefontaine, whose image adorns Jonas's bedroom wall. His father tries to ignore the stunt by focusing on the girls running laps.

"He dreams big," someone says to the elder Price.

"Yeah, but the bigger you dream, the bigger you can crash too."

Just then, Jonas runs straight up to his dad and puts the "Lil' Pre" sign right in his face. Price laughs and swats Jonas lightly on the back of his neck. Jonas playfully punches his dad on the shoulder, and the two take off running, amid squalls of laughter from the boys' team milling about.

Molly has filled out a poster, too, and shows it to Mister. It reads: "Let Molly Run."

Saturday

By 5 a.m., everyone is on the bus—if not fully conscious. Mister has practically ordered the runners to sleep for the two-hour trip to Lake Sammamish State Park, where 57 teams will be racing at the Bellevue Invitational. Eisenhower's varsity runners will not be competing until later in the afternoon, but school district policy dictates that teams must travel together. Mister, ever detail-oriented, has bought 40 sandwiches, cases of water and Gatorade, and energy bars to keep his team nourished throughout the long day.

Bellevue boasts a different format from most meets, one that Eisenhower also employs at the Sunfair Invitational. There is no single "varsity" race but, rather, a series of "flights." The Nos. 7 and 8 runners from each school race each other, then 5 and 6; 3 and 4; and, finally, late in the afternoon, 1 and 2. In the end, a team total is crunched by the computer timing system, but the main emphasis in this meet is the individual matchups.

No race is more anticipated than Jonas and Rogelio's, in which they face other top boys in the elite flight, the final race of the day. Neither Central Valley nor Lewis and Clark, both of which had handily beaten Eisenhower the week before, is competing in the meet, but Tahoma High, the other team that handled Eisenhower at Fort Steilacoom, is back, and Ike runners in each flight were on the lookout for Tahoma's blue jerseys on the course.

Earlier in the day, the boys receive solid, if not spectacular performances, from Jesus, the seventh runner, and Tony, the fifth. Angel, the fourth man, who was sick and missed the two big workouts earlier in the week, has a poor showing in the third and fourth flight, but Fonzi runs in the lead pack for two and a half miles before fading and finishing third. Fonzi wants to win, of course, but he just doesn't have the burst of speed on the backstretch. "I'm doing a lot better now, and that's all I'm worried about at this point," he says. "As long as I'm getting faster. . . . Me being in the front makes it feel like the old me again. It felt great not being in the middle, feeling like an average runner. It's a confidence boost."

The girls, sans injured Molly, struggle again. The biggest disappointment to Mister is Dantzel, who finishes 14th in the flight pitting the teams' third and fourth runners. As he would later write in the meet analysis spreadsheet he distributed to the team, Dantzel had "an uninspired run. Went through the motions, did not even sprint at the finish. . . . Can do better!"

Erica does do better. But as soon as she knew Issaquah High would be racing, she knew her chances of winning were slim, because freshman phenom Julia David-Smith was running. David-Smith won at Fort Steilacoom, and she wins again at Bellevue, wire to wire. But, this time, Erica starts too slowly, 21st at the first mile. Both Mister and Erica's parents along the course route shout for her to move up faster. Eventually, by the second mile, she does and picks off several runners to finish seventh, two seconds faster than her race at Bellevue the previous fall.

"She played it too safe; it was like the tentative Erica of old," Mister says. "She had to play catch-up against some very good runners and wasn't able to do it. I was hoping she'd moved past that way of running."

If Mister fails to get Erica to fully embrace the race plan, he isn't going to make the same mistake with Jonas in the boys' elite race, which features five of the top distance runners in the state, all juniors or seniors. Among them is a 9:12 two-miler, Riley McDowell. As McDowell's father retreats to the sidelines after the final race instructions, coaches from Tahoma and Kamiakin High ask him who he thinks might win the race. McDowell mentions three runners besides his son. Then, almost as an afterthought, he adds, "Maybe the Price kid."

Mister has walked the course, point by point, with Jonas, as he does with all of the runners. The plan is to stay Velcroed to the lead pack for the first mile and then start picking up the pace just after Mile 2 and a stretch of sand that the runners must traverse next to the lake and then make a definitive move on a series of subtle but taxing rolling hills at two and a half miles.

Oh, and Mister has one last piece of advice: "Go for the win, Jonas!"

Jonas executes the plan well. He is fourth after the first mile, which the pack runs in 4:58. He is shocked that it all feels so effortless. Has he really run a sub-five mile and not even felt winded? That effortless feeling lasts until a long backstretch before Mile 2. That's when pain and dead legs set in, but Jonas pushes through. Emotional Intelligence and all that. He knows he'll have to rally his energy for the hairpin turn, followed by the stretch of sand running just past the two-mile mark.

Meanwhile, Rogelio is enjoying the race of his life through two miles. He is in the top 10, the second pack of runners, after a 5:12 first mile and then he starts passing people and throws down a 4:56 second mile (three seconds faster, it should be noted, than Jonas's second mile). But the swift pace catches up with Rogelio, and no amount of mustering Emotional Intelligence can keep him from slowing to a 5:30 third mile, but, in a gritty kick, he finishes 12th in 16:08.

While Rogelio is still 100 meters from the sand bog, Jonas takes control in that stretch. "I was thinking, 'These kids do not know how to run in the sand,' Jonas says later. "I'm looking at them, and they are kicking sand back, and I was thinking, 'I can get them after this.' Riley was still ahead of me at that point, but I knew I had him."

A gutsy thing for a sophomore to think, but Jonas sticks to his strategy and surges past McDowell on the small rolling hills. By the time the runners emerge from the trees and head for the long backstretch toward the finish, Jonas opens a significant lead on McDowell. Jonas looks up briefly when he hears an Eisenhower supporter along the backstretch shout, "You've got a 50-meter lead, Jonas!" But then, a few meters on, he hears the unmistakable voice of his father, video camera to his face, yell out, "No time to let up. Go now!"

He wins by four seconds, a big margin by cross-country standards. In the finishing chute, Eisenhower boys high-five Jonas and slap him on the back. His father, too, has people come up and congratulate him. Later, the elder Price would crack, "The only thing I did was on Valentine's Day about 16 years ago," meaning his contribution to his son's conception.

Mister, postrace, keeps his cool reserve. Privately, though, he is thinking that Jonas could be a favorite to win the individual title at State, a year or two earlier than most figured. Jonas's mother, Lisa, lingers around the Eisenhower tent while Jonas goes on a cooldown run afterward, saying how surprised she is with the win. But Robert Price stays silent. He knows what Jonas is capable of, and he knows no other kid in that race has the same burning desire to win as his son. How does he know? Because he has to live with Jonas, the kid who stretches the bounds of obsessiveness about running, driving his parents nuts.

"This makes Sunfair (next week) more interesting," Robert says on the bus. "He wants to run under 15. The course record is 14:48, and the school record is Drew's [Schreiber] 14:55. I ran 14:56 there back in the day, so I know he wants that."

The elder Price smiles. One of the courses he teaches at Eisenhower is psychology, so he knows all about that Oedipal stuff that might, subconsciously, be going through the mind of "Lil Pre."

"If he needs any extra motivation to run under 15, that's it—to beat my 14:56," he says. "That's just fine with me."

Meanwhile, the bus is delayed because the coach from Pacific Lutheran University is chatting with Rogelio and his parents about the possibility of Rogelio running for the college next year. When Rogelio boards the bus, he looks down in embarrassment. Mister smiles, thinking of the chubby version of Rogelio who hated running four years before.

FROM HEAVY TO HEALTHY

Summer, to the 14-year-old Rogelio Mares, meant long, lazy hours lounging on the couch, staring hypnotically at a video game screen while swigging soda and munching chips. Good times.

His mother, Leticia, thought otherwise.

The kid was sluglike, motivated only to get to a higher level against other gamers. The Mareses were a reasonably fit family; Rogelio's older sister, Cassandra, had run at Eisenhower several years before. But Rogelio? Walking to the fridge was all the exercise he cared to do. And it showed. He graduated from middle school in 2014 weighing about 170 pounds, pushing toward 180 after a few big meals. He was tall for his age, 5-foot-6, but, still, he was overweight for a 13-year-old, sporting a waist size of 34. Not dangerously overweight. Certainly not morbidly obese. But Leticia knew changes had to be made. Rogelio's health depended on it.

So one evening in early June of that year, the summer before Rogelio's freshman year at Eisenhower, Leticia made him change into a T-shirt and shorts, found his little-used pair of running shoes and made him put those on. He wasn't happy, may have whined a bit. But he complied. Then she drove to Wilson Middle School (Eisenhower, that summer, was being rebuilt) where the first day of summer cross-country workouts was about to begin.

Rogelio stayed cemented to the backseat. He gazed out the car window at Mister walking among the gaggle of runners, all thinner than Rogelio and presumably in much better shape. He had never participated in a sport, didn't really feel a compulsion. He knew all about cross-country, though, having been dragged to meets to watch his sister run.

"I watched her and said, 'Heck, no, I don't want to do this,'" Rogelio recalls. "It was tiring and looked boring."

But now he sat in the backseat, and his mom was adamant. He would try this sport, if just to get his body moving and get healthy. Leticia wasn't expecting her son to be a top runner or even enjoy himself much, but she sure as heck wanted to get him away from the video-game screen, if only for a few hours each day. Rogelio dug in and stayed put; Leticia was equally headstrong.

"Sometimes," she says, "you have to push him. Rogelio's a great kid, but he needs motivation. Going into that freshman year, he was chunky, and I think at that time he was OK with it."

Finally, Rogelio relented, "only because she literally wouldn't leave until I got out of the car, and it started to be a little embarrassing just sitting there."

He left the car and joined the runners. It did not go well.

"I finished behind the girls—I mean, all of them," he recalls, wincing at the memory.

When Leticia picked him up after that first workout, she found her son in tears. "When he came in last, that was horrible for him," she says. "He cried and cried. He said he never wanted to feel that way again. So he came back and started improving."

The pounds came off that first season, not rapidly but steadily. His times improved by the end of the season as well. He went from running a 3.4-mile late August "time trial" in 29 minutes 35 seconds (8:42 pace, dead last among his 14 male teammates) to running 21:27 in a 5K at the Bellevue Invitational. Not blazing, but not dead last either. By Rogelio's sophomore year, he had made the varsity team and, in 2016 as a junior, he became one of the team's top five. He cut more than 10 minutes off his time in that same time trial he had struggled even to finish as a freshman.

Now that Rogelio is a senior, the story of his stark transformation has almost become local cross-country lore, a punch line, a good-natured needling, among teammates. But Mister uses Rogelio's metamorphosis as a motivational tool. He tells the tale every summer at the White Pass camp attended by runners from throughout the state. He tells it at the parent meeting at the start of the season and at the banquet at the end of the season. And, this fall, he had Rogelio stand before 2,000 of his classmates at the fall sports assembly and told the story once more, hoping to inspire more Rogelios.

"I want to focus on one kid, and there's a lot of *you* in this one kid," Mister spoke at the assembly. "He is Rogelio Mares. Stand up, Rogelio. Rogelio Mares is one of our top runners, an elite runner in the state, and he can compete in [college] Division 1 when he leaves Eisenhower next year. Here's what a lot of you need to know. When he came out as a freshman, he wasn't participating in any school activity. His mother threw him out of the car. He was a chunky little boy. The first workout, there was nobody he could beat, not even the slowest JV girls. Nobody was slower. I saw a three-legged dog outsprint him on the way to Randall Park. Here he is now an elite runner who did it with hard work. So if you don't think you can do something, look at this guy. He has transformed his life. A lot of you sitting here, today, can do the exact same thing if you want it, if you're dedicated enough to do it."

Though not every out-of-shape teen—Eisenhower has nurtured more than a few, as has every prep cross-country team—will make such a dramatic leap in ability and lose as many pounds as did Rogelio, his transformation serves as motivation on the Eisenhower team. But neither Rogelio nor his mother says there was any weight-loss secret. Combine healthy eating with the 50 to 70 miles a week a varsity Eisenhower runner logs during the season, and you can understand how Rogelio has gone from wearing pants with a 34-inch waist to ones with a 26-inch waist.

"He stopped eating junk food," Leticia says. "Doesn't eat it at all anymore. But the big thing to emphasize is that he doesn't drink pop. He used to be a big pop drinker and chips eater. We don't keep that in the house anymore. He drinks water now, a lot of water."

"Snacks," Rogelio added, kind of wistfully. "No more snacks. Now I'll eat an apple. I try to have a more balanced diet."

One vice remains, though. Rogelio still is an avid video-game player, like most of the rest of Eisenhower's boys' team. But with twice-daily workouts in the summer, he doesn't have the time or the energy for marathon gamer sessions.

"He's so tired after running," Leticia says, "that he doesn't have time to play all the time or get in trouble—or gain weight. I haven't had any trouble with my kids in that way, and I think it's because I made them get active and play sports. We have a lot of farmworker families, and they leave their kids at home all summer with all the fast food and macaroni and cheese they can make themselves. There's not a lot of Hispanic families get their kids involved in sports. At least not the ones I talk to. Why? Maybe it's not a priority. But they don't realize it's not healthy for their kids."

★ ★ ★

A significant portion of the teenagers in Yakima sadly resemble the "before" picture of Rogelio Mares, and as results from several surveys and studies suggest, they may never even attempt to strive for the "after" picture.

The statistics for childhood obesity in Yakima County are jaw-dropping. According to the Washington State Department of Heath, 31 percent of Yakima County children can be categorized, using body-mass index figures, as obese. But it's not just the children. Their parents, too, struggle with weight problems and the concomitant health issues. More than 37 percent of Yakima County adults are categorized as obese, nearly 10 percentage points higher than the state average. For Yakima County kids, the prevalence of obesity is trending upward; in other words, they are getting fatter and unhealthier. In 2006, 29 percent of Yakima 12th graders fell into the categories of obese or overweight; in 2016, that number rose to 34 percent.

A 2016 Washington Healthy Youth Survey questioned high-school students about their eating and exercise habits as well as factors such as "food insecurity" via poverty and time spent in front of a screen. Among high schoolers, 58.5 percent of respondents identified as Hispanic, higher than the 48.3 percent Hispanics in the county's population as a whole. Nearly 67 percent of the respondents received free or reduced lunch at school, and 25 percent who fell into the obese category reported experiencing "food insecurity" compared to other youth.

Poverty's role in Yakima's obesity problem, of course, cannot be overrstated. But the Healthy Youth Survey also pointed out a significant lack of physical activity and time spent in front of a screen as major contributing factors. Among 12th graders, 79 percent reported that they did not meet the required 60 minutes of physical activity seven days a week; 60 percent, however, reported that they spent three hours or more with screen time, either video games or TV; and 70 percent did not participate in school physical education classes. What's more, many students were barely moving at all. Some 73.9 percent reported never having walked to school, and 93 percent never having ridden a bicycle to school. More telling are the students' dietary behaviors. Although only 12 percent reported buying sweetened drinks at school, 83 percent said they drank sugar-sweetened drinks in the past week and 59 percent consumed chips or snack foods at school. An even 50 percent do not eat breakfast, and 51 percent responded that they do not usually eat dinner with their family.

Alarming statistics are one thing, but the full extent of Yakima's obesity challenge hits home traveling its streets, many of which not only do not have bike lanes but lack sidewalks as well. The city's parks, especially on the heavily Hispanic east side, are in various levels of disrepair. In many areas, convenience stores greatly outnumber full-service grocery stores.

But the really stark visual, one that rankles the county's health-care providers and healthy-eating advocates, comes on a three and a half block stretch of 1st Street, not far from downtown Yakima. That retail corridor plays host to a cornucopia of fast-food eateries—at least two per block. It's a litany of neon signs offering the citizenry cheap caloric options, dizzying in their ubiquity: McDonald's; Burger Broiler; Sonic; McDonald's; Baskin-Robbins; Burger Ranch; Panda Express; Chipotle; Mod Pizza; Five Guys Burgers; Burger King; Carl's Jr.; Taco Time; Taco Bell; McDonald's; Jack in the Box. It is no exaggeration to say that nearly every strip mall in the city, as well as in the neighboring suburb of West Valley, is anchored by one or two fast-food emporiums.

Attitudes may align with one's political leanings, and assigning blame set along party lines, but to those who study obesity among lower-income populations, particularly heavily Latino populations, the effects of poverty cannot be downplayed. Dr. Gino Aisenberg, director of the Latino Center for Health at the University of Washington, says the poverty in Yakima, particularly on the less affluent east side, affects children in several deleterious ways. Chief among the problems is dietary choices.

"Because there aren't big supermarkets in poor areas, access to fresh fruit that is not costly is a real limitation," Aisenberg said. "You have corner markets whose prices aren't competitive. And they don't have a healthy selection. They pay a higher price not just in terms of dollars but the variety and the fresh quality of products. That is an everyday lived experience in low-income communities like in Yakima."

Beyond food choices, the east side of Yakima also has fewer parks than the rest of the city—and those they have are not as well maintained and have had problems with crime and drug use within them, as civic activists have told the Yakima City Council on several occasions.

"Access to and the state of parks is very important in curbing obesity," Aisenberg says.

For years, Yakima has neglected parks on the east side while pouring much of the city's limited resources in the parks and recreation budget toward the west side. In early 2017, though, the city council vowed to allocate funds to improve 20 parks on the east side but, as the *Yakima Herald Republic* reported, the $350,000 set aside annually would only provide enough money to build three playground structures and make rudimentary repairs to restrooms and picnic areas targeted by vandals. In the past decade, two pools on the east side have been closed due to budget cuts while a new aquatics center is being planned at the spacious and verdant Chesterley Park on the west side.

But as Aisenberg points out, improving the parks doesn't necessarily mean people will use them. Among some of Yakima's Hispanics, Aisenberg says, making sure their children get enough exercise is low on the priority list when more immediate financial and, in some cases, immigration issues persist. In addition, Aisenberg says the culture doesn't emphasize physical activity as much as other racial groups. In fact, they may perceive excess weight as a sign of health.

"There are families that hold to the sense of providing food for the family and having chubby partners, spouses, and children is a sign of love and health," he said. "If a child in Yakima is coming from Mexico, they may see how life is portrayed in this country via the media and be influenced by TV commercials. It's not like Coke doesn't exist in Mexico, but here it's become the norm. . . . Our concern in this population is that the [high level of] obesity heightens risk of Type 2 diabetes, metabolic syndrome, cardiovascular disease, and kidney disease. The health consequences are major."

★ ★ ★

The fruit basket front and center at the reception desk was empty, nary an apple or banana there for the plucking. It was more a testament to the popularity of Yakima pediatrician Dr. Yamileth Cazorla-Lancaster's idea to offer healthy options as "treats" for her young patients than from a lack of interest. Forget lollipops for kids after getting shots at a well checkup; these Yakima children get a ripe pear or sweet cherries plucked from orchards within only a few miles. As she leads two toddlers and their harried mom out of an exam room and toward the front desk, Cazorla-Lancaster winces as she sees the empty bowl.

"Looks like we're out," she says, bending to address the kids eye-to-eye. "But we do have some all-natural applesauce in the fridge. Let me run get it."

Since moving to Yakima from Ohio eight years ago, the Panama-born Cazorla-Lancaster has been on a mission to improve the diets and overall health of her young patients. She admits that when she first arrived in Yakima, she was shocked at the level of obesity among youth. First at a nonprofit community health center and now in her own pediatric practice, she promotes healthy eating and spends a considerable number of her off-hours educating the public, especially among her Hispanic cohort. As Cazorla-Lancaster sees it, the biggest problem is just getting parents to recognize that their children—and, often, they themselves—are seriously overweight due to poor nutritional choices.

It can be a delicate subject to broach.

"I don't want to put any blame or fault on anybody, because this is already such a heated topic," she says. "People here already feel so ashamed when people [describe] Yakima as an 'obese city.' We are moving into consciousness that we need to change something. The easiest way in for me is when I start to see their children with health problems. At least that gets to the parents, and they say, 'We need to make a change,' after it's pointed out their children are approaching obesity or high blood pressure or having chronic abdominal pain. Every opportunity I have to inch a mom toward a healthier lifestyle is a step. The moms need to get their heads in line first, and it starts with the head of the household, and a lot of times it's the mom making the food decisions. When she starts to say, 'I'm going to change my diet,' it trickles down to the rest of the family. She is the gatekeeper of the habits of the family. I spend a lot of time empowering mothers."

When she worked in community health, Cazorla-Lancaster dealt primarily with "underserved Spanish-speaking families." She saw from personal experience what social organization program directors such as Aisenberg speak about in generalities: Poverty leads to poor food choices.

"It's not just poverty with these poor Latino families; it's stress, anxiety, and depression—all are factors," she says. "Those mothers, just like any other mother, love their children so much and want the best for them. However, some of these moms are working two or three jobs. They are barely sleeping. Imagine if you're overworked, stressed, worried about money, anxious or depressed, barely getting enough sleep, and your child is easily appeased with food. Food can seem to be the only bright spot in the day for these families. Families see food as that way out of their problems. It's an escape. It's so easy to access."

She pauses and smiles wryly.

"What I see here commonly is things like Hot Cheetos and soda. Hot Cheetos—it's like a food group here in Yakima."

Cazorla-Lancaster concurs with Aisenberg's observation that Hispanics in America think of food and body types differently from people from other cultures—even low-income people from other cultures. Moving from Panama to Texas when she was young, Cazorla-Lancaster herself grew up in an environment in which, to a large extent, health meant girth. And although she is hesitant to try to impinge on people's cultural heritage, the negative result (namely, obesity) can be damaging.

"It starts with mentality and [the result is due to] the addictive nature of junk food," she says. "You see it all the time. Even the terms of endearment [used in the Latino community], calling kids 'gordo' or 'gorda' [Spanish for "fat"]. It's cute as a kid. But, of course, there's a magical time when these kids transition from being cute to obese.

"I think it has to do with the fact that the mom emigrated here from Mexico, and that their children might be first-generation here. Those mothers still remember a time when access to calories was difficult, and you ate whenever you had the opportunity to avoid [starvation]. . . . I have moms come in, and their chief complaint is, 'My child won't eat.' OK, so I do a body-mass index, and the kid's in the 75th to sometimes 90th percentile for BMI. Serious weight-gain issues."

In recent years, Cazorla-Lancaster says, she has had a few Eisenhower cross-country runners as patients. And although she applauds their low body mass that comes, for the most part, from running 50 to 70 miles per week, she wants to improve even athletes' diets to keep them healthy later in life.

"I'm not saying exercise isn't important; it is," she says. "But it's food and food choices that's the real problem. You can't outrun a bad diet."

* * *

Six o'clock on a late June evening, the temperature hovering just under 100 degrees and a scrim of smoke in the air from the remains of a fire on the scorched hills north of town, and the Eisenhower runners seem annoyed. They want to get the run in, in and done. They wait for Mister to give them the workout, speculating in murmurs whether it will be a hard or easy day. Mister occasionally likes to keep them guessing. They gather in the shade of the shed, where Ivan Alfaro is scooping ice into the water containers. With this heat, it figures to be a four-container evening. Mister, however, is around the corner, speaking with Rogelio, who takes a piece of paper out of his backpack and hands it over. After a few minutes, both enter the shed. Mister clears his throat in that way he has to snuff out any lingering conversation.

"Some of you who've been in the program for a while, you know how important this is," Mister says, holding up the printout. "This is Rogelio's blood analysis for his ferritin level. I can't tell you how important this thing is."

He raises the paper and shakes it.

"If you are anemic, now is the time to find out before we go further into the season, so you can do something about it. If you are low, it's going to take about two months to get those levels up. If you go into the season and you are low, essentially, guys, your season is over."

He pauses a beat, for emphasis.

"There's nothing you can do about it then. It's too late. You're done. So take care of it right now. Get a test. If you're good, that's great. If you're low, we need to talk. Any questions on that?"

No one raises a hand. They have heard this speech before. For the seniors, it may seem repetitive, having received the same lecture for four years. Even for the newcomers, this isn't new. They heard much the same talk three weeks earlier on the first day of summer workouts.

"What it is is a blood test," Mister goes on, "and you're going to have to go through your doctor to get it. Your parents need to ask for it. You have to understand. We've got data here going back 20 years now. When they find out your ferritin level is low, you have to deal with it. If you take a chance on it, say, 'I'll be OK,' by the time October rolls around, you are low. We've had people on the team, both boys and girls, who have gone through this. The new numbers coming out from University of Washington sports medicine department say if you're ferritin levels are below 35, they see that as anemic. Used to be 25. Also, ask your doctor to test Vitamin D levels as well. Don't worry. I'll be letting your parents know about this."

He nods curtly, and then the team goes about its workout. But Mister will make good on that promise, giving the runners' parents the same message in late August at the season kickoff parent meeting. And the runners, too, will hear it later in the summer; ferritin is one of Mister's nightly lectures to the participants at the White Pass camp.

Unlike the bulk of youth in Yakima, the Eisenhower runners hardly need to worry about staving off obesity. The sheer bulk of mileage they put in, week in and week out, assures that. In fact, the opposite is true.

"We need to make sure these kids get enough calories for everything they are burning off," Mister says a few days after the late-June ferritin speech. "It's not necessarily that the Hispanic diet is bad, it's that *all* teenagers eat poorly. We know anemia is endemic to this population across the state. And it's good that some of our highest level of iron comes from the Hispanic families. A big part of their diet—meat and beans—that helps. But it's the junk food all kids eat, that's the problem. When we tell the parents about ferritin, they become aware and are supportive of ensuring their kids get a better diet. Rogelio is a great example. The transition from where he started to where he is now is impressive. It can be done."

That sheet of paper Mister was waving contained Rogelio's ferritin score: 66. That's well within the normal range. Mister held the paper aloft, like a proud parent showing off their child's A+ assignment.

"I wish all kids scored that well," he says. "I could tell you horror stories I hear from other cross-country coaches about runners suffering from this."

In high-school cross-country, anemia and eating disorders are issues nearly every team faces at some point. English and Bryson-Driver say incidences of anorexia have been few at Eisenhower, but the coaches remain vigilant. It is one reason why the coaches have closely monitored Dantzel's calorie intake and ferritin levels since her freshman year, when she fell seriously underweight and complained of fatigue. What's more common among Ike runners, Mister said, is eating the "wrong foods," eschewing the iron-rich protein from meat and leafy-green vegetables that build up healthy ferritin numbers that in turn increase a runner's strength and endurance amid weeks and months of hard training. A change in diet often can bolster ferritin numbers, but often athletes must also take iron supplements.

Ferritin, put simply, is stored iron in the blood, which transports oxygen to the muscles. As explained in a recent study in the *North American Journal of Sports Physical Therapy*, "The formation of hemoglobin and the body's subsequent ability to transport oxygen from the lungs to the tissues will be impaired in the athlete who is iron deficient. Additionally, athletes who are iron deficient may experience the following symptoms: nausea, frequent infections, shortness of breath during exercise, respiratory illness, fatigue, weakness, pale appearance, lack of energy, and exhaustion." Another study, in the journal *Physician and Sports Medicine*, reported that 82 percent of female cross-country runners are iron-deficient. Runners low in ferritin often don't recover fast from hard workouts and are more prone to stress fractures as well as illness.

One Eisenhower runner, Kayli Carl, essentially has had her once-promising career reduced to barely being able to keep up with the back of the pack because of low ferritin. Her first indication was slow recovery from a stress fracture in her leg. She had her ferritin checked. It came up at

18—extremely low. At one point, her ferritin dipped to 4, and Mister forbade her from running. This led her to see specialists in Seattle and receive iron infusions.

You might think Carl's plight, so publicly played out around her fellow runners, would spur the rest to take Mister's ferritin admonitions to heart. But the coaches say getting teenagers to be disciplined in their diets is a constant battle. Hence the periodic ferritin lectures and hectoring about eating enough to replenish their bodies after hard workouts. At Mister's urging, nearly all of the runners have eliminated sodas and other sweetened beverages. At practice, Gatorade and other sugared "energy" drinks are discouraged. Water, however, is plentiful. At the September parents' meeting, he hands each parent an example of what it takes to consume 3,000 calories a day—3,000 *healthy* calories, that is—based on the meal plan adopted by the UC San Diego cross-country team, which has worked with sports nutritionists. Parents' eyes bulge at the graphic. Three large meals *plus* three significant snacks?

"It's a constant battle with kids not eating enough food," Mister tells the parents. "Even the smallest girls on the team probably need between 3,000 or 4,000 calories. Some of our guys are up to 5,000. You cannot have any type of machine unless you provide the fuel. If the fuel isn't there, then that engine, whether it's biological or manmade, just won't go. That is a huge deal. That is a lot of food."

Because many Eisenhower runners come from low-income families, supplying enough food for a runner burning several thousand calories a day can be a financial burden. Eisenhower's low-income status means all students qualify for free breakfast and lunch, and nearly every member of the cross-country team routinely heads directly from the morning workout to the breakfast line.

"What these guys need are calories," English says. "That won't be enough for them, so I've seen then eating other kids' lunches. What we've done is started giving kids food, feed them before they leave practice at night in case they aren't getting enough at home."

The refrigerator in the team's shed is stocked with rows of cans of chili and Progresso soup with beef and chicken. Chimichangas are popular and go quickly. Runners can pour the soup in bowls and microwave it while icing their legs or pocket the cans and take them home. Bags of cheese ravioli and pasta will be replenished, and the crispers are well stocked with fruit, such as ubiquitous Yakima Valley apples. Lining the fridge's side shelves are jars of supplements, ranging from iron and vitamin D pills to magnesium and potassium, with a bottle of Pepto-Bismol and a mustard container thrown in for good measure.

But it isn't all health-store offerings. Every Friday during the season, Mister flings open the freezer after practice and treats the team to "ice cream." Why the quotation marks? Because Mister never allows real ice cream to pass his runners' lips.

Rather, Mister offers sugar-free, naturally flavored fruit Popsicles.

But everyone just calls it ice cream. Call it a collective delusion, but after a hard workout, they taste better than Ben and Jerry's. And everyone indulges, even Rogelio.

SUNFAIR INVITATIONAL

Mister proffers the apple, but Dantzel will not partake of the forbidden fruit. Sophi tries to get Dantzel to take it. All the girls do, in fact. Still, Dantzel resists. Still, she will not bite.

The girls have just finished another Rez run, this time eight miles of steady effort on the rolling dirt-and-gravel roads hugging the apple and pear orchards. Mister has parked his truck in the usual spot, the six-mile turnaround for the boys, who are running 12 miles on this day. And, while he waits, he wanders toward the first few trees, the ones growing Gala apples hanging big and red and fat, heavy on the branches in this last week of September. So, as he has done for decades at this spot, Mister picks some. He finds a few good specimens on the ground to liberate as well. By the time he is done, about two dozen apples will serve as a postrun snack.

This being Sunfair Week, a high-stress point in the season in which Eisenhower hosts its own huge invitational, Mister has been working the runners hard. Nerves are on edge, anxieties high. The team wants to run well before the home crowd, but it also is in the midst of heavy training because early November, the state meet, remains the important goal. Mister has been more intense than usual in practice, even though his added responsibility of getting Franklin Park ready for Sunfair has kept him "in and out like a fiddler's elbow." But he makes an effort to reward the runners for their efforts, as well. Hence the apples. Hence, later in the week, postworkout ice cream at the shed.

But Dantzel now simply will not eat an apple. Her face scrunches up in almost physical pain when Isaiah Lopez, one of the JV boys who ran with the girls on this day, places one in her hand. Dantzel tries to look nonchalant as she discards the apple on the open back gate of Mister's truck.

"C'mon, Dantzel," Mister says, his manner lighthearted. "Remember the 20-minute rule of recovery after a hard workout. Eat something in that 20-minute window, when your body is open to absorbing nutrients."

"They're really good, Dan," Erica says, chewing a hunk so big it looks as if she has a wad of chewing tobacco in her cheek.

Dantzel shoots a glance at Mister and then looks at the ground.

"I can't eat it," she says. "It's stealing. Really, these aren't our apples."

Dead silence from the team. Then Mister, who regularly has reminded Dantzel to consume at least 3,000 calories a day during heavy training, speaks up.

"Oh, c'mon, we've been doing this for years. Here, let me call up John Borton, I know him, and have him tell you it's OK."

Mister takes out his phone as if to punch up his contacts. He does not speed-dial Borton, whose name is on the side of all of the apple crates the runners' pass. He puts the phone away, no longer amused.

"We've talked about this," he says, an edge to his voice. "You've got to replenish the calories after a hard, hard workout."

Dantzel almost never brings up her Mormon faith around the other runners, none of whom is overtly religious. But religion plays a big role in her life, in who she is. So in her moral universe, stealing even one apple is not just a crime but a sin.

"I don't think it's fair or right. That's a whole backseat full of apples you took."

"It's not about *that*, Dantzel; it's about you eating—"

"I've got a nectarine and a bar back at the shed, Mister," she says, walking away.

In the truck, heading back to the school, Mister worries about Dantzel's attitude toward food. Her poor and listless race at Bellevue is only the latest sign that her fitness is flagging. A week before, Mister had all of the runners, boys and girls, get weighed to make sure they were not losing weight during this hard training period. The weigh-in was done privately, the numbers not divulged. Dantzel, he says, did not want to participate.

"That's a red flag," he says. "And another red flag is not wanting to eat in front of her team. And you can just see by how fatigued she is. That's a red flag, too. She ran poorly at Bellevue. We were hoping she'd turned a corner by her good race at the league meet. We've been dealing with this with her since her freshman year. She just has to keep herself healthy. And to do that, she needs to eat. I don't know what we're going to do. We'll see how she does at Sunfair."

Back on campus, at the shed, Dantzel eats her nectarine on her way to doing core exercises with the girls. Later, she reflects on her deteriorating relationship with Mister. She has bristled at his insistence that she eat more, and she isn't thrilled that Mister, on three occasions, has talked to her father about her caloric intake. And then there is Mister's written criticism of her Bellevue race, which Dantzel says didn't take into account that she was running while suffering from a head cold.

"I just don't take him too seriously now," she says. "My freshman year, anything he said either built me up or tore me down. It was *everything* to me. But as you grow with him, you learn. He's a really smart guy who sometimes does stupid stuff. Says stupid stuff. He doesn't realize how mean he's being to a girl, right? To someone who's sensitive. I now take it, like, this is what he's trying to say. I don't think he's attacking me personally."

Dantzel does have the self-awareness to know that, occasionally, she does not eat enough. Or get enough sleep, for that matter. She has a busier schedule than most on the team. She is one of the state's top high-school violinists, part of the Yakima symphony, and hopes later in the year to be picked for the state ensemble. And although her classical music auditions do not ramp up until winter, a month after cross-country season ends, Dantzel still has lessons and rehearsals two nights a week. She does not attend morning cross-country practices because she has a Mormon seminary class before school five days a week.

"For me, it's always been a struggle," she says. "Like, I don't know, eating tons of food is hard. Three thousand calories! That is so much food. And I'm not someone who just loves eating food. It's not like I love to sit down and eat. And I'm so busy all day that it's hard for me to consume that much food on a daily basis. I try; and I know it's important; and I know, like, today, I'm down on calories, so when I go home tonight I'll stock up. But it's definitely a struggle."

And to think that Dantzel has always turned to running as a stress reliever. Now, what has been a fun diversion is making her wrought up with worry.

"I get so nervous for violin. When I get out there on the starting line for cross, it's like, hilarious. Everybody's so geared up. But I'm looking around thinking, this isn't pressure. With running, I'm more confident with my body and I'm not judged as much as I am in violin. Technically, I know every mistake I make on the violin. You spend hours and hours on the same concerto, and you know every note you did wrong. Whereas, in running, I just go run as hard as I can. It's like you don't notice as much when you're off your form."

But Mister notices. He always does. And Mister is worried, not only about Dantzel's contribution to the team but also about the state of her health.

★ ★ ★

Under a purple, predawn sky on Monday morning, six days before Sunfair, the boys and girls are running in two packs round and round the soccer fields behind the team shed. It is a standard morning workout, two sets of 20-minute steady runs, the last five minutes of each increased to speedier, near tempo, pace. The groups lope along seemingly by rote muscle memory while Mister stands off to one side, arms folded and squinting to get a better look, and Price stares down into the glow of his smartphone.

Suddenly, as the boys' group heads close to Mister, Jonas speeds up and veers from the pack. Tears stream down his face. He runs, at near full speed, directly at his dad, yelling, "It's all your fault." Then he keeps running out the gate and onto 40th Avenue. Mister gives a sidelong glance but does not intervene. He coached his own kids, so he knows how home life and team life can bleed into each sphere. The timing of the Price family episode seems curious, coming just two days after Jonas's breakout victory at Bellevue.

"They will work it out," Mister says.

By the end of morning practice, Jonas has returned. Dry-eyed, he does the leg squat drills with his teammates but speaks to no one. He does not make eye contact with his dad. It is a stark change to the voluble Jonas his teammates expect.

Later that afternoon, Jonas's sullenness seemingly has permeated the team. He sits off by himself in the shed before practice, and Fonzi, Jesus, and Jonathan are similarly subdued, not even partaking in their new favorite time-killer, the *Clash Royale* video game. Then again, the quietude could be because Mister has scheduled another session of mile repeats—six, with a time goal of five minutes, four minutes of rest in between—and is tacking on four sets of 800-meter (half mile) repeats at 2:30 pace immediately following.

A sense of dread descends as the boys sit on the grass at Chesterley Park, changing into their racing spikes. Pain is coming. Mile repeats at near full effort are never fun, but unlike last week's session, this time Mister makes it clear he wants them to hit their time goals—or, at least, come damned close.

"Church time," he shouts, as he leads the boys to the orange cones that serve as the start. "You're on a mission from God! Anyone remember what movie that quote is from?"

No one answers.

"*The Blues Brothers.*"

The film came out in 1980, before some of the younger runners' parents were even born.

"Guess I'm dating myself," he tells the team. "Great movie."

He claps his hands together.

"OK. This is where the Emotional Intelligence quotient comes in again. You gotta have the presence of mind to push through that discomfort for six seconds, OK?"

The always-affable Rogelio, the only varsity boys' runner not brooding, raises his hand.

"My arms are hurting, Mister. I've been using them too much."

"That's because you've never used them before in 17 years."

Mister resets his stopwatch and yells, "Hit it."

Rogelio beats Jonas by a second in the first repeat, and the two finish neck-and-neck on the second one. They are within seconds of the five-minute barrier. On the third repeat, Fonzi joins his two teammates, and all three cross the line at 5:05. Halfway through the next repeat, though, Fonzi pulls up limping, sits on the grass clear across the park from Mister, and takes off his left shoe. Then, gingerly, he walks back.

"My left arch, Mister," he says, out of breath. "Hurts."

"I'll tape it."

Fonzi doesn't ask to end repeats early, and Mister doesn't offer. The tape job gives the other runners an extra minute to rest. Back for the final two repeats, Fonzi wins both by a single second over Rogelio and Jonas.

"Best workout Fonzi's had since last year," Mister tells Price.

But it isn't over. There are still those four 800s to run. Three repeats in, the boys are bent over, hands on knees, stomachs undulating with deep breaths.

"Mister, there's no way I can take your test tomorrow," says Rogelio, a student in Mister's anatomy and physiology class. "I'm too tired to study. I'm just going home and going to sleep. Let me take it Friday or something."

"Nice try, Rogelio."

But then Mister reconsiders. He sees that his team had put in a hard, honest effort. And they do look spent. He needs to do something to get them through the rest of the workout.

"Tell ya what. You run that last 800 [repeat] in 2:23, and you won't have to take the test until Friday."

This gets the boys excited. Even Jonas perks up.

"We'll pace you, Rogelio!" Jonas says.

"Yeah, boys," Fonzi adds. "Let's do this."

Rogelio takes off like a shot on the last 800, leaving his pacers, Jonas and Fonzi, in the dust. About 400 meters in, Mister looks at his stopwatch.

"Making good time," he says.

Then he turns to Price and Bryson-Driver and says, "What Rogelio doesn't know is that I wasn't planning on giving the test tomorrow anyway."

The three have a good laugh. But Rogelio keeps coming. The watch reads 2:02 when he makes the final left turn and has about 50 meters left. Rogelio is struggling, though. The girls and JV boys have finished their workouts and are cheering Rogelio on. He pumps his arms and churns his legs, but his pace is slowing. He crosses the line at 2:25 and collapses flat on his back, arms outstretched. Told his time, he only groans.

The next afternoon, as he walks to the shed before practice, Rogelio is asked how his anatomy test turned out.

"Oh, it was great," he says. "Mister didn't make us take it. He told the class it was because I did so good in the 800s."

Mister's kindheartedness extends only so far, though. At that day's workout, a fartlek run in which the boys alternate steady running with 150-meter bursts of speed, he doesn't like the lackluster effort.

"Fartlek!" he barks. "That's Swedish for 'speed play.' I see a lot of playing and not much speed. Lazy. Remember, Sunfair may be the most technical course you run all year. You need these bursts of speed. Now do it again."

★ ★ ★

Practice, this week, is almost a relief to Mister. Since Wednesday, he has been spending nearly all of his free time supervising the stark transformation of Franklin Park into a fenced-in, flagged-off, certified three-mile cross-country course. A substitute is teaching his classes; in fact, it is a sub who finally makes Rogelio and the rest of the anatomy class take the test on Friday.

"There's a lot of things to coordinate," Mister says, poring over a three-page to-do list. "There's a lot of logistics to pull together in using a city park. But we've been doing this so long that we've got it down."

Mister has been the meet director at Sunfair for 38 years, so nothing much can surprise him anymore. Still, things crop up occasionally. Such as, this year, Mister tries to unlock the Franklin Park swimming pool with his master key to all of the locks in the park and discovers that someone has changed the locks. He doesn't take it personally. After all, he is grateful for the free use of the park from the city—by contrast, the meet director of the Bellevue Invite has to pay close to $2,000 to rent a part of Lake Sammamish State Park for a day—but he needs to get in that pool area. So he calls the city, and a worker drops everything and runs over with a new key.

"So I say to the woman, 'I'll get this key back to you first thing Monday,' and she says to me, 'Oh, it's OK, Mister, keep it. Just give it back to us when you retire.' Incredible."

Mister acknowledges that he has a pretty good thing going at Sunfair. The Eisenhower cross-country team keeps all of the proceeds (five dollar admission plus concession and T-shirt sales, etc.). It is the team's only fund-raiser all year. As Price tells the runners several times in the days leading up to the race, each kid will have a job on race day because "this race makes sure you and your parents don't have to sell a whole bunch of crap so that you can get nice things like hotel rooms on road meets and cruiser buses, things a lot of cross-country kids don't get."

But Mister is more comfortable being a coach than an event manager. And he is back two days before the race addressing the team before practice about strategy and form. As he speaks, he notices that Jonas is not seated among the runners in the stands of the football stadium before the workout. Suddenly, Jonas emerges from the shed carrying a bouquet of white roses and a poster. He takes the stadium stairs two at a time until he nears where Julia Johnson, a freshman, sits. He holds up the sign, which reads: "Julia, With Your Brains and My Brawn, Let's Tackle HOCO together." She smiles and accepts, to hoots and applause from teammates. Papa Price captures the whole "ask" on video. Mister holds up both hands to quiet the crowd.

"Now, Julia," Mister asks, "why on Earth do you want to go to Homecoming with *him*?"

She reddens.

"Why not?" she says in a small voice.

The boys erupt in mock derision at Jonas, who is smiling more broadly than even after he won the Bellevue race.

"You don't have any 'brawn,' Jonas," Fonzi cracks.

"That's the advantage of having a co-ed team," Mister says. "You always have a date."

Indeed, in addition to longtime couple Angel and Nayeli, Izzy is dating Isaiah Lopez, and Fonzi has asked Antonia Harrich, a German exchange student on the JV team, to the Homecoming dance. Rogelio, after a week or two of hemming and hawing, and with moral support from Izzy and her sidekick, Madi, has finally followed through and asked a nonrunner, a girl in one of his classes, Angel, to Homecoming. Izzy has recorded "the ask" on video and replays it at practice for teammates, to much amusement. Rogelio may be aggressive on the cross-country course, but he seems downright cowed when making the romantic overture.

Homecoming is still more than a week away—after the Richland Invitational. Sunfair still beckons, and Mister wants the team to focus on that.

★ ★ ★

The great thing about Sunfair is that it goes a long way to "bond" the oft-cliquish girls' team. The girls, Erica included, meet at Molly's house to make ribbons for their hair and posters that they will tack up at strategic points along the course. And now, on race day, those posters are a hit with the more than 600 runners and nearly as many spectators milling about.

• A half mile into the race: "UR Not Almost There!"

• At the top of the Terraces, a steep 100-feet elevation gain near the one-mile mark: "Ooof."

• At a smaller hill the runners must traverse three times: "Don't Quit!!! This might end up on YouTube!"

• Near the two-mile mark: "WTF: Where's the Finish?"

• Near the finish: "Slow and Steady Is Not Going to Get You Anywhere."

Molly had done one more sign, one that the girls wanted to put at the base of the steep Terrace climb—"This Hill Is Your B★#!&★"—but Mister worried that some spectators could be offended, so Molly kept it propped up at the team tent.

Even without the banned poster, there is plenty of buzz among the Eisenhower runners at Sunfair. The marquee race figures to be a rematch from the Bellevue Invite between Jonas and Glacier Peak's Riley McDowell. Adding to the intrigue, both runners' fathers had squared off against each other in the 1984 Sunfair, Robert Price of Carroll (14:56) beating Bruce McDowell of Columbia River (15:02).

But Mister really isn't worried about Jonas. He wonders whether his boys will fair any better against the 3A powerhouse Kamiakin, the team that beat them handily at Bellevue. The race format—seven "flights," for the Nos. 1 through 7 runners—is similar to Bellevue's setup and is the last time Eisenhower will race in the nontraditional format all season. Will Fonzi continue to improve and place high in the No. 3 runner flight? Will Angel bounce back from a poor showing in the No. 4 runner race? And, on the girls' side, will Erica go out fast enough early on to contend in the top-runner race? Can Molly's sore foot hold up on the hilly Sunfair course in the No. 3 race? And which Dantzel will show up in the No. 2 race: the strong runner from the league race, or the weak runner at Bellevue?

Kamiakin's boys, as expected, dominate early on, but Eisenhower gets a lift when, in the No. 7 runner heat, Jesus Gonzalez finishes second in a strong effort, making up for disappointing showings by Tony and Mo in the Nos. 6 and 5 races, respectively. Mister is pumping his fist and cheering when Angel redeems himself with a strong third-place finish, and Fonzi gives the Kamiakin lead runner a battle before settling for second.

Back at the tent, Fonzi is not totally pleased by finishing second to the same runner who beat him the week before, but this time he is only four seconds off Rogelio's time in the No. 2 race (Rogelio had also finished second.) "I feel like I'm getting stronger every week," Fonzi says, biting into a hamburger his mother thrust at him. She also tries to get him to eat a blueberry muffin the size of a dinner plate, and Fonzi says, "Mommm!" When Mo overhears and offers to take the muffin off of Sonya Cuevas's hands, Fonzi perks up. "No, Mo. That's mine," he says, laughing.

"Guess what?" Fonzi's nine-year-old sister, Caris, still wearing her race bib number from the morning's elementary-school division run, says to him, "I beat a sixth grader."

"Getting her started early?" someone within earshot asks Sonya.

"Mom," Fonzi interrupts, "you gotta start her in soccer first, then running later. That's the way it's done." At least, the way it worked with Fonzi.

"OK," she says, "Eat your muffin, Alfonso."

The girls' side of the tent is not so jocular. Molly has raced well, despite a noticeable limp she tried to hide from Mister. She finishes seventh in the

No. 3 race, two seconds off her personal record on the Franklin course. Erica once again goes out too slowly and cannot work her way back up to the lead pack, finishing eighth in 19:12, three seconds off her Sunfair mark as a junior. Dantzel runs an even poorer race than at Bellevue. It does not go well even before the start. She forgot to wear her race bib number and, if Eisenhower had not been the meet host, she probably would not have been allowed to run. She hovers near the top 10 in the first mile but then drops well off. Her second mile: 8:32, a jog. She finishes third to last at 21:55—2 minutes and 9 seconds slower than her Sunfair time the previous year. Back at the tent, she coughs repeatedly, showing lingering effects from her cold that has lasted two weeks.

Bryson-Driver seems perplexed—then again, not really—with Dantzel's showing.

"She's not recovering from workouts," Bryson-Driver says. "She can't put in the effort. And that all comes down to energy and that comes down to calories. She's not eating enough. She's got to do that, eat, to recover even from that cold she's had. I don't know what we're going to do."

Mister knows.

"We're going to have a long talk with her mom and dad and Dantzel," he says. "Kind of an intervention."

Dantzel's finish and Erica's lower-than-expected finish mean that the girls fall to ninth. The boys, on the strength of Angel, Fonzi, and Rogelio, are pretty much assured a second-place team finish behind Kamiakin going into Jonas's race.

Racing at home in front of friends and extended family and reporters from the local newspaper and TV stations, as well as publicly stating that he is shooting for his dad's Sunfair PR of 14:56, Jonas has a lot of pressure on those narrow, bony shoulders. The race goes off as expected, a tight pack of seven runners moving almost as one over the terraces and past the one-mile mark. Included are Glacier Peak's McDowell; Nicholas Russell of Bishop Kelly, in Boise, Idaho; and Kamiakin's Jonah Franco, the latter of whom finished well behind Jonas the previous weekend at Bellevue.

Well into the second mile, the pack remains, and the pace is slower than Jonas had anticipated. It feels too easy for him. So, on an out-and-back section at the top of the Terraces, just before the two-mile mark, Jonas makes a surge, unsure whether the pack will follow. For about 10 meters, the pack lets Jonas take the lead and then it picks up the pace and reabsorbs him. At this point, Jonas settles in and figures it will be a kicker's race. He has been working on his kick and his strength to pull it off. But, only a sophomore and weighing all of 115 pounds, he cannot keep up with Franco, a senior, six inches taller and much more muscular, when he makes his decisive move with about 300 meters to go. Franco wins, going away.

Back at the team tent, Jonas patiently answers questions from the local TV reporter and then accepts high fives from teammates. His performance ensures that Eisenhower will finish second overall with 24 points, well behind winner Kamiakin (8) but well ahead of 4A rival Glacier Peak (34).

Eventually, Robert Price wanders by. He and Jonas exchange a hug. They seem to have settled whatever differences they had earlier in the week, when Jonas stormed out of practice. Mister has been proven right about his refusal to intervene in a family dispute. Jonas now clings to his dad's side. The two walk silently back to the tent. Nothing more, really, needed to be said.

RICHLAND INVITATIONAL

Fonzi's insouciant swagger has returned. At least, glimpses of it. There he stands, busting dance moves in the middle of the maelstrom of competition on the field outside the track shed. His smile, absent often during what for him has been a season of frustration, beams like klieg lights.

"Three-and-oh, baby," he says, waving three fingers above his head. "Three. And. Oh."

It is the day before the Richland Invitational, the last major face-off between many of the state's best teams before State about a month hence, and the Eisenhower boys and girls are fully engaged in a matchup every bit as heated and competitive as the next day's race would be—Mister's annual Conkers Tournament.

Each October, before the final push for the district and state titles takes hold, Mister devotes half of a practice to the game from his Irish youth: Conkers. The team collected the bulbous, brown-burnished horse chestnuts at Fort Steilacoom, and now Mister has drilled holes through nuts, threaded a string through them, knotted the things, and then given them to runners to face off and do battle. The objective: Take turns swinging your conker at the opponent's outstretched conker dangling from the foot-long string. Knock the other kid's nut off, you win.

"Today is the most important day of the year," Mister says with mock sternness. "Today is the Conkers Tournament."

The runners clap, enthusiastically, not dutifully. They seem pumped to compete. Or maybe the tournament just means an easier workout day.

In any event, they are slapping hands and talking trash. The winner earns the coveted Conkers Trophy—a runner holding two strings of conkers—a Brooks running jacket, and $10 from Mister's wallet. Jonas, last year's champion, stands and takes a mock bow. He is shouted down.

"Listen up," Mister continues. "This was a serious game when I was growing up. It often led to fights at school and at home, believe you me. We had all sorts of tricks. Some people put the conker in salt overnight, thinking it gave them an advantage. I trust you'll all play fair."

And so the games begin. Fonzi is on fire. He eliminates Mo in four direct hits. He takes out Rogelio in an intense exchange between the two friends. Then he sends Jonathan packing in short order. Then comes this dance interlude. Fonzi's confidence may have been waning on the cross-country course, but at Conkers he is exerting domination.

Mister, watching with arms folded, laughs at Fonzi's antics. "Don't celebrate too soon," he says. "This isn't even the finals yet."

Mister has seen Fonzi's mood lift in direct proportion to his running performance. He still isn't back running within 15 seconds of the times he had logged at meets in his breakout sophomore season, but at the previous two meets, Bellevue and Sunfair, he showed signs of the Fonzi of old, the pre-injury Fonzi, the Fonzi who found pure joy in running and everything else. Mister hopes the brooding Fonzi, the withdrawn and subdued one, won't return any time soon, because in Mister's mind, Fonzi's troubles now are as much a matter of confidence as running mechanics and injuries.

At Sunfair, Fonzi's time was only a few seconds shy of Rogelio's. Fonzi didn't go so far as to say he was satisfied, but in practice earlier in the week, he confided that he is starting to feel like his old self. A whole year, when you are a teenager, can feel like an awfully long time; and, for Fonzi, his 2016 sophomore season felt like a geologic age. All week, he has been eager, and slightly impatient, to test himself sans his orthotics. Over the summer, when Mister first insisted Fonzi wear the custom-made insoles to correct his foot pronation and prevent his worsening ankle injury problems, the two made a deal. Late in the season, if all went well, Mister would consider letting Fonzi race without the orthotics, a much heavier insole than those found in racing spikes.

And, apparently, now is the time for Fonzi to make the ask. A few days before the Conkers Tournament, during a break between interval sets, Fonzi breaks free of the group. Smiling slyly, he trots over to where Mister, who is wearing a black T-shirt bearing the message "I Yell Because I Care," stands.

"Excuse me, Mister," Fonzi says head bowed slightly, as if deferring to a schoolmaster. "Can I try running without the orthotics in my spikes?"

"What? At Richland?" Mister seems taken aback.

"No, here. The next set."

"Not now, Fonzi. Let's think about this."

Fonzi lopes off, and Mister sighs.

"He needs those orthotics. They help with his foot plant. But they are a little heavy, so he doesn't like racing in them. The plan we agreed to was to have him race most of the season with them in."

For the next set of intervals, on the grass, Fonzi takes off his trainers and, instead of changing into the racing spikes, runs barefoot—an option Mister affords most runners. He breezes through the next set, easily running stride for stride with Jonas and Rogelio. In Fonzi's mind, the advantage of racing in ultralightweight spikes is mitigated by the bulky leather and plastic orthotics. To him, it is like running with ankle weights attached. Then again, Fonzi trusts Mister's judgment implicitly, so he accepts that he will race at Richland three days hence with the orthotics in place.

"I wanted to test running in spikes," he says. "But, at the same time, I'm scared because I've been running with the orthotics the entire time this season. I'm just trying to get back to the old me."

The old Fonzi is present at the Conkers Tournament. It turns out that his celebrating is, indeed, premature, because he is subsequently eliminated by a JV runner, Jason Martinez, who would go on to lose to Kayli Carl in a spirited final match. Yet Fonzi does not mope at his Conkers loss. He makes the rounds to cheer others on, including German exchange student and JV runner Antonia Harrich, whom he will be taking to the Homecoming dance the evening of the Richland race.

Later, at a boys' team meeting convened to go over strategy for the Richland Invite, Mister stresses the importance of the meet.

"Tomorrow will be like a dry run for State," he says. "All the teams are straight-up really competitive. It's highly unusual for us to get a State preview like this. Yes, we still have a month of training to get ready, but this will be a good test."

As the meeting breaks up, Jonas shouts, "The story is . . . our top five under 16 [minutes] at Richland, yeah!" To which Fonzi turns back and adds, "The story is . . . the return of Alfonso!"

★ ★ ★

Among the people duking it out with reckless abandon in the Conkers competition, laughing and trash-talking with every swing of the nut, are Erica and Molly. Erica made it to the finals the previous year before losing to Jonas, but she really doesn't seem hell-bent on avenging her loss. In fact, when Molly's direct hit on Erica's conker splits the nut nearly in half and ends the match, Erica laughs. She doesn't drift off by herself afterward, as is her wont during breaks in workouts; rather, she hovers close by other matches and cheers for any girl matched up against a boy.

In recent weeks, the thaw in the relations between Erica and the rest of the girls' team has been noticeable. At first, when Mister decreed that Erica would do drills and "easy" workouts with the other girls, she chafed and couldn't wait to join the boys for harder workouts. But Erica gradually has softened. Now she occasionally is encouraging other girls in workouts, an upgrade from her previous curt nod at teammates and a perfunctory "Good job." And the girls, for the most part, have responded. Molly has even gone so far as to cheer on Erica as she pounded out repeats with the boys, telling her, "Great job, Ric," and imploring her to "watch that right elbow flying out."

The season has proven to be something of a revivification of the friendship between Erica and Molly, the only two seniors on the varsity. When they were freshman, they described themselves as close, but as Erica's performance skyrocketed, she withdrew from the girls, which made Molly (and others on the team) feel left behind. The nadir in the relationship, Erica had acknowledged, had to be the team meeting—"bitch session," several called it—at the White Pass camp.

"Things have changed," Molly says. "Everyone is supportive of everyone now. I think she [Erica] has changed. She's accepted that the rest of us are trying to improve. It's not that we're dogging it, like she thought, because we aren't as fast as she is."

Molly, almost by default, has assumed leadership. And Erica has not only accepted it but has embraced it. She never wanted the responsibility in the first place. When it came time for the girls to gather in a "bonding session" before the Bellevue meet, and Molly decided they should make identical decorative ribbons to tie up their ponytails, Erica volunteered to have the meeting at her house. When Molly wanted the girls to make funny posters to be placed around the Sunfair course, Erica did three of them herself.

For her part, Erica is matter-of-fact about the change in team chemistry.

"Things have improved. It's not that I've decided to make more of an effort; it's that I *have* to, what with me being around them more [at practice]. But it's not like I'm saying, 'Oh, no, I *have* to.' Don't get me wrong."

The thaw between Erica and Molly has not totally trickled down. Sophi, a junior who has served as a buffer between the older girls and a group of sophomores, says tensions remain.

"I, myself, get frustrated because we are a team, and that's like a family to me, so it's hard when someone puts themselves above the rest of us," she says. "I get the workouts, and I encourage Ric to be the best she can be, and if that's running with the boys, then go for it. But she still sets herself apart other times. That part still needs work."

But even Sophi and Erica share a laugh at an otherwise tense team meeting going into the Richland meet. After Sunfair, Mister has ordered both teams to chart their eating habits over a three-day period, to make sure they are consuming enough calories to combat the calories expended by their twice-daily workouts. His goal: a minimum of 3,000 calories consumed per day. The meeting convened in the middle of day 2, and most of the girls had fallen somewhat short of the 3,000 goal, Sophi coming in at 2,997.

"We need, like, those bars from *Mean Girls*," Erica says. "Mister, you know the movie, *Mean Girls*? They get the mean girl, Regina George, to eat these energy bars they serve to starving people in Africa to gain weight."

"Yes!" Sophi exclaims, "that's what we need!"

Mister seems clueless as to the pop culture reference, but he has another point to make, a point mostly directed at Dantzel, but applicable to all.

"Trying to increase calories in these three days wasn't the goal," he says. "The goal was to get a good reading on where you stand. The good thing about it, with good nutrients in a short amount of time, like, 10 days, you can absolutely turn your body around and feel a huge difference. An old coach reminded me of a phrase we used a long time ago, 'Good nutrition and good nutrients—iron, magnesium, zinc, and all that—that's like being on steroids.' It gives you that much of an advantage; you may not realize. That's how big a deal it is. If you're not getting enough calories, then you can't expect your body to perform.

"You have to be responsible for your own health. If you want to be in denial over how many calories, what does that tell you? We can't force you to eat, right? You are fooling yourself, and in the broader picture you are hurting your performance and hurting the team as well. If you don't want to do it for yourself, try to do it for the team. You can solve this issue if you choose to do it."

In the lull that follows, several girls glance sideways at Dantzel, sitting cross-legged, suddenly very interested in the patterns of the grass at her feet. But then Sophi breaks the awkwardness.

"Mister, can we have a girls' fridge, because the boys eat all of our food?"

"No, Sophi, you're not going to have a girls-only fridge."

Molly: "But last year, the boys ate everything. They hid a mac and cheese from us."

Erica; "And remember that box of granola bars they took?"

Molly: "They hid it in the closet."

Erica: "On hard days, we'd be out there working, and people going through [injury] rehab would go in the fridge and gorge."

Sophi: "You're right, Ric. We got back from Fechter hill [training] one day in track last year, and Alex [a sprinter] is sitting in there with a Hot Pocket in each hand. I'm like, 'Are there any left?' He said, 'No.' I said, 'Can I have one? You have two.' He said, 'I actually had a workout today.' I said, 'Our easy days are your hard days, so give me the freaking Hot Pocket.'"

Everyone busts out laughing, even Dantzel.

★ ★ ★

Dantzel lingers on the periphery of the Conkers hubbub. She played one round, losing to Sophi, but really didn't seem too into it. She mostly keeps to herself, wandering the field of battle to take in other matchups. The only sound she makes is the coughing that has persisted for nearly three weeks.

Perhaps she is subdued because, not 15 minutes before the tournaments, Mister called her out of team drills for a private talk. Dantzel has been around long enough to know that, for Mister to interrupt drills, it must be something important. It was. He and Bryson-Driver talked about the calorie thing again, wanted to know why she wasn't eating more. It wasn't so much the calorie consumption that dogged Dantzel; it was that cold she couldn't shake and the sleep deficit she had racked up by having violin lessons two nights a week after practice, Mormon seminary each morning, and a steady stream of homework.

By the time she emerges from the conversation, the girls have started an easy run, and Dantzel chugs along after them, her expression noncommittal, her affect flat.

"We're holding Dantzel out of Richland," Mister says. "She's not mentally or physically ready to race. I really think our decision was a relief for her."

"She was wishy-washy on whether she even wanted to race," Bryson-Driver adds.

When Mister asks the results of her calorie counting, she tells him she consumed 2,700 calories on each of the first two days, 3,300 on the last. She comes close to the minimum, but Mister was hoping she would have eaten more.

"We don't know if we can believe her," Mister says. "In any case, that's not enough for the kind of exercise we ask these kids to do."

Mister's doubts are fueled when one of the girls who regularly eats lunch with Dantzel reports to him that, one day earlier in the week, Dantzel threw away half of her brown bag, uneaten. Upon being told, Mister makes it a point to hang around the team shed after a hard practice that afternoon to see whether Dantzel will abide by his mandate to refuel with food from the fridge. Mister has even gone so far as to stop by the grocery store and pick up three boxes of Popsicles to go with the $300 of food—everything from chicken taquitos, to pizza pockets, to ramen noodles—he previously picked up at Costco. While the others hover around the fridge, Dantzel keeps her distance, sipping from a blue Nalgene bottle. Eventually, she goes to her backpack and takes out a Ziploc bag. Sophi, dipping hard breadsticks into Nutella spread, approaches her.

"Want one, Dan?"

"No, I'm good," she replies, lifting up the baggie.

"What is it?"

"Whole wheat pancakes, from home."

She tears off a bit and nibbles on it.

"Do you at least want to microwave it?" Mister asks.

Dantzel shrugs.

Eventually, the crowd around the fridge and microwave thins, and many runners go home, Mister reminding them to eat a well-balanced, "nutrient-dense" dinner. Danztel is one of the last to leave, and Mister makes it a point to stick around. He wants to see whether she will, indeed, take a Popsicle. Every other kid did. Eventually, Dantzel rummages around the freezer and takes a raspberry Popsicle, then takes her car keys from her backpack and leaves without a word.

Now, on Conkers day, word has slowly spread among the girls that Dantzel will not be running the next day at Richland. The news does not go over well. Teamwise, Eisenhower figures to have an uphill battle against top teams at Richland. Competing without its No. 2 runner will make it that much harder for the girls.

"It's pretty frustrating," Molly says. "We've tried to talk to her. Tell her, you should be eating that. She kind of lied to me this morning. I asked, and she said, 'I got 3,000 calories.' I could tell she hadn't. It's frustrating to hear her say, 'I want to get better, and I don't understand why I'm not getting faster.' I'm like, 'Dan, it's staring you in the face. *Eat.*'"

Erica says she didn't even try to appeal to Dantzel, calling her "stubborn" and saying that "she'll never improve as a runner" until she gets healthy and starts eating right.

"I tried talking to her last year, because this has been an ongoing problem," Erica says. "I remember saying, 'I'm frustrated that you cannot just suck it up and eat something.' She didn't say anything. I mean, I hope she will run for us, but I'm not sure now how much it'll help."

Mister says he will not let Dantzel compete until she is physically and mentally strong enough to do it "safely and healthily," even if it means that the girls lose the district title for the first time in a decade.

"Dantzel's health is more important," he says. "I told her to stay at home and rest."

★ ★ ★

Three of the four 4A division teams ranked ahead of Eisenhower's boys are running at Richland, and it turns out that two of them, Central Valley and Lewis and Clark, set up their tents within spitting distance of the Eisenhower encampment. As if Ike needed a reminder of the stiff competition on this day.

The boys' and girls' varsity races are the final two of the day, meaning several hours of waiting. Fonzi, nervous, spends considerable time away from the tent, even with race time approaching. Jonas jogs around, the hood of his sweatshirt concealing him. Eventually, the boys gather at the tent to change into their racing spikes. Fonzi, as in the previous five races, carefully transfers the orthotics from his trainers to his spikes. His race face is a rictus of concentration, his furrowed brow making him look 16 going on 60. Rogelio takes a Popsicle stick and breaks it in half. He will race, once again, carrying the split stick to remind him of arm placement. It has become a crutch, sure, but it has worked for him. Angel has a knot in his right calf and asks Mister to "rub it out" using the pungent Tiger Balm from the medicine bag. Maybe no one says much because they are wary that Central Valley's runners may overhear. It is at that precise moment that Mister, out of character, launches into an inspirational speech directed toward Angel, the No. 4 runner whose inconsistency has been consistent all season.

"Be brave, Angel," Mister says, kneading Angel's calf. "No second thoughts. Go out hard. Go out hard early. Race like a madman, Angel. You can do this. Keep your eyes focused on Rogelio and Fonzi. Be there with them. Push yourself, Angel. Be brave."

Minutes later, Eisenhower lines up at the starting line, two boxes away from Lewis and Clark and right next to Central Valley. The gun goes off, and a mad dash ensues.

"Man, this is going to be a fast race," Drew Schreiber, the former Eisenhower star runner who is helping out at the meet, says from behind the starting line.

It is. The lead pack of 10 runners whooshes by a half mile in. And by the one-mile mark just after the first of two major hill climbs, the pack has been reduced to six, Jonas right there among them. The pack's collective one-mile time of 4:38 seems insanely fast, even to the coaches cheering from the flagging and checking stopwatches. Only five seconds behind Jonas comes Rogelio, his fastest mile ever in a cross-country race. A second behind him is Fonzi, arms pumping furiously. But where is Angel? He finally shows up at the first mile 14 seconds behind Fonzi. Though it appears to be another slow start for Angel, he actually comes through at 4:55, very fast for him. The second mile takes its toll, but only slightly, on the lead pack, which comes through in 5:09, Jonas in fourth position. Even that pace is too much for Rogelio and Fonzi. Rogelio drops back to 13th place and Fonzi six seconds behind Rogelio among a cluster of runners in the top 30. Fonzi's form looks strong, and his arm swing and knee lift as robust as always, but his face looks strained. He fears losing more ground in the final mile, and that's what is happening. Angel, meanwhile, catches a second wind. He is passing runners in the last half mile, living up to his nickname of "The Snake" for his knack of slithering around dying runners in the final meters of a race.

In the stretch, Jonas cannot stick with the leaders and, despite running a 4:57 final mile, places fifth, sprinting a little early to make sure he finishes ahead of Central Valley's top two runners, Ryan Kline and Romney, four seconds behind him. Rogelio, clearly spent from his fast start, holds on for 19th, but by that point Central Valley and Lewis and Clark each already have three runners cross the line. When Fonzi emerges, in 42nd place, Lewis and Clark have all five of its runners across the finish line; and Central Valley, four runners. The best Eisenhower can hope for at this point is to best Bellarmine Prep for third among 4A division schools. And Angel helps the Cadets' cause by finishing only six spots behind Fonzi. However, it is a long wait for Eisenhower's fifth and final scoring runner, Mo, who places 84th, 16 places behind Bellarmine's fifth runner.

The boys finish sixth overall and fourth among 4A schools—in the spot where they are ranked in the most recent state coaches' poll. But the Eisenhower runners are far from satisfied. Jonas is one of five runners to break the course record (14:45) on this speedy day, but he is not pleased.

He turns to his dad and says, "That kid who won [Hanford's Caleb Olson]? I destroyed him in track [season]."

The elder Price shrugs. He, too, remembers that Jonas had easily beaten the Olson kid last spring during track season.

"Well, what are you gonna do about it?"

Rogelio hovers nearby, still not believing that he ran 15:18, a huge personal record for a three-mile race. Ivan stands next to him, holding out a clipboard on which he charts every time, including mile splits, from every race. He taps his finger on the board to get Rogelio's attention, and when Rogelio's eyes bug out as he sees his time, Ivan breaks into a big grin. "I just tried going with Jonas, be as close as possible," Rogelio says. "It didn't seem that fast, but I'll take it."

Just after crossing the finish line, Fonzi hangs his head. When he emerges from the chute, he rips off his bib number and tosses it. When he finally looks up, tears mix with sweat on his cheeks. His time, 15:44, is 26 seconds slower than his time at Richland last year. So, on a day when most of his teammates set personal records on this course—and Jonas breaks the course record—Fonzi is left wondering what has gone wrong, again.

Schreiber walks him back to the team tent, trying to give the inconsolable Fonzi a pep talk.

"You can't expect to repeat how you ended the season last year in the middle of this season," he says.

Fonzi nods.

"It doesn't work that way. It happened to me when I ran."

Another nod.

"You have to let the season unfold, Fonzi. Look to the next race. It's league. It's [in] Wenatchee, where it's really flat, the easiest course there is. You'll be sub-15 there, I know you will."

Fonzi stares straight ahead. When he reaches the tent, his mother comes to console him as well. He waves her off, and Sonya quickly turns on her heel and returns to where a group of parents stand talking. She should know by now to gauge Fonzi's postrace mood before approaching.

In her mind, her son looked good out there. Sure, he was a dozen or two runners behind where he finished at Richland last year, but how was she to know he was 26 seconds slower?

Back at the tent, Jonas praises Angel's performance—"sub-16, Angel, I told you, I told you that you could do this!"—and Fonzi murmurs, "Great job, Angel." Richland runner Riley Moore, who finished just in front of Jonas in fourth, approaches Eisenhower's tent. Fonzi and Moore had struck up a friendship last fall during cross-country season, when they battled in several meets. They started following each other on Instagram and ran together on cooldowns after several races.

But on this day, Moore heads right to Jonas, standing five feet from Fonzi.

"Meet me back at my tent; we'll cool down," Moore says to Jonas.

"Yeah! OK!" Jonas says.

Fonzi keeps unlacing his shoes. Last year, Moore came up to *him* after races. Now, apparently, he no longer ranks. His mother stops by once more. He sends her away with a shake of the head. Asked about his race, his eyes well.

"It's just . . ." he pauses.

"It's hard for me right now . . ." "comparing what I did last year to this year and . . ."

He turns his head and is unable to finish the sentence.

Schreiber, walking back toward the starting line for the start of the girls' race, isn't sure what to make of Fonzi's slump. During his celebrated Eisenhower career, Schreiber had a few off races, but nothing like this. He concurs with Mister that Fonzi's form still needs some tweaking, but to his way of thinking, there is more wrong.

"Confidence," Schreiber says. "He needs, like, one great race to get it back."

The girls' race, sans Dantzel, is moments away from starting. Making Eisenhower's task tougher is the fact that Erica had a flare-up of an old injury to her right ankle and shin earlier in the day. Mister taped it, but Erica still has problems extending her foot and ankle and pushing off each stride. She remains in the top 10 through two miles but fades badly in the third, limping at several junctures. She finishes 21st in 18:37, 30 seconds faster than the year before, but as Erica brutally notes, she didn't run well the year before either. Molly runs strong, finishing 43rd in a season-best 19:22, but the final three scoring runners for Eisenhower are more than 30 places behind her. The team places 12th out of 17 teams.

On the jouncing bus ride back to Yakima, empty of all but a handful of runners because many had left with parents to get ready for the Homecoming dance, Mister tries to put the performance in perspective.

"I was actually fairly pleased with the boys," he says. "I liked how they competed. They ran well, but the problem was the other teams ran *really* well. We've got our work cut out for us in the next month."

Mister doesn't mention the girls. But a typically blunt four-word comment by Erica sums it up: "We are falling apart."

Two days later, back at practice, nobody talks about the Homecoming dance. Strange, because these teens talk and talk, incessantly, about their lives. Could it be that they are . . . shy? They always are talking, bitching about homework, ranting about who cheated at a video game. But when it comes to romance, they clam up. Jonas, who escorted a freshman, Julie Johnson, to the dance, keeps his distance from her the first day back at practice. Even Fonzi is closed-mouth about his evening courting exchange student Antonia Harrich. Rogelio shows a smartphone photo of himself posing with his date, who is not on the girls' team, but nobody pays it much mind. It is back to the grind, back to thinking about getting ready for the league championships and district finals—and, of course, State.

LEAGUE CHAMPIONSHIPS

The usual pre-practice milling about carries a little extra charge on this afternoon. Ike runners, as is customary, hover near the cubby where, a few minutes before 3 p.m., Mister deposits copies of that day's workout, which they peruse and, almost invariably, commiserate over, especially on days when they would be doing hard interval training. Mister likes to keep them guessing, to ward off complacency, to keep things fresh.

But here it is three weeks before State, the meet the team has been training for all fall, and word has gotten out that Mister has something new planned. Specifically, a new toy. A new science experiment. What are they, runners or lab rats? Talk is that it has something to do with blood testing, again. Not ferritin levels this time, but a gizmo that tests blood levels. Mister has been fiddling with it in his room during the school day, trying to figure out how it works. Will this new training twist distract the runners from the task at hand: to win the league title in a meet scheduled later in the week and then take the district title a week after that before zeroing in on State? Or—and this is what Mister fervently hopes—will the use of cutting-edge technology enhance the training, give Eisenhower an edge on the competition? Whatever it is, Fonzi hopes it won't involve needles. Fonzi hates needles.

When Mister's red truck pulls up near the shed, he emerges with the usual stack of papers (that day's workout) and a small object cupped in his hand. It is the size of a credit card and about as thick as an early-generation iPhone. A cord and an attachment that clamps onto one's index finger dangle from his hand.

"OK, let's get going," he barks, and the runners dutifully trudge to the bleachers for what usually is a brief pre-workout talk. But now, Mister is in teacher mode. He talks about how a British cycling team in last summer's Tour de France used a device, called the Ember, to measure the hematocrit levels of each cyclist before each stage to determine fitness for competing. Testing takes only 90 seconds and gives immediate feedback and, no, Fonzi, it requires no drawing of blood. That article, Mister tells the kids, got him thinking he could use the device to determine the blood oxygenation levels of his runners each day, to know whether they are healthy enough to complete a strenuous workout. It is, he said, the closest thing he can get to real-time readings of ferritin levels, the closest inkling of possible anemia in his runners. So, in the next few days, he says, everyone will stick her or his index finger in the device and get tested.

The team seems satisfied with the explanation. Nods all around. But Mister needs to explain further. Mister wants to pontificate on how important oxygenated red blood cells are to running success. And he has a captive audience.

"Let's take one red blood cell," he continues. "For all the world, it looks like a doughnut without the hole. Obviously, much smaller. And I know Rogelio has no problem imagining this: Imagine that this doughnut is covered with sugar sprinkles. Can you envision that, Rogelio?"

In the first row of the bleachers, Rogelio lowers his head and smiles. Mister winks at him and resumes.

"That's the picture we need in your mind. Those sugar sprinkles: those are the hemoglobin molecules on the outside. These things—and there are literally thousands of them in every red blood cell—they have a strong affinity for oxygen. If oxygen is present, it hooks on to each one of those. So, the number of red blood cells you have and the more sprinkles you have on each red blood cell means you'll have high hemoglobin. The key to making hemoglobin is iron. That's why we have you taking all those supplements. Hematocrit, then, is a percentage of red blood cells you have to the rest of the fluids in your circulatory system. If you take your hemoglobin level, multiply it by three and take it up to the next whole number, that's your hematocrit level. Low hemoglobin is almost always the function of a poor diet. The more you exercise and eat right, the more hemoglobin will increase over a long period of time. The acceptable levels for the kind of exercise we do is 40 for girls and 45 for boys. Anything lower than that, and we've got a problem, might have to adjust your workouts.

No one else is doing this, far as I know, but this can really give us an idea as to where we stand."

The runners squirm in their seats. They have heard enough. But Mister needs to say more, to provide historical context.

"Of course, you've heard about blood-doping in distance runners. What do they do? The old way they did it—the Finnish way, long ago—they'd take blood out of their body and store it."

"Eww," come a few replies from the runners near the back of the bleachers.

"So they would be running two-thirds less blood and training very hard. Then, two weeks before the competition, they put the highly oxygenated blood back in, see, and gave them a big advantage."

Jonas raises his hand, nearly jumping out of his seat.

"Mister, I'd be down to do that."

Price, standing behind Mister, rubs his eyes in mock despair.

"It's *illegal*, Jonas," his dad says.

"Ah, man. I'd be down for that."

"You gotta do what you gotta do for a state trophy," Fonzi kicks in, needling Price.

Mister raises both palms to quell the uprising.

"Back in the '70s, that was the technique," Mister continues. "Then they came up with a chemical way called EPO. It makes red blood cells. Scientists say if you're on EPO, you increase your aerobic ability to deliver oxygen 15 percent. That is gigantic. Huge advantage."

"I totally want to do that, Mister!" Jonas says, jokingly.

"No, no. It's *illegal*."

"There's no testing in high school, Mister. No blood testing. Just sayin'."

"But there's a *moral* aspect to it, Jonas. In any case, we are not doing it."

"He has no morals, Phil," Price cracks.

"Gotta do it for the win, gotta do it for the 'dub,'" Fonzi teases the coaches.

"We will do it the natural way—with a really good diet."

★ ★ ★

After practice, Mister sets up a table in the shed and then opens his laptop to record hemoglobin scores. The device lay next to it. Some runners line up, eager to find out where they stand; others hold back. Dantzel lingers on the periphery and, in the midst of the hubbub of testing, grabs her car keys, hoists her backpack over her shoulder, and ducks out.

Molly, it turns out, is the highest-scoring girl. (Erica is home sick with a chest cold and isn't tested.) Molly's hemoglobin level of 15.9 translates to a hearty 47.7 hematocrit score. "Not surprised," Mister tells her. "You're running well." Kayli Carl, the JV runner who for four years has battled severe anemia and routinely travels to Seattle for iron infusions, scores 14.3, which calculates to 42.9, within the limits.

"You're kidding," she says. "Do you think the infusion affected it, Mister?"

"Oh, I have no doubt."

The boys, of course, make it a competition, as they do with everything. To the highest scorer come bragging rights and the unofficial title of Hematocrit Hulk. Fonzi eyes the device warily and then sticks in his finger. The reading pops up: 17.1. He flexes his biceps, superhero-like. But, as has been the case all season, Rogelio comes out just a bit ahead: 17.9, highest on the team, translating to a 53.7 hematocrit rating.

"Must've been the three tacos and four tamales I had at lunch today," he says.

Jonas then rolls up his sleeve—not needed for the test, but perhaps a show of seriousness—and inserts his finger. The 60 seconds it takes for the score to calculate seem an eternity to Jonas. His teammates ring the table around him, leaning in. They want to see what the fastest kid on the team—and one of the fastest in the state—will score.

Up comes the number: 13.4, lowest on the team.

"Oh. My. Gawd!" Jonas shouts. "Mister, are you gonna limit my workouts? Huh, Mister?"

"Don't worry about it right now, Jonas."

"Let me do it again, Mister. Right now. Let me do it again. I can do better."

"It's not a matter of 'doing better.' The number is what it is."

"Oh my God. I eat, like, tons of protein three times a day. God!"

His teammates laugh, a few slapping Jonas on the back.

Two days later, after practice, Mister keeps his word and retests the runners. Jonas is one of the first in line.

"He's been driving me crazy for two days at home about this thing," the elder Price says. "He's convinced that Phil's going to limit his workouts. I finally just said, 'If you're so worried, call Mister yourself.'"

Jonas's score this time: 17.1, translating to a 51.3 hematocrit percentage. He smiles broadly. "Yeah, baby!" All is right again in Jonas's world. Mister corrals Dantzel for the test. He also takes her aside and weighs her, as she missed a weigh-in a few weeks prior due to illness. She has dropped nearly two pounds, from 116 to 114.3, which actually is encouraging to Mister. He had thought her 5-foot-6 frame had been looking more gaunt than that. Her hemoglobin score, however, registers 13.2, which translates into a hematocrit percentage of 39.6, slightly below the threshold to be held out of workouts.

Even before the scores confirmed it, Mister had decided to hold Dantzel out of the mile repeats and hard fartlek interval sessions, just to give her body time to recover. But she will race in the upcoming league meet. The girls' team needs her.

★ ★ ★

As for the boys' team, Mister has two ongoing concerns.

Jonas and Rogelio are running well, but then there is the continuing case of Fonzi and his flagging confidence, which showed in his poor effort at Richland. Mister still maintains that Fonzi just needs one or two great workouts, in which he would push Jonas and Rogelio, to get his sophomore groove back. That, and vigilance about his running technique, especially his foot plant.

The other concern is getting the boys' pack to move up closer to the top three runners. That "pack-running mentality" is what, to this point, separates Central Valley, Lewis and Clark, and Bellarmine Prep from Eisenhower. Central Valley, for instance, had only a 45-second difference between its first and fifth runners at Richland. Eisenhower: 1 minute 43 seconds.

"Working on their form is the fastest way to close that gap and gain improvement in the time we have left before State. And the thing is, we don't have much time left. This is an important week of heavy training before we cut back."

★ ★ ★

"OK, gentlemen, are you ready to find some religion?"

Mister is in motivation mode on a partly cloudy afternoon at Chesterley Park, arms clasped behind his back, stalking back and forth between the orange cones that serve as the starting line for another dose of six one-mile repeats for the boys' team. The girls are on the other side of the park, running eight 800-meter repeats, this time with Schreiber pacing them.

"Are you ready for a revival meeting?"

The boys are not in a joking mood. They have heard this Mister routine—intervals as religious experience—many times before. They are all business, silent if not sullen, getting ready to deal with the pain of running all out for a full mile six times, with four-minute rest periods between each attempt.

"This first mile, I want you top guys (Jonas, Rogelio, Fonzi) to go 4:50. The rest of you, you can't let the leaders go. You've got to keep near them, get them to pull you through. We've got to work on our gap. You guys ever heard the expression in the UK, 'Mind the gap?' No? Well, remember it. Mind the gap."

The first mile repeat goes almost to Mister's expectation. Rogelio leads the way at 4:44, Jonas one second behind, and Fonzi at 4:51. More important, Angel stays reasonably close, finishing at 5:08, with Mo at 5:10 and Jonathan Valenzuela at 5:11.

But is Mister satisfied?

"You need to *push* each other," he chides. "You're not *competing*. In this workout, these guys are not your friends. Angel, Mo: they hate you. Jonas: they want to knock you off. Rogelio: he'd cut you, man. He is not your friend out here."

Even breathing hard, even with hands on knees, the boys manage smiles.

Jonas and Rogelio pull away in the second and third repeats, with Fonzi holding on and finishing at 5:00 and 5:02, respectively. After the third one, Fonzi collapses, rag-doll-like, to the grass. The runners in the back struggle even more, Diego Vargas staggering to a trash can to throw up not once but three times.

During the break, Mister falls back on his Emotional Intelligence speech. He is pulling out all the stops today in trying to goad the boys into a quality workout.

"Remember, mentally, the EI quotient. If you can endure the pain for six seconds, that feeling will pass, and you'll go to Never-Never Land, where sheep and daisies are. You'll go beyond the pain if you have the Emotional Intelligence to get through it."

And then Mister looks straight at Fonzi.

"You've got to be harder on yourself, Fonzi. Where is that aggressive guy we saw as a sophomore? Where is that guy? You've got to be mad.

You've got to *want* it. You need your eyes on Jonas and Rogelio, eyes stuck on them. Be a hunter, Fonzi."

Fonzi scrunches his brow, runs a hand through the sprouting curls atop his head (he needs a haircut), and nods ever so perceptively. But he still cannot break five minutes in the final three mile repeats.

As the group walks, more like staggering, to the other side of the park to finish the workout with four sets of 800-meter repeats, Mister and Price huddle.

"Fonzi, I think, is close—*this close*—to getting it back," Mister says. "I really think so."

Fonzi is way out of earshot, but it almost seems as if he could hear Mister's prediction. He gains a second wind in the 800 repeats, running stride for stride out front with Rogelio the first two sets and then beating everyone in the final two. As the boys sprawl on the grass and change out of their spikes and back into trainers to jog back to the school, Fonzi seems buoyed by the workout.

"Pain is temporary," he shouts to no one in particular. "Glory is eternal."

The next day, at a team meeting, Mister makes it a point to praise Fonzi, part of his new plan to improve the kid's confidence as much as he keeps trying to improve his running mechanics.

"Yesterday, you looked like the old Fonzi," Mister says. "But you've got to be harder on yourself. Yesterday showed you are back and just as good as last year. In fact, I don't think you had a workout last year as good as the one you had yesterday."

Rogelio punches Fonzi in the arm, and Fonzi beams.

★ ★ ★

The first Saturday of the season without an invitational to run does not mean an easy day for the runners. In fact, Mister and Price have something new planned—a fartlek workout at the school, but not just any fartlek, a "random" fartlek. Price, holding a megaphone, will start and stop the runners at sometimes wildly different times—say, 50 seconds of hard running, then 20 seconds steady state recovery, then 40 seconds hard, 30 seconds recovery, and so forth.

"This is a takeoff on a workout I did with the Kenyans at WSU," Mister says, watching the ebb and flow of effort by his runners as Price blows the horn at random intervals. "They never know when Price is going to hit the siren. It simulates surges in the races where you need to answer that surge or get left behind. You know the recovery is coming, but you don't know when. It's also good to promote pack running. We're going to try to keep them running together as long as possible. I remember doing this workout with the Kenyans at WSU. We did it for 12 miles. God, I hated that workout. But I remember I got really mad and forced myself to go with them until they'd back off the pace. I remember after that workout, the Kenyans said to me, 'Irishman very strong today.' That was the only compliment I ever got out of them."

Then Mister turns his attention to the torture taking place.

Before the second of the four sets of 15-minute random fartleks, Price calls the boys to one side.

"There's no reason why we can't do this Tuesday [at the league meet in Wenatchee], for God's sake," Price said. "You guys need to stay together, run as a pack. No more watching the top three take off. No more riding at the back of the bus."

Mo, the team's lone black runner, feigns outrage. Jonas, too, feigns mock indignation at his dad.

"Hey, that's not right to say," Jonas tells his dad. "I'm the civil rights leader on this team."

The eight Hispanic runners standing behind Jonas howl.

Price turns to his son and says, "No, *you're* the minority on this team, buddy."

Mister is not in a mood to josh, though. All business. He wants the clump of runners going all out to stay a clump, not dissolve into a line of wounded soldiers.

"Don't let them go, Mo!" he shouts. "You can't let them go. Stay with it, Tony. Control. Remember the EI. Six seconds of pain."

The girls have problems running as a pack, and this is without Erica taking it out fast and leaving them behind. Erica has missed a full week of practice with a chest cold. Dantzel, too, is not participating in the workout. Mister feels she still isn't strong enough to run hard, so she slowly jogs laps around the field.

Early in the fourth and final set, Price projects into the megaphone: "Be ready for some surprises . . . because I'm *psychotic!*"

Then he hits the siren for them to pick up the pace and doesn't stop them until a minute has elapsed. Twenty seconds later, he sounds the siren again, and off they go.

Afterward, the runners linger by the shed, assaulted by lassitude borne from a truly hard workout—their last before the league meet in Wenatchee.

Mister and Bryson-Driver made a Costco run a few days ago, and now the kids gorge themselves on microwaved chimichangas and mini-pizza appetizers. Jonas scarfs down a couple of microwave burritos, perhaps worrying about the current state of his hematocrit level.

★ ★ ★

Erica boards the bus for Wenatchee, wearing a mask that extends from under her chin almost to her eyeballs. She still has a rattling cough, but no way is she going to miss her final league meet. After all, she has won league titles as a sophomore and junior, and she has no plans to abdicate her throne due to the common cold. Her father, Eric, pulls his truck up behind the bus 15 minutes before it leaves, knocks on the door, and gives driver Rick Glenn a foot-long Subway sandwich to pass along to his daughter.

"It's sort of a tradition we do for league meets," he says, sheepishly.

Erica says her dad likely will miss these rituals once she graduates. "He's joking that he's going to retire next year," she says, "and he'll drive to wherever I go to college and set up a kitchen and make me pre-meet steak dinners like always, both for me and my new teammates." She rolls her eyes, but it is clear that Erica, too, will miss her dad's daily involvement in her running after all these years.

The boys' team files onto the bus, en masse, all wearing masks like a gang of Old West outlaws. Fonzi is silent, staring straight ahead. Jonas takes off his mask and grabs a Jimmy John's sandwich his mom has dropped off. Extra meat for the hemoglobin.

Eisenhower is the overwhelming favorite to keep both of its league winning streaks—10 years for the girls, 9 for the boys—intact, but Mister is taking nothing for granted. He doesn't like the blasted wind that is supposed to buffet Wenatchee that afternoon, 30 miles an hour with gusts up to 50. And though he isn't fretting about winning, he is fretting about how his runners will perform. Specifically, will Fonzi bounce back from the Richland disappointment following a strong week of workouts? Will the boys' fourth and fifth runners stay close to the leaders and narrow the gap? Will Dantzel regain the form that, earlier in the season, made her the team's No. 2 runner?

The afternoon begins on a positive note. Despite a sometimes dicey bus ride through the wind-tossed Columbia basin, the team arrives at the course on the banks of the Wenatchee River to find strong but hardly daunting winds. Things continue to brighten when the JV races produce two individual victories for Eisenhower. Senior Diego Vargas easily wins the boys' JV race, leading Mister to lament once more that he wishes he had the kid, who would graduate in a few short months, for another year because he could turn him into a standout varsity runner. And, in a surprise to everyone, especially herself, Kayli Carl wins the girls' JV race. It is an emotional moment for Kayli, who wasn't even sure she'd be able to compete at all due to her chronically low ferritin levels and her many forays into Seattle for treatment. But just a few days after her latest infusion—and after acing Mister's hematocrit test—Kayli holds off a Wenatchee runner in the final sprint to win the first race of her life. She raises her arms at the finish line and, after breaking the tape, wraps it around her neck like a scarf.

"I can't believe I won," she keeps repeating. "I'm so happy. It feels so good to feel good enough to run hard. I mean, it's great to feel tired during the race—the normal tired, from running hard, not the fatigue from not having energy from low iron."

No surprises in the girls' varsity race. Erica dominates, taking the lead near the one-mile mark and cruising from there. Molly finishes a strong third overall, a personal best, and Madi and Sophi both run sub-20 minutes to crack the top 10. Eisenhower has a wait for its fifth runner, Dantzel, to finish, and she labors to the line in 14th place at 20:31—1 minute 20 seconds slower than she ran on this course the year before.

Jonas, no longer freaked by his hematocrit level, dominates the boys' race almost as thoroughly as Erica did in the girls' competition. But the real race takes place behind him.

Two Eisenhower runners, early on, easily secure the second and third positions. But here is the change: Almost from the starting gun, Fonzi goes out strongly, a full five meters ahead of Rogelio. Only this time, Fonzi does not fade. In fact, he gains strength as the race progresses, gaining five seconds on Rogelio at the two-mile mark. Mister jogs to various parts of the course, exhorting Fonzi to "keep your eyes up" and "plant that foot, push off." Heading into the home stretch, Fonzi's arms pump, his knees lift, and his eyes are focused not on the clock ticking off the seconds but on the finishing chute. He beats Rogelio by eight seconds for second place, the first time he has bested Rogelio all season. More encouraging to Mister is that Fonzi's time of 15:38 is three seconds *faster* than his time on this course the previous year, when he had his breakout season.

So, is Fonzi back?

Mister is cautiously optimistic. "I think he's peaking at the right time," he says. "He'll need another couple of good workouts before State to convince him of that."

Back at the team tent, Fonzi is animated, joking with Jonas and trying to cheer up Mo, who had a poor race and was beaten by Jesus for the No. 5 spot among Ike runners. When someone tells the boys of their times, Fonzi raises an eyebrow at his 15:38—he knows to the millisecond what he ran the year before—and Rogelio turns to him and pokes him in the shoulder once more.

On the bus ride back to Yakima, in the pitch dark, Fonzi's voice echoes through the otherwise silent bus. He is rapping. Then he is regaling seatmates with tales of learning to drive and his mom's freak-out at his early attempts. Then he helps a couple of girls with some math homework.

"Nah, nah, it's easy, you're almost there," his voice rings out. "Just move the decimal point and round up. Yeah. Easy."

On this night, at long last, things have come easily for Fonzi. He has missed that feeling, and now he wants to make sure it will stay.

POSTSEASON

DISTRICTS

State is two weeks away. State looms. State is on everybody's mind, the expressed reason behind the increasingly taxing workouts the runners endure. State becomes the subtext for every word coming from Mister's mouth.

State, too, means adopting some drastic measures, such as this whole surgical mask-wearing thing that Mister now strongly enforces for everyone, lest any stray germs invade the sanctity of the team's collective body and, insidiously, result in a chest cold or the flu at the very time his runners need to be at full strength, inviolable, tuned up like a performance race car.

Heading into the postseason, then, the Eisenhower runners don masks, much to the bafflement (and amusement) of many of their classmates. Well, actually, not so much bafflement. By this time, most Ike students know that the masks mean it is getting on to the end of October, a time when many dress up for Halloween but the cross-country kids always cover their faces with masks like patients in a 19th-century tuberculosis ward. One might suspect that, if Mister had his way, he would quarantine the team for these final two weeks leading to the state meet, keep them hermetically sealed, only to be unwrapped each afternoon for practice.

But there is this thing called school, and Mister really is all about education first. It's just that, you know, teenagers spending seven hours a day at an enclosed campus, well, they could turn the place into a petri dish of contagion. So, two days before the District 9 meet that would determine the qualifiers for State, the boys' and girls' teams take masks from a fresh box Mister opened after the morning practice and dutifully comply. They are allowed to take off the masks to eat breakfast, of course, and on this morning, the boys and girls at their usual conjoined tables scarf down cereal, bananas, breakfast burritos, and an egg-and-sausage sandwich concoction so stale that when Molly drops it on the table, it thuds.

In the half-hour lull between the end of school breakfast and the start of first period, most runners congregate in Room 633 of the science wing—Mister's room. There, they study and chat, store their running backpacks, and raid the refrigerator in the back—a separate fridge, it must be noted, from the one in which Mister keeps science experiments. Jonas and Nathan watch a YouTube video on one of Mister's laptops; Dantzel, sitting next to Oscar Mendoza, reads a book and nibbles on a bagel; Diego sits off by himself, engrossed in the screen of his phone; Rogelio, Erica, and Kayli study the spinal column of a skeleton in preparation for their fourth-period anatomy quiz in this very classroom; and Fonzi reaches into his backpack to take out his notebook and packet to cram for a second-period psychology test.

"Dang," he says. He brings both hands to the side of head in disbelief, his teammates at first thinking he is joking again. "I left the notebook at home. I think I'll be all right. I'll remember it."

But the longer Fonzi sits there on a stool with furrowed brow, the more anxious he becomes. He starts shaking his right foot, clad in a black Converse All-Star, and looking for help from both directions. Then he spots Jonathan Valenzuela, who sits next to him in psych class. Jonathan tosses Fonzi flashcards he had written the night before to try to memorize neuroanatomy.

"Frontal lobe," Fonzi reads off the card. Then he closes his eyes and blurts out, "Emotional control."

"Temporal lobe . . . the center for auditory."

"Occipital . . ."

And here Fonzi scans the room, catching Molly's attention. She bugs out her eyes, a hint.

"Your vision!" Fonzi exclaims.

"Parietal lobe . . . I got this—memory!"

One by one, the runners trickle out and head to first period. Only Jonas and freshman Julia Johnson stay, because they are taking Mister's first-period biology class. Jonas sits at the far end of the first row, his mask covering half of his neck and nearly hooding his eyes. None of his classmates give him a second glance. He is wearing his usual school attire—a Nike Oregon Project sweatshirt, jeans, and a shiny pair of Nike Pegasus running shoes that look fresh out of the box. He exhumes a three-ring binder from his Nike Oregon Project backpack and opens it to the sheet of paper on which he had scribbled the lab results from the previous day's measurement of pectin in applesauce. But before he can review it, the bell pings, and a female voice rings out from the speaker over the room's door. After the Pledge of Allegiance, student announcements commence: the debate team has a meeting; the diving team is holding tryouts; the newly inducted National Honors Society members are congratulated.

Then comes this: "Thursday at Franklin Park, Eisenhower hosts the Big 9 District cross-country championships. Will Erica Simison defend her district title from last year? Can anyone beat Eisenhower super sophomore Ronan Price . . ."

Jonas pulls down his mask and groans, "Oh. My. Gawd."

Mister laughs. The announcement has mistaken Jonas's older brother, since graduated, for him.

What Jonas does not know is that Mister has written that announcement himself and e-mailed it to the school office. He eventually confesses his mistake to Jonas.

Mister the teacher is pretty much the same in demeanor as Mister the coach. The man brooks no nonsense in his class. When he points to the jugular notch or the hyoid bone at the head of the spinal column during an anatomy lecture, students had better be quick with an answer. Those two girls in the back chatting during a presentation regarding the scapula are silenced with little more than an arched eyebrow and the admonition, "On my time! If I'm talking, you're not." In the classroom, though, he often ratchets down the intensity and lets his softer side emerge. When a girl in the back stares at the skeleton and asks, "Do only males have a coccyx?" Mister barks out a laugh.

"I've been teaching this course for 26 years and have never been asked this question," he says. "The answer is, yes. That reminds me. One question I get asked a lot is: Is there one less rib in the female body? The answer is no."

Mister's quirky side shows itself in his penchant for adding weird, off-topic extra-credit questions to tests. His extra-credit question on this day: "Let's say you go to college, and let's say you want to major in something unusual, not business. You could major in limnology. That's the question: What is limnology?" Blank stares and poised pens from the students, but then Mister goes easy on them and makes it a multiple-choice question: "A: The study of glaciers in Lima, Peru; B: The study of the features of

fresh water; C:The study of the pee of milking cows—milking cows only."
Two-thirds of the class choose the correct answer—"B"—and Mister
playfully chides a brash boy slouching in the back row who admits he
went with Lima's nonexistent glaciers.

"Really?" he tells the student. "*Really?* You guys, c'mon."

This is Mister in mentor mode. Partly compassionate, partly challenging. All caring. And in the days leading to the District 9 meet, the
cross-country team will see other sides of Mister too. Namely, Mister the
father confessor, the former altar boy turned nurturing quasi-parental figure who cares more about a runner's health than performance, and Mister
the rabid drill sergeant, who shows flashes of that famous Irish temper.

★ ★ ★

"Dantzel, where are we with the eating?"

"What do you mean, Mister? I eat every day."

Mister runs a hand across his jowly cheeks, exhales. He wants to
ease into this latest conversation with Dantzel—and a conversation he
most assuredly wants it to be, not a confrontation or inquisition. In the
week following the league meet, he and Bryson-Driver have mulled over
holding what the two call "an intervention" regarding Dantzel's general
sloth on and off the racecourse, her weight loss (three pounds in as many
weeks), and reports that she has been dumping food at lunch in the school
cafeteria. Most troubling is a report Mister received from two of Dantzel's
teammates and a mother of a runner concerning Dantzel's behavior at a
girls' team bonding dinner at Sophi's house the night before the league
finals. The girls dined on baked potatoes, with taco meat, cheese, sour
cream, vegetables, and condiments, and cheesecake served for dessert. Mister had been told that Dantzel ate a few bites of her potato, excused herself
to go to the bathroom, returned shortly thereafter, and dumped the rest
of it, leaving early.

Given that information, it is no surprise to Mister, after the fact, that
Dantzel had run poorly in the league meet. He would need an energized
Dantzel at Districts and State, but more important, he wants a healthy
Dantzel for the sake of Dantzel's health. He is worried, too, that in a con-
versation with her last week, Dantzel had told him that she fasted one day
a month (the first Sunday) as an observance of her Mormon faith.

"I'll even consider not letting her run if we can't get this under control," he tells Bryson-Driver as he walks to the fitness lab, where the girls'
team is doing drills.

The three meet in an office adjacent to the lab. Dantzel sits with her arms crossed, her left leg slung over her right. She stares at the drab gray carpeting. When Mister brings up the potato report, Dantzel denies it. She says she ate most of the potato and had to leave early for violin rehearsal with the Yakima Youth Symphony.

"Dantzel, I think you're tricking yourself into thinking you are eating nutritiously when in fact you are not. Would you agree with that?"

The tone he adopts exhibits both tenderness and resolve, a tricky combination for someone normally as blunt-spoken as Mister.

"I think I'm eating. It's not like I skip meals."

"But what I'm hearing from other people, kids and others, is that you're dumping your lunch."

Dantzel quickly uncrosses her legs and then recrosses them. She kneads her left calf, digging her thumb deep into the tissue. Then she looks Mister in the eye.

"Well, I'm not a snake, first of all. But I could turn this on all those other girls. I watch all the other girls, and I don't tell on them. Because I'm not the only one. But I *am* the one that has all the flak. But there are other girls that do the same thing."

"They are concerned about you."

"Nobody on this team eats perfectly, Mister."

"You are right, nobody's perfect. Listen, you're an honest person and great kid, but sometimes I don't think you're honest with yourself. Would you agree with that?"

She rolls her eyes.

"Sure."

"No, either you agree or you wouldn't. If you wouldn't, please tell me, why?"

"OK, I know sometimes I'm not honest with myself."

"Do your parents talk to you about eating as well?"

She smiles. "Oh, everyone does!"

"Does your mom do the cooking at home?"

"Yeah."

Bryson-Driver leans forward and asks, "And your mom is vegan, right?"

"She's 89 percent vegan. We don't eat a lot of meat. We just eat vegetables and beans."

"So, if you want meat, do you have to cook it yourself?" Mister asked.

"Yeah. Well, sometimes [her mom] does, but we have to get it out of the freezer."

"Who is 'we'?"

"Me."

"Is it possible for your mother to have meat there almost every night?"

"This is what she'd say: 'My daughter is *available* to meat every day. She just has to cook it herself.' Somewhere in the freezer, I'm sure there's some meat. We're just not a meat family. I'm less apt, in my busy schedule, to be like, 'OK, I'll pull out this chicken and cook it, whatever.' I don't think about it, and I don't want to waste my time spending more time eating food."

"She won't cook it for you, your mom?"

"It's hard for her to cook something she's not going to eat. Especially when I first joined cross-country. The consumption of food that I'm supposed to eat compared to what she's supposed to eat is, like, opposite."

A pause, not so much awkward as fraught with tension, ensues.

"So, what's the way forward, long term, Dantzel? What's the solution?"

"I don't know. I don't know how to consume more than I'm already consuming."

"What about changing the content of the food?"

"That would be a lot more time than what I'm already taking out of an already busy day. I'm an AP student. Think about it. I get home at 6:30 [p.m.]. If I want to be home at a reasonable hour, that's not that much time, by the time I take a shower and do my honors and AP homework. Cook my own food? It's hard to find time to do everything."

"That's probably the issue. You have all these things you want to do. Something has to give, and what has been given up is your eating. Think of it this way: The violin is your instrument of choice. What if I taped your three middle fingers together for tonight's performance? What would you say to that? Do you think you'd be able to play proficiently?"

"For orchestra? Of course not."

"But now I want you to compare that to not eating enough and running. That's the comparison. You wouldn't dream of having me tape your fingers, would you? But the same should be true for your running. You are talented, but that talent has been totally suppressed because you are not fueling the body. In that way, you are not being honest with yourself."

Dantzel keeps kneading her left calf.

Bryson-Driver: "Not fueling your body, Dan, is also impacting your violin and your studying and classes as well. It's not just impacting your running. The reason you haven't bounced back from being ill is that you aren't bringing in enough energy. Your body is having a hard time healing itself because it's tired.

If you take the time when you get home to make something of quality to eat, you'll make up that time in energy for study time and violin time."

The meeting has lasted a half hour. Mister starts to sum up.

"There's nothing that we're going to say that will change where you are right now. The only thing I can say is that you need to be honest with yourself. I think you are an honest person with people, but I don't think you're honest with yourself. Every night, going forward, we're going to feed you meat here after practice, maybe some type of soup. There will be times when I say, 'You're not leaving until you eat this particular thing.' It's not punishment. Don't take it as that. OK?"

"OK."

"OK then. You're the best. Be happy, Dantzel."

The three walk out together.

Later, after the workout, Mister microwaves her a bowl of chicken noodle soup. Dantzel takes it from him without comment. She eats.

★ ★ ★

Mister manages to hold it together, barely, as he watches the boys' varsity run the first of the six mile repeats, the last really hard workout of the season. He has told the guys as much as they line up at the orange cones. Last. Hard. Workout. He is hoping it might inspire them to run in a pack and stay close to Jonas, Rogelio, and Fonzi up front. Eisenhower's only chance of improving on its No. 5 ranking and making the podium will be if its fourth and fifth runners, most likely Angel and Mo, can close the gap and finish closer in time and place to the top three. They hadn't done so at the league meet, prompting Mister to muse in a subsequent team meeting that Central Valley and Lewis and Clark certainly didn't have a minute, or a minute and a half, gap between their first and fifth runners. Eisenhower shouldn't either.

But now, here come the leaders, Rogelio, Jonas, and Fonzi, around the final turn in the first mile, but where are the others? It is just a mile, for heaven's sake, not even a three-mile cross-country race, and here comes Mo some 20 seconds behind the top three. And finally, near the back, comes Angel, Ike's fourth runner all season, a full 30 seconds behind the front-runners.

Mister watches the stragglers finish and then lowers his head and stomps on the grass back to the starting line. His nostrils flare, bull-like. His face flushes. Here is a man ready to explode. And when he does, it comes all in a rush, loud and menacing.

"If you don't do it here, you're not going to do it in the meet," he says, not quite yet at full volume. "And that's all we've seen. After the state meet, you guys'll need to explain to each other why you COUGHED it up. This is it! There is no other practice. THIS. IS. IT. What are you waiting for? You guys drop off again, we're going to send you to the 8s [800 meters, with the girls' team]. There's no other point in doing this. This has to have a quality to it."

He pauses and scans the boys up and down the line. Only Jonas and Mo make eye contact. This seems to set Mister off even more. He gesticulates wildly, as if he might take flight at any moment.

"Stop thinking about how HARD it is," he yells. "Put your mind in a place that makes you competitive."

Then he focuses on Angel, who scuffs at the grass with his spikes.

"Angel, you've got to explain to your teammates why you are a half minute behind," he says. "You're not even *trying*. You are making *no* effort. You're the strongest kid here. Get your eyes on Rogelio and *stay* with him."

As Price starts counting down to the start of the second mile, Mister sends them on their way with a final thought ringing in their ears: "There's nothing left after this! This is your last chance!"

The second and third mile repeats go slightly better for the pack. Mister is far from satisfied. If they run like this at State two weeks hence, they won't have a prayer. And, even though he senses his team knows it, as well, it needs to be verbalized. Mister lowers the volume before the fourth mile.

"This is state meet *simulation*," he says. "You've got to start thinking about *team* and not *yourself*, not how much you are hurting. Just use technique and drive your arms. Get past the hurting. Think: Team. Team. Team."

At least three runners get the message—not the three Mister was worried about. Fonzi, Jonas, and Rogelio run together and log their second-fastest mile of the afternoon, 4:52. The rest of the pack lags behind. Mister hustles over to the far side of the field, about 600 meters in, and spurs them on. When Angel passes, gait flagging, Mister crosses his arms.

"Right now you are No. 8, Angel," he yells. "You are a No. 4 runner. Get moving."

Before the sixth and final mile, even the top three runners are spent. Fonzi had collapsed in a heap after finishing the fifth mile and was still breathing hard as he walked back to the starting line. Angel clutched both sides of his rib cage. Even Jonas, who normally tries to goad his teammates to finish the interval workout strongly, seems too tired to exhort. Mister, however, is not.

He loses his temper once more, speaking so rapidly and loudly that saliva flies out. He is, to coin a phrase, spitting mad.

"Guys, a lot of you are refusing to let your mind go where you need to be to run hard," he shouts. "A mile left in the state meet, and you are just playing it safe, just doing self-preservation, just going for the least amount of pain possible. If you don't let your mind go there, then we've lost the battle. You have to be willing to go out hard and get past the pain in the state meet. That last mile means everything. Are you going to be there?"

Price has already counted down and sent off the runners, but Mister isn't finished. He cups his hands around his mouth and shouts at their retreating figures, "Don't be afraid of it! Don't be afraid of it!"

"They've got to somehow believe they can do it," he says, voice hoarse but softening now. "That's our only hope. We'll see how they respond at Districts."

★ ★ ★

Smartphone poised, its camera zooming in on the crouching figure of her daughter at the starting line, Eric Simison has no time to think that this will be Erica's final race at Franklin Park, that it will be the last time he will see her traversing the rolling hills and chugging up the steep terrace, that after today he will not enjoy the sight of watching her turn the corner and fly down the finishing chute, usually in the lead.

He will contemplate all that later. Right now he is just concerned about getting the start perfectly focused on the video. He wants to preserve the moment and add to the family's vast collection of footage and photographs of Erica from the past 11 years, from that picture of the tiny seven-year-old at the Sunfair Invitational to today's attempt to defend her district title.

His finger hovers over the red button, shaking just a little. And when the starter's gun sounds, Eric taps the phone, guiding it left to right as the runners take off, en masse, along a grassy embankment.

"Go get 'em!" he shouts, but with the crowd noise, the pistol-shot reverb, and the pounding of footsteps, Eric knows she probably didn't hear his encouraging words. Perhaps it does not matter. Perhaps Eric is saying it as much for himself as for his daughter.

Immediately after the runners flee into the distance, Eric hustles to his next spot on the course: along the gentle downhill backstretch that the runners will traverse three times before finishing. Most spectators gather on the side closest to the start area, but Eric always heads to the far side, where no parents or coaches will either block his view or outshout him. Properly positioned, he takes out his phone again and peers up the hill, awaiting the pack. When the pack starts heading toward him, Eric feels a brief jolt of panic. "Where's Erica?" he says to no one in particular. She usually is out front. He scans the runners, still about 40 feet away, and, momentarily, cannot find her. The red singlet of a runner from Moses Lake, Camille Carpenter, is out front, and Davis senior Ada Naranjo, runner-up to Erica last year, is in second. Erica, meanwhile, has positioned herself to the far right and is cruising in third place, a step or two behind the leaders. Eric hits the red button.

"Let's go, babe!" he yells to her as the pack whizzes by.

Eric turns to a guy next to him and shakes his head.

"Boy, that Moses Lake girl," he says. "She took it out the same way last week [in the league meet] and died, but it still, it gets to me, that sight . . ."

The next time the runners emerge, the red singlet has faded. Now it is just Erica and Ada, who have raced each other since junior high, running in sync, step for step.

"OK," Eric says, tugging on his ball cap. "Here we go."

He watches from a distance as the two runners start climbing the steep terrace that leads to the one-mile mark. Slowly, incrementally, Erica puts some space between her and Ada. By the time she crests the hill, Erica has a 10-meter lead and is pulling away. Eric rushes back to the backstretch to reposition himself, but his wife, Pam, pauses. She seems pleased.

"Well, Erica's in a good position now. It's good she had somebody to race with that first mile."

"Erica tends to pull away from Ada on hills because Ada doesn't recover from the climb as well as Erica," Eric says.

When Erica makes the second pass by him, Eric keeps the smartphone camera on her and yells, "That's a girl, babe. Keep it up." He allows himself a brief smile now, a smile of relief and of pride. Even this early in the race, before even the second mile, Erica has things well in hand. So Eric stays put in his viewing position. He is worried, frankly, about the rest of the team. Molly passes by him in eighth place and Dantzel in 15th.

"Let's go, Dan!" he shouts.

"Does Davis have their third runner before us?" he asks two men next to him. "We can't lose Districts in Erica's senior year. We can't."

Just then, Sophi and Madi, Eisenhower's fourth and fifth runners, the final two team scorers, pass, in the middle of a large pack.

"They've gotta be farther up," Eric mutters, then pumps his fist and shouts, "Sophi, Madi, you gotta go. Now!"

The final mile turns out to be something of a victory lap for Erica. When she passes Eric on the back straightaway, she has perhaps a 200-meter lead on Ada.

"Good job, babe," Eric yells. "Close hard."

Then Eric notices that Molly and Dantzel have moved up considerably on the field, and he breathes a little easier.

"Think we'll be all right," he says; then he takes off for the finish line to witness Erica's coronation.

By the time Eric positions himself three feet from the finish line, the PA announcer intones, "And around the corner comes our leader, Eisenhower senior Erica Simison, at about 18:05 . . ."

The proud dad beams. His smartphone follows Erica all the way to the finish, as several hundred people lining both sides of the finish line cheer. Erica finishes 29 seconds ahead of Ada, her time of 18:41 a 25-second personal record. Then Eric turns and walks away—opposite where Erica will emerge from the finisher's chute in a minute.

Breathing hard but walking briskly, Erica makes her way back to the finish line area to see how her teammates fared. She is stopped along the way by parents and students congratulating her. A school board member, Don Davis Jr., in a three-piece pinstriped suit, high-fives her. But Erica is preoccupied.

"How'd we do? Did we win? I saw Davis girls behind me. Are we OK? Did we win?"

Eisenhower has, indeed, won its seventh straight district title, thanks to a third-place finish by Molly, an improved 11th-place run by Dantzel, followed by Sophi in 13th and Madi in 17th.

"Thank God!" Erica says, when informed the team title is assured. "Where's my dad? I bet he's off somewhere crying."

Back at the team tent, Pam Simison has a surprise for her daughter: a new puppy, a French bulldog that Erica immediately names Winston. The family has two pugs at home, but this one will be Erica's dog. She seems infinitely more excited about Winston than about winning another district title.

★ ★ ★

Whatever the boys' race lacked in obvious drama—by the first mile, Eisenhower has positioned itself with a big team lead, Jonas already gapping the field—it makes up for in several intriguing subplots that Mister is eyeing with interest.

How will Angel and Mo, his fourth and fifth scorers, fare? Will they go out aggressively and try to maintain and finish strongly, or will they hold back, play it timidly, and then scramble madly to make up ground and pick off runners?

And which Fonzi will show up: the strong, confident runner who placed second behind Jonas the previous week at the league meet or the tentative competitor from earlier in the season who battled shin pain and an acute crisis of confidence? The fact that Fonzi, despite the mask wearing, is fighting another cold and vomited the night before, does not bode well.

On those counts, Mister doesn't like what he sees early on. Fonzi has let Jonas and Rogelio go in the first 800 meters and is barely leading West Valley's talented freshman Brayden Packard nearing the first major climb, the terraces. Halfway up, though, Packard passes Fonzi and opens up a five-meter lead.

"It almost looks like Fonzi's stopped running," Mister says. "He gave up—right there."

Things aren't looking much better for Angel and Mo in the first mile. Angel was 16th and Mo 19th at the one-mile mark, far behind where Mister wants them at that juncture. If they don't pick up the pace, and pronto, Eisenhower's eight-year reign as district champions could well end.

Mister's body language speaks volumes: arms crossed, eyes narrowed.

But things do improve, somewhat. Fonzi never catches Packard, but neither does he fall apart. He is obviously struggling, as the grimace on his face shows, but he easily holds onto a fourth-place finish—two seconds slower than his time on the same course at Sunfair a month earlier. And Angel and Mo, as they often do, rally in the final mile. By the second-mile mark, Angel has moved to 10th and Mo, 17th place. On the final straightaway, both start passing runners, Angel slithering by stealthily while opponents can definitely hear long-legged Mo stalking them from behind. Angel's ninth-place finish and Mo's 13th easily clinch the victory for Eisenhower. It is not the strong "pack-running" performance Mister was shooting for going into State, but it will do. When he pauses to analyze the results, Mister notices that four of his top five runners had set PRs on a difficult Franklin course, the only slower finisher being the ill Fonzi. Jonas's time of 15:37 is the fifth fastest in Eisenhower history on the course.

Once the heat of competition simmered, and Mister had a chance to reflect on what he witnessed, he felt more encouraged. He may even have been caught smiling a few times.

"The times weren't stellar across the board, which is a good thing," he says. "They weren't supposed to be after doing the hardest workout of the year on Monday [three days before]. It's still a fairly dominant performance. Everything these past two weeks has been geared toward State. There have been years when we ran so-so at Districts and then did very well at State. We're cutting back now on our training for State. Their bodies are going to be so much recovered. They'll see what it's like to run with fresh legs. I guarantee you they'll feel the difference."

Lingering near the podium, Mister's mood brightens even more. He catches sight of Dantzel nibbling on a paper plate of street tacos her parents have brought her. She ambles over, slyly smiling and offering up the plate.

"Here, Mister, you need to eat," she says, smiling.

Mister takes a taco and bites into it lustily.

After the formal awards ceremony, both Eisenhower teams, in possession of the championship trophies and hoisting the gnome aloft, clamber atop the awards podium for a group photo—all 32 blue-clad runners grinning madly, some flashing victory signs and others trying not to let Mister see them horsing around.

"That's a pretty good picture there now, isn't it?" Mister says with customary understatement.

As the runners scramble back down off the podium, someone drops Dwight the gnome. The mascot's left arm—the one with the taped wrist and message "courage" written across it—snaps off.

"Hope that doesn't mean we've lost our courage," Price jokes.

"Ivan, you gotta fix it before State," Jonas implores, not amused in the slightest.

"I didn't break it," Rogelio offers, when teammates point the finger at him. "Nobody saw me break it."

Not even the gnome's injury can dampen Eisenhower's spirits. Whatever might happen a week hence in Pasco, they can take pride in knowing that both teams have once again defended their turf and won yet another district title.

STATE

The bus doors whoosh open, sounding like a nervous exhalation, and the Eisenhower teams file out to see . . . a mostly deserted golf course in the early stages of being transformed, by the next morning, into the nexus of cross-country in the state.

Mister, as usual, has gotten the team to the Sun Willows Country Club at least five hours before most of the hundred other teams that will compete at State arrive to check in and check out the course. Got to get the lay of the land before too many teams crowd them. Got to walk all 16,404 feet of the 5K course, which at this early stage is marked only with a white chalk stripe and not the flagging that will guide runners at race time. Got to point out every undulation, every indentation, every slight slant in topography and every change of surface. Got to point out when to surge and when to hold back, when to swing wide and cut inside on turns and when to run a straight Euclidean line, the shortest point possible. Got to pick up the race bib numbers and other official materials before the horde descends. And, as tradition dictates, got to reserve the same spot on the driving range to make homesteading claim and erect the team tents, the on-course base of operations for the next two days.

Only a half dozen other tents are up by the time Eisenhower arrives and, thank goodness, no one has dared to take Ike's usual spot—just to the right of the 175-yard ball marker.

At other, less high-profile races, Mister usually hands over the boys' team course-walking duties to Price. But for State, he does it himself. And he is typically precise and exacting, right down to the number of warm-up strides the boys should do at the start area (5) and the type of joke that Rogelio, team cutup, should tell just before the gun (something clean and appropriate, but funny enough to quell the guys' nerves).

"OK, everyone got golf balls? Good. Let's go."

Ike runners will not, of course, be playing golf here. Mister decides to go public with this training exercise the team has performed in secret most of the season, the gambit of placing a golf ball under runners' chins as they run either up or down hills to promote forward lean. He figures some coaches might look at this unusual practice and wonder, *What's that crazy Irishman doing this time?* But Mister likes the golf-ball drill. It works. Helps the runners' form, keeping their chins down. And here at State, he knows the boys will need every advantage if they hope to improve their station and make the podium.

"See that little downhill up there?" he says, pointing to an undulation several hundred feet away. "You can't blast down that. Too soon. It's all about saving energy that first mile."

And with that, Mister takes off, jogging the course, his team like a pack of ducklings following behind.

"Hey, Mister, *arms!*" somebody in the back, maybe Jesus, chides the coach, just as Mister is always on the boys' case about arm swing.

"Oh, it's much too late for me," he says, smiling.

Then he turns serious.

"We've got some rolling up and downs, so take the golf balls and do a few repeats on these. The whole purpose is to give you a feel for what your body needs to do at this point in the course."

On it goes for the next two miles, about 45 minutes of running commentary, interspersed with some hill repeats and drills just off the greens. It isn't all strategizing, though. Mister has stories to impart, tales of past triumphs meant to inspire or serve as a cautionary tale for the boys.

At the one-mile mark: "See this tree, right at this turn when you'll run toward this massive, screaming mob of fans? This was where back in Robbie Barany's senior year [early 2000s], he got caught too far inside— be careful of that—and he had to hurdle over the race worker who was still putting up the flagging."

At a long stretch that parallels a fence separating the driving range from a fairway: "Run wide, on the outside, because there are ruts. I remember one year, one of the Dominguez brothers stepped in a hole and rolled his ankle. Stay clear of that."

At the crest of a hill approaching the two-mile mark: "If you're feeling good at this point, you can pick up a lot of time. When Aleah Thome won the state title [1994], she was running head-to-head with the other girl for the lead. She used this stretch to surge and open a 20-second lead. The race was over. She won."

At a dogleg before the 2.5-mile mark: "At this stage, you will be tired. It was here in 2010, when [German] Silva, [Timothy] Cummings, and [Santos] Vargas were spent, absolutely dead on their feet from going out too fast. That's when Jaziel Rodriguez passed them. And the reason we won the state title was because, through effort, those three dead runners pressed on. They showed tremendous EI and got past the pain and followed in Jaziel to the finish. If you're not feeling it here tomorrow, remember that. Emotional Intelligence for six seconds, get beyond the discomfort."

Rather than furtively rolling their eyes at Mister's EI-6 pronouncement, the boys nod like novices learning the tricks of the trade. There is very little smack talk or bravado, false or otherwise, among the guys on this walk-through. They jog behind Mister and take his words to heart.

It isn't all fond memories from Mister either. He imparts specific advice to specific runners. Since Jonas's stated goal is to win the individual title, Mister makes it a point during his stops to tell him what position among the field he should be in at that juncture. For most of the course, Mister advises him simply to stay in the lead pack, biding his time and showing a patience that sometimes eludes him. But when the group stops at a dirt-road crossing at 2.5 miles, Mister catches his breath and looks Jonas in the eye.

"Cross this road, Jonas, and take the race over from Maton, right here," he says, referring to Camas High's star, Daniel Maton. "Maton will go with you initially on that hill, but you've got to keep pushing and break him. Then, on the downhill, you've got to fly. This is where Fonzi took advantage last year. He just flew."

Jonas nods. Fonzi, to Mister's right, stares into the distance. Mister has no grand strategy for Fonzi and Rogelio for State, other than to stay as close to the lead pack as possible throughout and finish in the top 20, at least.

Quite frankly, Mister is more worried about Angel and Mo, his fourth and fifth runners, the all-important final scorers and, perhaps, the difference between a third- or fifth-place finish. If Angel can keep within striking distance of Fonzi and Rogelio, the team will be in good shape. And Mister is hopeful. Angel currently is in the best shape of his four years on the team, but he has this nagging habit of losing focus—"spacing out"—during races. And Mo? Well, he tells Mo he needs to start picking up the pace halfway through the second mile, not near the end. Such a late rallying, Mister tells Mo, might work in the league or District meets. Not so at State, where the swift competition will bury him early if he doesn't maintain contact.

"This is the part I call 'Reality Check Hill,'" Mister says, looking at Angel and Mo. "Turn around and look at how much you've gained getting to here. Now, Angel and Mo, this is the time to move. You've got to be racing these rollers, running hard. I want to see you passing guys along this stretch."

Eventually, Mister jogs them to the high point, the crest of the final hill. They stop and stare at the finish line arch 50 meters down below. He doesn't speak for a long while. Everyone stares at the banner reading, simply, *FINISH*. Finally, Mister breaks the spell.

"This is where EI-6 is key, getting you over the top," he says. "OK, put in the golf balls and run that last downhill and see the finish line."

See the finish, he means, not run through it. The boys know it is bad luck to cross the finish line during a walk-through. Mister stays behind and joins the girls, whose walk-through is led by Price and Bryson-Driver. He repeats the EI talk before the girls, too, run down the final hill and then repair back to the team tent.

Mister tries to make it back to the tent promptly. But, as usual, he keeps being stopped by people he knows. Fellow coaches, mostly, but also race officials and runners, lots of runners, many of whom have attended his summer camp at White Pass. In a single 20-yard stretch, the coaches from Sehome, Glacier Peak, and Snohomish Highs all chat Mister up. Those who call him "Phil" are mostly the veterans, Phil's peer group; younger coaches—and all current runners—invariably use the more deferential "Mister" moniker.

"You watch," Bryson-Driver says, half joking, "these coaches saw us using the golf balls out here, so next year, everybody's going to come with golf balls to State because Mister did it."

By the time Mister frees himself, the team is itching to go to lunch and then to the hotel, a 25-mile drive back to the small town of Prosser, where few teams stay. Mister wants the privacy so his runners can focus. He wants to avoid the crowds of runners milling about Pasco hotel lobbies. Nothing good can come from schmoozing. They are not here to socialize, after all. They are here to run.

★ ★ ★

The Best Western Hotel in Prosser is expecting the team. There's a standing reservation, the first weekend in November. State means Eisenhower will invade the space. In the hotel kitchen, the vats of pasta are aboil, the tureens of marinara sauce bubbling, by the time the team checks in. Mister has reserved a private dining room for the last supper, paid for at school district expense. Another tradition. Ideally, Mister would like to have seen a little more protein on the menu, some meat, but this will do. The hotel chef tosses a giant bowl of salad and bakes a few loaves of bread, as well. Off to the side, shrink-wrapped, is a tray of cookies.

The runners encamp at a long, rectangular table stretching at least seven yards, boys on the left side, girls on the right. The coaches sit at an adjoining table. The conversation is subdued, strangely quiet for this chatty bunch. Mister makes a mental note of it. He will need to calm nerves, give reassurances, later that night at the team meetings and one-on-one race-planning sessions.

Mister is the last to fill his plate and has just started tucking into his pasta when a presence hovers over his left shoulder.

"Uh, Mister?" It is Jesus, looking a bit sheepish.

"Uh-huh."

"Can we have—I mean, we were wondering—could we have a cookie?"

Mister's brow furrows in puzzlement.

"Of course, you can have a *cookie*, Jesus."

"Well, we were just wondering because, like, the Halloween candy thing."

Bryson-Driver smiles. She recalls the kids' reaction just before Halloween when Mister told them they were forbidden from eating candy because of how all that sugar negatively affected a runner's pancreas.

"I don't think one cookie is going to shut down your pancreas," she laughs.

Mister bristles. "I'm never gonna hear the end to the 'pancreas thing,' am I?"

The team snatches up the tray of cookies. Even Dantzel indulges.

An hour later, back in Room 278, which Mister shares with Ivan, the mood is far more somber. Mister is holding shortened versions of the one-on-one meetings he had with each runner at Camp Ghormley. He completed the girls' tête-à-têtes back in Yakima, but the boys' team still needs briefing. One by one, every five minutes, they cycle in.

"Mo, this course suits you as long as you are aggressive on the downhills. It's OK to be back in the first mile, as long as you are moving. You've got to be racing, not just striding out. You will be back a ways in the first mile. That's OK. Then, you gotta *go* . . ."

"Listen, Angel, you are the type of kid that, if you can focus on the job at hand, can produce extraordinary results. And that's what we need tomorrow. You've got to get top 45 and fly by those people. We need you, Angel. If Fonzi and Rogelio start struggling, you need to step up and help them. Don't be drifting. You need to focus . . ."

"You've had a great season, Rogelio, wouldn't you agree? Tomorrow, you can't get locked into a super-hard early pace. You need to run even-paced. Hard but even. I know both you and Fonzi want to qualify for the Border Clash [a postseason showdown, sponsored by Nike, pitting the best runners from Washington against those from Oregon]. I can see a top-15 finish for you. You can do it. Go out in the top 25 and then start passing people in the last mile . . ."

When Fonzi walks through the door, Mister notices right off that the boy is stressed—again. That brow is wrinkled, furrowed big-time. Mister begins what almost has become a catechism between the two.

"So are you feeling confident or unsure about tomorrow?"

"I'd say I'm really unsure."

"How are you feeling now compared to a year ago?"

"Different."

"In what way?"

"I'd say not as confident."

"The thing is, your workouts are every bit as good as last year. Where does this lack of confidence come from?"

"Just from my performance in races and watching videos, because my form was a lot better then. Every time I think I'm doing better, the videos show the same."

"A lot of that is just growth. You may be one of these guys who won't get the technique down until they stop growing. But this time last year, did you think you were going to finish fifth at State?"

"No, not at all."

"Again, I'm saying to you, your workouts now are every bit as good as last year. You don't finish fifth at State by accident. That's talent and training. Last year, you didn't worry so much. You just went out and raced. What the hell are you worrying about? I think that's hurting you. Just race. Stop thinking, 'If this happens, if that happens.' You're building scenarios, Fonzi. Just *race*. The races you had earlier this year are no indication of what's going to happen tomorrow."

"Yup."

"Do you really believe that? Yes or no."

"No."

"You don't believe me?" Mister's voice rises in surprise and irritation.

"No."

"Whatever happens tomorrow, you can't give up in the middle of it, because the team needs you. Run for the team."

"Yup."

"And stop being a worrywart. I want freshman Fonzi back. What happened to that guy?"

"Gone with the hair," says Fonzi, whose curls were much more pronounced two years before.

"You don't have to be perfect tomorrow. Just run, Fonzi. All right? Go bring in Jonas."

Jonas strides into the room a few seconds later and sits at attention opposite Mister.

"What are your thoughts going forward here, Jonas?"

"I want to win, Mister."

★ ★ ★

Race day dawns cold and dank, temperature hovering in the high 20s. It looks as if it might snow. Mister, finishing his scrambled eggs along with the team in the Best Western's continental breakfast room, just shrugs. Everyone has to run in the same conditions, after all, and it may warm up before Eisenhower's races in the early afternoon. And, besides, his kids are tough. So tough, in fact, that Mister is going ahead with the planned morning conditioning drills in the hotel's back parking lot. The runners throw on an extra layer or two and start doing their high-knees march, back and forth, puffs of steam coming with every exhalation. They draw a few puzzled looks from big-rig truckers pulling into the McDonald's next door. Mister doesn't stick around. He walks across the road to the 24-hour Subway to order 31 sandwiches for the runners to eat for lunch a couple of hours before their races.

Later, back inside the warmth of the hotel, most runners flounce on their beds, spending the final hour before the bus departs playing video games on their phones (the boys) or watching TV and chatting (the girls). Mister leaves the door to Room 278 ajar so that runners can come and go to get a prerace massage. Guests on the second floor must be wondering what is going on down the hallway. They can breathe in astringent whiffs of Tiger Balm, the menthol, mint, and clove ointment the coaches use to "rub out" knotted muscles. And they can hear squeals of pain and peals of laughter coming from inside the room, perhaps not knowing whether to call the authorities or join the festivities.

Fonzi goes first, lying facedown on the bed, his left calf being kneaded like bread dough by Mister. Though he tries to endure the pain in silence, Fonzi cannot help himself. He yelps and groans and writhes as Mister digs a thumb deep into his knotted calf. At one point, when Mister really bears down, Fonzi starts laughing and shaking his free leg, the right one, uncontrollably. Mister chortles, "My God, Fonzi, my dog does the same thing. You scratch her ear, and she shakes her leg."

Bryson-Driver, cutting Popsicle sticks in half for those who run clutching them, looks up from the bed and says, "Whatever helps the kid get through it."

Rogelio follows for some therapy on his shins, then Dantzel for her calves and hamstrings. Mister doesn't even break a sweat. He holds up his hands and flexes them. He doesn't say what he usually says at such moments, but the words by now echo in everyone's head: "These are strong cow-milking hands from back in Ireland."

★ ★ ★

The bus pulls up to Sun Willows Country Club and, this time, the whoosh of the doors opening is like a gasp of astonishment. The golf course has been utterly transformed, as in that scene in *The Wizard of Oz*, black-and-white to Technicolor. An armada of yellow school buses and fancier white charter coaches lines a two-block stretch of the main road. Runners, clad in every color in the Crayola box, jog either exaggeratedly slow in flocks or dash around in preparation for racing. More than 1,500 runners from schools with enrollments as large as 5,000 and as small as 200 are competing in 11 races, and by the time Eisenhower's bus arrives, four of the races already have been completed; the hubbub of activity is in full roar.

Per Mister's instructions, Ike runners walk directly to the staging area to pick up the electronic timing chips they will affix to their shoes and then proceed to the team's tent at the driving range, which now looks like a tent city for natural disaster refugees, with plastic water jugs and torn-open boxes of energy bars and splayed banana peels strewn all around.

The plan is to lie low and avoid the horde until it is time to warm up in their secluded spit of grass outside the facility. But the runners cannot help but gawk at the sheer number of people swarming the driving range, folks leaning over fences to shout encouragement as racers fly by, sprinting like mad to another part of the course to get a glimpse of the pack and then sprinting back, shouting to friends and family members, "He's moving up," or lamenting, "She's getting passed!" A new race starts every half hour, and those in the driving range can only tell by the thunderous roar of a crowd after the gun, followed by a stampede heading from the starting line to the part of the fence with good views of the one-mile mark. Strangely though, while many fans are in feverish states following a race's progress, others seem completely oblivious. The only lines longer than the one for the Dutch Bros. coffee truck are the ones for the 22 portable toilets. By day's end, savvy fans know to avoid standing downwind from the porta-potty area, the stench becoming so strong that no amount of urinal cakes can mask it. Almost as ubiquitous as the toilets are the inspirational slogans found all over—on tents ("Running Is Mental and We Are All Insane"), on the back of T-shirts ("Our sport is your sport's punishment"), on runners' calves written in a Sharpie's scrawl ("Harder. Faster. Stronger.").

The backs of Eisenhower's warm-up shirts bear two words: "MISTER'S ARMY."

★ ★ ★

On the starting line, in box number 5, the girls have done their allotment of five strides and have shed most of their warm-up clothes. Erica, steely-eyed, looks straight down the fairway as Bryson-Driver rips off athletic tape and wraps it around Erica's slender wrist. Erica, more than any runner, doesn't need this visual reminder to swing her arms, but she offers up her wrists dutifully. Neither Bryson-Driver, former State champ, nor Erica, hoping for a top-10 finish, says a word to the other. Both know what is at stake. And both know Erica is ready. Sophi, already taped and fully hyped up, walks over and wraps Mister in a hug. Dantzel looks over and smiles wanly. Can Dantzel salvage a difficult season here with a good run at State? She told Mister two days before at her one-on-one interview that her season has "not been a staircase; it's been a roller coaster," but that all of her troubles have made her realize how much she loves running, the sheer pleasure of physical movement. She is telling herself now not to overthink things, to run hard but steady, push back doubts that she might "die" in the final mile. And Molly? Molly is her steady self—focused but loose. Little fazes her. She seems most concerned about fulfilling her mandate from Mister—to tell the team a joke before the start, just to break the tension. What Molly produces—once Mister finishes taping Minelly Sereno's wrists and Sophi gives Bryson-Driver a hug—is not a joke but a funky kind of chicken dance. It does the trick. The girls break into nervous laughter.

Moments later, 161 girls take off down the fairway, the blue-shirted Eisenhower girls in a swarm, Erica alighting out front.

At the driving range fence closest to the one-mile mark, Eric and Pam Simison wait for the pack. They stare at the pair of leaf-bare trees marking one mile. Eric is dressed in his customary meet attire, a ball cap pulled low on his forehead, almost shrouding his eyes, and one in his collection of Eisenhower sweatshirts. Pam, strangely, is wearing an oversized rain slicker that bulges out in back, as if she were a hunchback. Strange because, though cloudy and a nippy 35 degrees, there is little chance of rain.

"Here they come," someone in the crowd shouts.

Erica is not among the four girls in the lead pack. Eric frowns. But here she comes in the middle of the chase pack 15 meters behind, that bobbing hair bun dwarfed amid a gaggle of lanky, long-legged girls. Her first mile clocks in at 5:43, not crazy fast. Good, Mister thinks, as he observes from a coaches' box in the middle of the course; she can move up later on. By the time Erica's chase pack makes a 180-degree turn and heads past the driving range lined with fans before disappearing toward the course's first significant uphill, Molly has just emerged at the one-mile mark in 6:08, Dantzel five seconds behind her and looking strong. Sophi and Madi, the team's final two scoring members, are running together well back in the field in 128th and 129th place, respectively, but Mister can see that they are *racing*, not merely running, so he isn't overly concerned.

The next time the fans can see the runners is at the crest of a hill nearing an extended downhill leading to the two-mile mark. The lead pack stays intact, but the chase group has been reduced to three, with Erica hanging on. She runs right by Mister, who cups his hands and shouts encouragement and strategy: "Arm swing . . . move on through . . . stay close . . ." Dantzel, gaining a second wind, catches Molly by the two-mile mark, and the two work together, running stride for stride in 75th and

76th place, respectively. Dantzel feels a jolt of confidence as she flies past girls who had beaten her, badly, at the district race a week ago, Davis's Grace Gerardi and Eastmont's Ashlyn Hill. She tells herself, *I can do this*, and for maybe the first time all season, she believes it. At two miles, Madi and Sophi still are running together, but they have passed six runners with the hoarse voice of Mister ("Move on through!") ringing in their ears.

Back near the front, at a dogleg leading to the 2.5-mile mark, the lead pack has been reduced to three, and it has opened a 20-second lead on the chase pack, which also is breaking up. But Erica maintains her pace, her dad saying, "Keep it going, babe," as she passes fans five deep along the course flagging. By this point, Erica has passed all three of the top runners from Issaquah High, the state's top-ranked team, runners who had beaten her in meets earlier in the season. Erica has moved into sixth place as she churns up the final hill before the long downhill sprint to the finish. Robert Price, videotaping the race from a portable ladder near the hill's crest, shouts, "Keep the arms going, Erica," before scurrying down the ladder and heading to the finish line to set up his video camera.

Farther back, on that last hill, Dantzel has now passed 12 runners in a half-mile stretch and has put eight seconds between herself and Molly. But she is feeling the burn of lactic acid building up in her muscles. She is in pain. She doesn't ignore it. She acknowledges it and keeps going, telling herself, *All right, here we go, you expected this.* A quarter mile—and about 25 runners—behind Dantzel, Sophi has pulled away from Madi. Madi has gamely tried to keep up, but fatigue is winning. Sophi is feeling it, too, but in the last half mile she moves up 18 spots and is now just trying to maintain her 102nd position.

Erica, by this time, has turned the corner and is flying toward the finish in sixth place, gaining on Skyline's Geneva Schlepp, who passed her just before the two-mile mark and spent the rest of the race trying to keep Erica at bay. Erica doesn't catch Schlepp but finishes a strong sixth—four spots higher than her 2016 State placing—and, at 18:03, 29 seconds faster than the year before. Erica's time is the fastest in school history for girls since the course was extended from three miles to a 5K in the 1990s.

Dantzel finishes 63rd, a minute and half behind Erica; Molly, 76th, nine seconds behind Dantzel; Sophi, 102nd; and Madi, 113th. Eisenhower finishes eighth as a team, the spot it was ranked, an impressive effort considering that, for most of the season, the girls had been unranked and in disarray.

Eisenhower runners, sans Erica, hug and walk together out of the finishing chute, exhausted but smiling. And where is Erica? She is being interviewed across the chute by a *Yakima Herald* sportswriter. Her family—most of it, that is—wait for her outside the chute as Erica tells reporter Scott Spruill, "A 30-second PR, that's crazy!" When she finally makes it out of the chute, Erica's family and friends cheer, and her mom, still wearing that oversized rain slicker, beams. Her boyfriend, Ronan Price, embraces her. Erica locks eyes with her mother.

"Did you bring him?" Erica asks.

"Why do you think I've been wearing this tent? I've been hiding him all day."

Erica squeals in delight and hustles around to her mom's back. She lifts the back of the rain slicker and scratches Winston, her French bulldog puppy, behind the ear.

"Careful," Pam says. "We don't want to get kicked out for having a dog in here."

"OK, Mom."

"Erica never texts me on the day of a race—never," Pam tells the group of well-wishers. "Today, she texted me three times. Not about me. Not about whether Ronan was coming. Or if Grandma was coming. It was, 'Do you think you'll be able to bring the dog?' 'Are you bringing Winston?' 'What about Winston, Mom?'"

Erica smiles. She closes the rain slicker and looks around.

"Where's my dad?"

She doesn't need an answer to the question.

★ ★ ★

The boys see none of this. They have gathered a quarter mile away from the girls' drama to stretch and warm up for their race. The boys' 4A, the largest division, always comes as the final race of the day—and always is the fastest and most contentious. Mister joins the team immediately after the girls' race. He likes to keep his runners as calm as possible beforehand, to quell nervousness. His laid-back attitude may be helping, but the boys still look anxious, teeth-grindingly anxious, as they drill and then change into their spikes. Jonas, clingier than usual, gets right up in his dad's face, whispers something, and then hugs him. Price pats Jonas on the back and tenderly calls him by a family nickname: "Jo-Jo. Jo-Jo, the monkey boy." Fonzi, face scrunched, stares at his spikes, and Rogelio asks Bryson-Driver for another set of Popsicle sticks. Price has Mo lie on his back while he stretches out Mo's balky hamstring, which is feeling pretty good for once. Angel, inscrutable as always, silently does knee-high drills, but he lights up when his older brother, Simon, who ran for Eisenhower several years before, stops and waves.

Fifteen minutes before race time, Mister motions for the boys to jog with him across two parking lots to the starting line. He has no final inspirational words, no further instructions. He is all talked out. He has been strategizing with the boys for more than a week now. If they don't know the nuances of the course by now, if they don't know the time splits and race strategies they've gone over, if they still need a kick in the ass for motivation at this late stage, well, there is little hope for a good performance. But Mister is feeling somewhat confident. *Jonas could win the whole damn thing,* he thinks. And Rogelio and Fonzi, they could well be in the top 20. Despite Fonzi's doubts, Mister has a feeling the boy might pull off something close to a repeat of his State performance a year ago. Strong efforts from the top three would make a podium finish possible, with one big caveat: Angel and Mo, the fourth and fifth runners, need to close the gap enough, pick off enough runners to put Ike over the top. That scenario did come to pass the previous year at State, with a slightly different cast of runners. It could happen again. But Mister cannot lie to himself. Strong performances from *both* Angel and Mo? That is a big "if."

Just before the coaches are asked to leave the starting area, Mister turns and asks, "What about the joke?"

Rogelio was tasked with telling the team a joke at the start line, but he has handed off duties to Jonas, who now stands before the team in box number nine and strikes a rapper pose, which already is amusing to his teammates. Lately, the team has been listening to a lot of Lil Pump, a teenage Hispanic rapper from Miami, whose song "Crazy" includes the lyric, "essketit," which never ceases to crack up the guys. So Jonas gathers them in:

"OK, so what does Lil Pump say after a delicious meal?"

"Exquisite!"

Mister looks puzzled. But the team laughs. No time to explain the joke and, frankly, Mister doesn't care to know. These guys have a race to run.

Ivan finishes taping Fonzi's wrists, Fonzi being the last to get taped up, and the team huddles in the box. Mo leans in and says, "We're looking out for each other out there." Then he fist-bumps Fonzi and says, "You're going to another level." Then he fist-bumps the others. Richland's Riley Moore walks by and shouts, "Hey, Jonas! Hey, boys!" Was it a psyche job or a friendly greeting? No way to tell. Jonas nods at Moore.

The gun sounds . . . and Fonzi does not fall.

But Mo does. Actually, Mo stumbles, badly, 20 meters after the gun, just as the horde of runners crests the first hill. He is falling forward, almost taking out Jesus in front of him, but Mo is able to right himself and avoid a tumble.

Still, not an auspicious way to begin.

Several of the girls' team members and parents, including Fonzi's mom and Rogelio's mom and dad, have scoped out the spots along the fencing with prime views of the one-mile mark. When the orange-painted lead vehicle rounds the trees, a tight pack of eight runners emerges. "There's Jonas!" someone in the back exclaims. He is in sixth place, smack in the middle of the lead pack. Then another voice: "There's Fonzi and Rogelio!" The two are in the chase pack, Fonzi 11th and Rogelio 12th at the mile, both clocking 4:57. So far, Ike's top three are running faster than anticipated, ahead of the leaders of the four teams ranked higher than Eisenhower. Mister checks the splits. He wonders whether Fonzi and Rogelio can maintain the pace, hoping all of those mile repeats he made them perform have prepared them for this type of swift race.

Still, Mister frets: *Where are Angel and Mo?* Runners stream past, and still no Angel and Mo. Elation has turned to anxiety, then exasperation. More runners make the turn, and still no Angel. Finally, with the clock reading 5:06, Angel's churning arms appear. By that time, all five scoring runners from Lewis and Clark have passed; none of the Central Valley runners has appeared yet, but Mister has figured that as a strategic move on CV's part, risky but potentially rewarding, to go out easy and run like mad from behind. Eisenhower has no such strategy. Mister needs Angel and Mo to run hard from the get-go and, geez, Mo hasn't shown up yet.

That is because Mo is hurting. The stumble near the start has hurt him, mentally and physically. His right hamstring is burning, the tweak now a more serious strain, and he adjusts his stride to compensate. But he feels broken by this point, in spirit too. *Have to move up*, he tells himself. *Move up.* And he makes surges. His body fails to respond. He hits the mile mark in 148th place out of 164—disastrous for Eisenhower's chances. The team stands in sixth place at the first mile split, after being in the lead when Jonas, Fonzi, and Rogelio hit the timing mat. If Mo cannot rally and Angel cannot move up, not only will Eisenhower not reach the podium but it might even finish outside the top five for the first time in four years.

Up front, things continue to look much brighter. Jonas cements his place in the lead pack, moving up to fourth at the two-mile mark. He is running sub-five-minute miles and not even feeling it. He is trying to be patient, as Mister and his dad cautioned, to hold back until that spot on the course, the dirt-road crossing near 2.5 miles, where Mister says to surge into the lead. Behind Jonas, Fonzi and Rogelio each clock a five-minute second mile and stay close, Fonzi moving into 10th place, Rogelio, 12th. Fonzi is hurting, lungs searing, but on a flat stretch he rallies and starts picking off a few runners to gain that 10th spot. Don't think; just run. For the first time, he feels like the runner he was last season. The old Fonzi has come back. Rogelio, who even after his vast improvement in his senior year still had the tendency to fade in the third mile of races, stares at the back of Fonzi's singlet and wills himself to stay close. The thought flashes in Rogelio's mind, *I'm dead. My legs are done.* But he pushes the thought away. Rogelio finds himself trying to push through the pain and stay as close as he can. And this EI stuff is working. He fades a little but stays strong.

Angel, however, falls back a few places in the second mile. All season, this has been the point of a race in which Angel picks up the pace. Called "The Snake" for his ability to slide by runners in the final meters, Angel now digs deep . . . and finds he has nothing. Truth is, he felt terrible even before the race. Not that he told anyone. Angel never complains. Angel never boasts. Angel just runs. But his placid exterior hides a welling of anxiety inside him. A new emotion. He didn't sleep much at all the night before. Hadn't all week. His mind played a continuous loop of what might happen at State, the soundtrack being the voice of Mister telling him how important his performance would be to the team's success. The pressure has gotten to him. When he tries to shift into "Snake" mode in the third mile, he gets passed instead of being the passer. All he can do is continue to grind it out, hope to rally. Mo, too, does not quit. He isn't running much faster in that third mile, but his fellow back-of-the-packers are slowing, so he moves up. But will it be enough to get Eisenhower to the podium? That thought keeps him going, despite his noticeable limp at this point.

When Jonas gets to the appointed spot where he'll make his move, he is in good position. Daniel Maton, as expected, leads by a step or two, and Lewis and Clark's surprising lead runner, Will Smith, is right behind him. Jonas shifts slightly left and surges. But Maton and the rest of the pack answer that surge. Mister has told Jonas to expect that reaction and to just keep pressing. And Jonas does, maintaining the surge into the horseshoe turn. The pack still follows. Jonas eventually falls back to fourth, not so much because he is tired but because the other lead runners have started sprinting. Coming from way behind and passing Jonas in the final 300 meters—just as he blew by Fonzi and Rogelio earlier in the third mile—is Central Valley's Ryan Kline, 95th after one mile and 15th after two miles. On that final downhill, as Jonas seemingly wraps up what would be a fourth-place finish, Kline stalks Maton, still the leader. Kline catches him two meters out, and Maton's dive at the line fails to make a difference. Jonas, meanwhile, is also outkicked by senior Nate Pendleton of Eastlake High. So Jonas has to settle for fifth, but his time of 15:16.60 is the fastest ever by a sophomore on this State meet course.

Fonzi, too, is being passed by hard-charging Central Valley runners Gabe Romney and Evan Peters in the final 600 meters. He tells himself not to panic and, most of all, not to give up. His personal goal for State, which he's kept quiet about, is to finish in the top 15 and earn another trip to the Border Clash, that Nike-sponsored all-star race in late November. But now that goal is in jeopardy, as Lewis and Clark's second runner, Carter Ledwith, sweeps by Fonzi as well. But it isn't as if Fonzi has slowed; others merely run faster. Fonzi finishes 18th at 15:43—only four seconds slower than his time in 2016—with Rogelio coming in three places and nine seconds behind him in 21st. By the time Angel (76th) and Mo (121st) have finished, tears are already streaming down Fonzi's face. No Border Clash for him. No podium for the team. Eisenhower finishes fifth as a team, even though the school stood in second place after its first three runners crossed the line. (Lewis and Clark edged top-ranked Central Valley by a single point for the team title.) The fact that Fonzi has run his best race, by far, of the season, that he has exhibited flashes of his old elite self, does nothing to assuage his disappointment. The tears flow. Teammates leave him alone. Rogelio, by contrast, is smiling and is wrapped in bear hugs first by his mom, Leticia, and then by his dad, Rogelio Sr.

Because of adolescence, that most fraught period of human development, those trying years between dependency of childhood and responsibility of adulthood, can elicit from teens a range of emotions from the very same event. Joy or sorrow. Sometimes, joy and sorrow mixed together. Such a range of reactions overtakes all of the team members in the first flush postrace. Mo squats and weeps. Angel cannot not make eye contact. Jesus looks dazed.

Yet to leave the chute is Jonas, clearly basking in the moment while recounting his run to reporters. When he finally emerges, his dad cuts through the crowd, comes up from behind, and lifts his son's scrawny frame into the air. His mother and brother laugh and clap. Jonas's face is a weird grimace of joy. Even the team's fifth-place finish cannot dampen Jonas's mood.

Fonzi, eventually, pulls himself together. But his brow remains furrowed. His mother and little sister, Caris, finally dare to approach him at the team tent, and Fonzi flashes them the saddest smile. He almost tears up again but holds it together long enough for someone to snap a photo of mother and son for Sonya's Facebook page. Later, when Fonzi and teammates go off for a cooldown run, Sonya reflects on what has been a trying season for her son. Fonzi will turn 17 the next week, still a kid in many respects, but Sonya says he has had to grow up fast this past year.

"At our house," Sonya, a single mother, says, "Alfonso feels like he's the leader for the other kids. He feels he's letting the other kids I take care of down when he doesn't run well. The first thing he's asked by them when he walks through the door is, 'How'd you do in the race?' And it was tough on Alfonso when he didn't run good. The kids at home, they don't have a lot, and they looked up to Alfonso. And this season, his pride got the best of him. I tell him to let it go, but he can't. I know why he was crying: Border Clash. He really wanted to go again. Alfonso's got very high expectations."

Cooldown run over, and with the late-afternoon shadows descending, Eisenhower packs up its tents and boards the bus back to Yakima. They wait for a good 15 minutes for Jonas, Mister, and Price, who are lingering at the Nike tent signing up Jonas for Border Clash. Tired of waiting, perhaps, driver Rick Glenn pulls the bus up in front of the road next to the Nike tent. (Erica, too, qualified for Border Clash and signed up after her race. She isn't on the bus, having gotten permission to leave early with her parents—and Winston.)

So the rest of the team sits there for another five minutes, watching Jonas sign forms and then tape an interview at the Nike tent. Fonzi makes a concerted effort not to look. Price eventually jogs over to the bus, and the doors open with a tired hiss. It has been a long day; it is time to go. But Price takes three steps aboard and shouts, "Fonzi, we need you over here." Fonzi stands, heart in his throat, mind reeling—*What's happening? Can this be?*—and follows his coach. Inside the tent, a Nike marketing representative reaches out his hand. Fonzi shakes it. At the bus, faces are pressed to windows.

"We need to double-check the numbers tonight, but it looks like you've qualified," the Nike rep says, and a dazed smile freezes on Fonzi's face. "We take the top 15, plus the next three fastest times. At the very least, you'll be an alternate. Congratulations. Take this release home and have your dad and mom sign it, OK?"

A full year has passed since anyone has seen such a luminous grin on Fonzi's face. When he steps back onto the bus, his teammates burst into applause. He smiles broadly, but he does not cry. "Border Clash—*yeah!*" he exclaims.

★ ★ ★

The next morning, Yakima and nearly all of central Washington wake to an inch or two of snow coating the streets and dusting the hillsides.

Seasons change. Seasons end. Winter is descending, days shortening, those cursed smoky and stifling summer days of running without a shirt now a memory.

I needed to take a stand against this premature end to autumn, which fittingly, almost eerily, coincided with the end of cross-country season. So I bundled myself in three layers, grudgingly put on tights instead of my preferred shorts, and left the house for a long, slow run, snowflakes settling onto my exposed face and hair.

As I made the turn onto Chestnut Avenue and passed the Price house, I saw that the banner wishing Jonas good luck at State was still draped across the windows of the ballet studio. Somebody else, it seemed, wasn't ready for fall to end. I ran on, thinking that this talented Price kid, in two years hence, might indeed beat the long odds and run for his beloved University of Oregon. Then I thought of Erica and an upcoming college running career in which she would at last train among equals, or superiors. And then I thought of the team's large contingent of Hispanic runners, five of whom would be graduating in the spring. What would await them? And what of Fonzi and Dantzel, who, as seniors next fall, would seek redemption for difficult 2017 seasons?

I ran on, cresting a hill near Chestnut and 45th Avenue, heading down to the apple-processing warehouse shuttered on this Sunday morning. Up ahead a solitary figure came running toward me up the hill, swaddled in layers and wearing a ski cap that looked familiar. As we neared each other—I on the left side of the road, he on the right—I noticed that unmistakable arm swing.

Fonzi.

He waved and kept going. Chin down, eyes up, leaning in, moving swiftly. Running with ease, with grace. Running forward, ever forward, toward his future.

AFTERWORD

ERICA SIMISON and ROGELIO MARES both accepted athletic scholarships to run for the University of Montana, and Molly Stephenson accepted a scholarship to run at Lewis-Clark State College in Lewiston, Idaho. Six seniors from the boys' varsity team attended college. In the 2018 prep cross country season, Jonas Price finished second in the Washington state 4A championship race; Alfonso (Fonzi) Cuevas finished forty-eighth after an otherwise stellar season. Dantzel Peterson moved to Utah to complete her senior year of high school. In 2018, Coach Phil English was enshrined in the Washington State Cross Country Coaches Association's Hall of Fame.

2017 Eisenhower High School Cross-Country Team

Varsity Boys

Jonas Price
Alfonso (Fonzi) Cuevas
Rogelio Mares
Angel Cuevas
Moise Cook
Jesus Gonzalez
Antonio Heredia

Varsity Girls

Erica Simison
Dantzel Peterson
Molly Stephenson
Sophi Rodriquez
Madi Oliva
Minelly Sereno
Nayeli Barron

Junior Varsity Boys

Jonathan Valenzuela
Diego Vargas
Isaiah Lopez
Oscar Mendoza
Fernando Cornejo
Nathan Valenzuela
John Campos
Victor Xu
Michael Edmonds
Jason Martinez

Junior Varsity Girls

Yesenia Rodriguez
Kayli Carl
Isabel (Izzy) Gutierrez
Anai Manzo
Julia Johnson
Luisa Molina
Antonia Harrich
Kaitlyn Ditter

Coaches

Phil English, Robert Price, Robin Bryson-Driver, Ivan Alfaro, Drew Schreiber (volunteer).

ACKNOWLEDGMENTS

THIS BOOK would not have been possible without the cooperation and candor of Coach Phil (Mister) English, who gave me full access to the Eisenhower program for six months and not once went "off-the-record." Thank you, too, to the Eisenhower runners, their parents, and the coaching staff for their patience and kindness, and to former runners who shared their memories of competing for Ike. Huge thanks go to Tom McCarthy, my editor at Lyons Press, and Charlotte Gusay, my agent, for believing in this project. Kudos to Lisa Norris, a great first reader, and Maya Zeller and Cynthia Mitchell for their input. Thanks to Central Washington University's English department for giving me the time to work on the book. As always, thanks to my wife, Beth McManis, for her unconditional support—and action photos.

ABOUT THE AUTHOR

Sam McManis is a former columnist and feature writer for the *Sacramento Bee*. He is a four-time winner of Society of Features Journalism awards and three-time Best of the West honoree. He also has been a staff writer and editor at the *San Francisco Chronicle* and a sportswriter at the *Los Angeles Times*. His profiles and essays have appeared in the *New York Times*, *Wall Street Journal*, and elsewhere. He is the author of a book of travel essays, *Crossing California: A Cultural Topography of a State of Wonder and Weirdness*. He lives in Flagstaff, Arizona.